AF557875

MARKETING OF TELECOM SERVICES

MARKETING OF TELECOM SERVICES

By

Dr. K. Rama Mohana Rao

M.Com., M.B.A., Ph.D.

Professor

Department of Commerce and Management Studies

Andhra University, Visakhapatnam

Andhra Pradesh, (India)

&

Dr. D. Srinivasa Prasad

M.B.A., P.G.D.A.S., Ph.D.

Management Consultant, Visakhapatnam

Andhra Pradesh

(India)

DISCOVERY PUBLISHING HOUSE PVT. LTD.

NEW DELHI-110 002

Published by:
Tilak Wasan
DISCOVERY PUBLISHING HOUSE PVT. LTD.
4831/24, Ansari Road, Prahlad Street
Darya Ganj, New Delhi-110002 (India)
Phone: +91-11-23279245, 43764432
Fax: +91-11-23253475
E-mail: parul.wasan@gmail.com
info@discoverypublishinggroup.com
web: www.discoverypublishinggroup.com

***First Edition:* 2011**
ISBN: 978-81-8356-718-3

Marketing of Telecom Services

Printed at:
Shree Balaji Art Press
Delhi

Dedicated to
Goddess SRI KANAKAMAHA LAKSHMI
Visakhapatnam

Preface

Marketing of Telecommunication services became a challenge to the public sector organizations in India due to the entry of private corporations to this sector. India is passing through mobile tele-services revolution since the beginning of this century. The growth of mobile segment overtook the age-old fixed line segment. It is evident from the fact that the demand for fixed line services is on the decline while the demand for mobile services is zooming year by year. Though mobile services provide greater convenience to the customers, the importance of fixed line services cannot be nullified. Fixed line service is not only economical but also connects all parts of the country particularly rural India. The public sector major BSNL is facing marketing problems with fixed line services. Therefore, a detailed study on the issue is felt necessary. The present study is a modest attempt to analyze various issues related to marketing of fixed line services and to suggest measures for the development of this business segment.

This book is divided into eleven chapters. *Chapter I* presents the historical perspectives of telecom sector in India, literature review and the research design. The growth of telecommunications in India, the competition scenario, planned development, the policies and organization system for the development of telecom sector are discussed in *Chapter II*. The organization system of BSNL and its performance perspectives are presented in *Chapter III*. The product mix, pricing policy and distribution system are analyzed in *Chapters IV*, *V* and *VI* respectively.

Chapter VII present internal marketing operations and *Chapter VIII* presents external marketing activities. The findings of the employees' opinion survey are presented in detail in *Chapter IX*, while the findings of consumers' opinion survey are shown in *Chapter X*. The conclusions and suggestions are presented in *Chapter XI*.

The work of this magnitude cannot be done without the help of many wellwishers. We take this opportunity to express our gratitude to the management and employees of BSNL, all the respondents, friends and family members for their help, support and encouragement. We thank Discovery Publishing House for bringing out this work in print form.

Dr. K. Rama Mohana Rao
Dr. D. Srinivasa Prasad

Contents

Abbreviations

1G	:	First Generation
2G	:	Second Generation
3G	:	Third Generation
4G	:	Fourth Generation
5G	:	Fifth Generation
ADC	:	Access Deficit Charge
AGR	:	Adjusted Gross Revenue
A & N	:	Andaman & Nicobar
APT	:	Asia Pacific Telecommunication
ATM	:	Asynchronous Transfer Mode
BTS	:	Basic Terminal Station
BSNL	:	Bharat Sanchar Nigam Limited
CCA	:	Controller of Communication Accounts
C-DOT	:	Centre for Development of Telematics
CDMA	:	Code Division Multiple Access
CUG	:	Closed User Group
CAGR	:	Compounded Annual Growth Rate
CMTS	:	Cellular Mobile Telephone Services
CPP	:	Calling Party Pays
DELs	:	Direct Exchange Lines
DoT	:	Department of Telecommunication
DHQs	:	District Headquarters
FDI	:	Foreign Direct Investment

FTS	:	Fixed Telephone Services
ECB	:	External Commercial Borrowing
GDP	:	Gross Domestic Product
GMPCS	:	Global Mobile Personal Communications by Satellite
GMPC	:	Global Mobile Personal Communications
GSM	:	Global System for Mobile Communication
HCA	:	Hour Call Access
IT	:	Indian Telecommunications
IT	:	Information Technology
ISP	:	Internet Service Provision
ITI	:	Indian Telephone Industries Limited
ISPs	:	Internet Service Provider
ITU	:	International Telecommunication Union
ITU-R	:	Radio Communication Sector
ITU-T	:	Telecommunication Standardization Sector
ITU-D	:	Development Sector
INTELSAT	:	Internnational Telecommunication Satellite Organization
INMARSAT	:	International Mobile Satellite Organization
ISDN	:	Integrated Services Digital Network
ISPs	:	Internet Service Provider
INSAT	:	Indian Satellite
ICT	:	Information and Communication Technology
ILD	:	International Long Distance
ISD	:	International Subscriber Dialing
LOI	:	Letter of Intent
LR	:	Licensing and Regulation
MTNL	:	Mahanagar Telephone Nigam Limited

NCAER	:	National Council for Applied Economic Research
NFAP	:	National Frequency Allocation Plan
NGN	:	New Generation Network
NTG	:	New Technology Group
NTP	:	National Telecom Policy
NLD	:	National Long Distance
OSPs	:	Other Service Providers
P & T	:	Post & Telegraph
PMRTS	:	Public Mobile Radio Trunked Services
PSPDN	:	Packet Switched Public Data Network
PWD	:	Public Works Department
PCO's	:	Public Call Offices
PSU's	:	Public Sector Units
QoS	:	Quality of Service
R & D	:	Research and Development
RRB	:	Radio Regulation Board
RF	:	Radio Frequency
RCPs	:	Rural Commnity Phones
RAX	:	Rural Auto Exchanges
SAS	:	System of Accounting Separation
SCP	:	Service Control Points
SDCA's	:	Small Distance Charging Areas
SACFA	:	Standing Advisory Committee on Radio Frequency Allocation
SCE	:	Service Creation Environment
SMS	:	Service Management Systems
SDH	:	Synchronous Digital Hierarchy
STD	:	Subscriber Trunk Dialing
SS	:	Secondary School

SWOT	:	Strength Weakness Opportunities Threats
SEZ	:	Special Economic Zone
SWANs	:	State-wide Area Networks
TV	:	Television
TDSAT	:	Telecom Disputes Settlement and Appellate Tribunal
TERM	:	Telecom Enforcement, Resource and Monitoring
TCIL	:	Telecommunication Consultants India Limited
TETC	:	Telecom Testing and Security Certification Centre
TEC	:	Telecommunication Engineering Centre
TRAI	:	Telecom Regulatory Authority of India
VSNL	:	Videsh Sanchar Nigam Limited
VPTs	:	Village Panchayat Phone
VTMS	:	Vigilance Telecom Monitorings
WPCC	:	Wireless Planning Coordination Committee
WLL	:	Wireless in Local Loop
WPC	:	Wireless Planning and Coordination
USO	:	Universal Service Obligation
USOF	:	Universal Service Obligation Fund

INTRODUCTION

Telecommunication is one of the prime support services needed for rapid growth and modernization of various sectors of the economy[1]. It has become especially important in recent years because of enormous growth of Information Technology (IT) and its significant impact on the rest of the economy. Telecom is the means of communication of the future and shall form a vital component of India's infrastructure. Communication Technologies are found to be contributing substantially to the development process. The process of socio-economic emancipation is now considerably governed by the quality of Information Technologies[2]. The role of telecommunications became pivotal in this perspective. This sector has undergone a total transformation throughout the world over the last two decades. Technological advances have revolutionised the quality and range of services available[3].

Telecommunications is one of the fastest-growing areas of technology in the world. Because of its rapid growth, businesses and individuals can access information at electronic speed from almost anywhere in the world. By including Telecommunications in their operations, businesses can provide better services and products to their customers. For individuals, telecommunications provide access to worldwide information and services.

The telecommunications is not a new concept. It began in the mid-1800s with the telegraph, whereby sounds were translated manually into words; then the telephone developed in 1876 transmitted voices; and then the teletypewriter, developed in the early 1900, was able to transmit the written word. Since 1960s, development of telecommunications has been rapid and wide reaching. The development of dial modem technology accelerated the growth rate during the 1980s. Facsimile transmission also registered rapid growth during this time. The 1990s have seen the greatest advancements in telecommunication sector.

Deregulation and new technology have created increased competition and widened the range of network services available throughout the world. This increase in telecommunication capabilities allows businesses to benefit from the information revolution in numerous ways, such as streamlining their inventories, increasing productivity, and identifying new markets and developing connectivity with customers.

Telephony was introduced in India in 1882. At present telecommunications system in India is the 4th largest in the world. India is having one of the fastest growing telecom networks in the world with its high population and development potential. India's public sector telecom company, BSNL, is the 7th largest telecom company in the world.

Historical Perspectives of Telecom Sector in India

The telecom sector is celebrating 150 years of Indian telecommunications. In the history of telecommunications in India, the first experimental electric telegraph line was started between Calcutta and Diamond Harbour in November, 1850. A year later the line was completed and opened for East India Company's traffic. The visionary behind this landmark was Dr. William O'Shaughnessy—credited to pioneer telegraph and telephone in India. The significant leap which really set the pace of telecom development was the establishment of Indo-Ceylon link. The Indo-Ceylon cable was laid in 1858. In 1865 the first Indo-European telegraphs communication was effected and two years later a new cable was laid between India and Ceylon. In 1873, Duplex telegraphy was introduced between Bombay and Calcutta. In 1875, ITD supplied the first private telephone line and two years later it erected telegraph line between Srinagar and Gilgit on behalf of Maharaja of Kashmir.

In the historical archives, the year 1888 has vital importance. It was in this year that the Indo-European Telegraph Department, which was later known as Overseas Communications, was merged with India Telegraph Department. Seven years later, India was gifted its first phonogram. In 1895, phonograms were introduced for the first time at Bombay and Calcutta. In 1902, the first wireless Telegraph Station was established between Saugor Islands and Sand heads and a year later, the departmental Wireless Telegraph was introduced.

The year 1905 can be termed as the cornerstone of today's telecom profile. It was in this year that the control of the Telegraph Department was transferred from PWD to Commerce and Industry Department except for matters connected with buildings and electricity. A year later, Baudot System was introduced between Calcutta and Bombay and between Calcutta and Rangoon.

In 1910, the technical branch came into being as a separate organization under Electrical Engineer-in-Chief. The next two years saw the introduction of Circle Scheme and decentralization, and two years later, i.e., in 1914, the Postal and Telegraph Departments were amalgamated under a single Director General. At the same time the control of the Postal and Telegraph (P&T) Department was reverted to PWD. The year also witnessed the opening of the first automatic exchange at Simla with a capacity of 700 lines and 400 actual connections. In 1920, Madras-port Blair route was opened for wireless telegraph and a year later National Cash Register were introduced in Calcutta CTO for the first time.

A major reorganization of the department took place when the accounts of the Indian Posts and Telegraphs were reconstituted to examine the true fiscal profile of the department. The attempt was to find out the extent to which the department was imposing burden on the taxpayers and brining in revenue to the exchequer and how far each of the four constituent branches, namely postal, telegraph, telephone and wireless, were contributing. It was also examined whether the rates charged for the public were inadequate or excessive.

Radio Telephone Communications between England and India were opened in 1933. Indo-Burma Radio Telephone Service started functioning between Madras and Rangoon in 1936. Burma and Aden Telegraph Systems, which were a part of Indian Telegraph System, got separated in 1937. Deluxe Telegrams with foreign countries were introduced in 1937. Bombay-Australian Wireless Telegraph Service and Bombay-China Wireless service were inaugurated in 1942. The Bombay, Calcutta and Madras telephone systems were taken over by the ITD in 1943. A Telecommunication Development Board was set up and Bombay-New York Wireless Telegraph Service was commissioned in 1944; Hindi telegram in Devangari script was introduced and 'Own Your Telephone' scheme was inaugurated in 1949.

The year 1950 saw the Indian Telegraph and wings across frontiers. The Indo-Afghanistan Wireless Telegraph Service, Radio Telephone Service between India and Nepal, Wireless Telephone Service between India and Indonesia and Private Priority Telegram were inaugurated. Besides these, "Own Your Telephone Exchange" scheme began to operate in 1950. In the following year, Radio Telephoto Service was started and wireless telegraph links to Thailand, Moscow, Egypt and Iceland were provided. These were followed by wireless telephone link to Iran and Japan and launch of telex service in Bombay. Later, the first coaxial route between Delhi and Agra and the first Subscriber Trunk Dialing (STD) route between Kanpur and Lucknow were commissioned.

In the 60s while the beatles wave was sweeping the world, the Indian telecom think tank was busy in introducing the microwave culture. The 1970s witnessed the installation of SPC Gateway Telex Exchange and introduction of International Subscriber Dialed Telex Service, the introduction of the first Digital Microwave System in Calcutta Junction Network, the setting up of Telecommunications Consultants India Limited and commissioning of the first Optic Fiber System for local junction in Pune.

The 1980s, completely established Indian telecom as the frontrunner. The first satellite earth station for domestic communications was set up at Secundrabad, Troposcatter system Link with USSR was inaugurated, the first SPC Electronic Digital Telex exchange and the first SPC Analog Electronic Trunk Automatic Exchange were commissioned in Bombay. C-DOT was established. The first mobile telephone service and the first radio paging were introduced in Delhi. The MTNL and VSNL were set up and the International Gateway Packet Switch System was commissioned in Bombay. The 1980s also saw the restructuring of the P&T Department into Department of Posts and Department of Telecommunications, the constitution of Telecom Commission and reorganization of at telecommunication circles with the Secondary Switching Areas as the basic units.

During 90s, breathtaking advances and value additions have taken place. The commissioning of I-Net Exchange to Voice Mail Service in Delhi and the announcement of National Telecom Policy to the setting up of Telecom Regulatory Authority of India are the major developments. Introduction of Cellular and WLL Telephone system to the commissioning of Indo-Nepal optical fiber link also took place during the decade.

In October 2000, Department of Telecommunications was corporatised as BSNL, the largest telecom company in India. BSNL rolled out its 'Cell One' Cellular Service in October, 2002. It emerged as the largest basic telephony network and the first largest mobile network operator in its licensed areas, and undisputed Telecom Titan in India.

Before 1990's, Telecommunication services in India were complete government Monopoly — the Department of Telecommunication (DoT). Government also retained the rights for manufacturing of Telecommunication equipments. Early 1990's saw initial attempts to attract private investment. Telecommunication equipment manufacturing was delicensed in the year 1991.

The telecom sector was entirely in the hands of the Central Government in the pre reforms period (prior to 1991). Due to absence of competition, the call charges were quite high. Further, due to paucity of funds, the government could never meet the demand for telephones. In fact, a person seeking a telephone connection had to wait for years before he/she could get a telephone connection. The services provided by the government monopoly were perceived as very poor. 'Wrong billing, telephones lying dead for many days continuously due to slackness on the part of the telecom staff to attend to complaints, cross connections due to faulty / ill maintained telephone lines, obsolete instruments and machinery in the telephone department were the order of the day in the pre reforms era'[4].

Several measures were taken to re-energise this sector during post liberalisation period. Certain measures like financial packages, formation of a telecom export promotion council, creation of integrated facilities for telecom equipment through SEZ and encouraging overseas vendors to set up facilities in India, are required for making India a hub for telecom equipment manufacturing and attract Foreign Direct Investment (FDI). The telecom sector has shown robust growth during 2000-07. It has also undergone a substantial change in terms of mobile versus fixed phones and public versus private participation.

Reforms in Telecom Sector since 1991

The specific measures initiated by the government of India to develop the telecommunication sector in India during the post liberalisation period are listed hereunder :

1991-92

1. The Government of India announced the New Economic Policy on 24th July 1991.
2. Telecom Manufacturing Equipment Production was delicensed in 1991.
3. Automatic foreign collaboration was permitted with 51 per cent equity by the collaborator.

1992-93

Private and Foreign players are allowed to offer on Value added services franchise or licence basis. These included cellular mobile phones, radio paging, electronic mail, voicemail, audiotex services, ideotext services, data services using VSAT's, and video conferencing.

1994-95

1. The Government announced a National Telecom Policy 1994 in September 1994. As per the policy the basic telecom services are opened to private participation including foreign investments.
2. Foreign equity participation up to 49 per cent was allowed in basic telecom services, radio paging and cellular mobile. For value added services the foreign equity capital was fixed at 51 per cent.
3. Eight cellular licensees for four Metros were finalized.

1996-97

1. TRAI was set up as an autonomous body to separate the regulatory functions from policy formulations and operational functions.
2. Coverage of the term "infrastructure" expanded to include telecom to enable the sector to avail of fiscal incentives such as tax holiday and concessional duties.
3. An agreement between Department of Telecommunication (DoT) and financial institutions to facilitate

funding of cellular and basic telecom projects has been arrived.

4. External Commercial Borrowing (ECB) limits on telecom projects made flexible with an increased share from 35 per cent to 50 per cent of total project cost.
5. Internet Policy was finalized.

1998-99

1. FDI up to 49 per cent of total equity, subject to licence, permitted in companies providing Global Mobile Personal Communication (GMPC) by satellite services

1999-00

1. National Telecom Policy 1999 was announced. The policy allowed private operators in multiple fixed services and opened long distance services.
2. TRAI was reconstituted. A clear distinction was made between the recommendatory and regulatory functions of the Authority.
3. DOT/MTNL was permitted to start cellular mobile telephone service.
4. To separate service providing functions from policy and licensing functions, the Department of Telecom Services was set up.
5. A package for migration from fixed licence fee to revenue sharing was offered to existing cellular and basic service providers.
6. The first phase of re-balancing of tariff structure started. STD and ISD charges were reduced on an average by 23 per cent.
7. Voice and data segment was opened to full competition and foreign ownership increased to 100 per cent from 49 per cent previously.

2000-01

1. TRAI Act was amended. The amendment clarified and strengthened the recommendatory power of TRAI, especially with respect to the need and timing of introduction of new service providers, and in terms of licences to a service provider.
2. Department of Telecom Services and Department of Telecom operations were corporatized by creating a new corporate organisation in the name of Bharat Sanchar Nigam Limited.
3. Domestic long distance services opened up without any restriction on the number of operators.
4. Second phase of tariff rationalization started with further reductions in the long distance STD rates by an average of 13 per cent for different distance slabs and ISD rates by 17 per cent.
5. Internet Service Providers were given approval for setting up of International Gateways for Internet using satellite as a medium in March 2000.
6. In August 2000, private players were allowed to set up international gateways via the submarine cable route.

2001-02

1. Communication Convergence Bill, 2001 was introduced in August 2001.
2. Competition was introduced in all service segments. TRAI recommended opening up of market to full competition and introduction of new services in the telecom sector. The licensing terms and conditions for Cellular Mobile were simplified to encourage entry for operators in areas without effective competition.
3. Usage of Voice over Internet Protocol was permitted for international telephony service.

4. The five-year tax holiday and 30 per cent deduction for the next five years available to the telecommunication sector till 31st March 2000 was reintroduced for the units commencing their operations on or before 31st March 2003. These concessions were also extended to internet service providers and broadband networks.
5. Thirteen ISP's were given clearance for commissioning of international gateways for Internet using satellite medium for 29 gateways.
6. Licence conditions for Global Mobile Personal Communications by Satellite finalized in November 2001.
7. National Long Distance Service was opened up for unrestricted entry with the announcement of guidelines for licensing NLD operators. Four companies were issued Letter of Intent (LOI) for National Long Distance Service of which three licences have been signed.
8. The basic services were also opened up for competition. Thirty three Basic Service licences (31 private and one each to MTNL and BSNL) were issued up to 31st December 2001.
9. Four cellular operators, one each in four metros and thirteen private companies were permitted with 17 fresh licences in September/October 2001. The cell phone providers were given freedom to provide, within their area of operation, all types of mobile services equipment, including circuit and/or package switches that meet the relevant International Telecommunication Union (ITU)/Telecom Engineering Centre (TEC) standards.
10. Wireless in Local Loop (WLL) was introduced for providing telephone connection in urban, semi-urban and rural areas.

11. Disinvestment of PSU's in the telecom sector was also undertaken during the year. In February 2002, the disinvestment of VSNL was completed by bringing down the government equity to 26 per cent and the management of the company was transferred to Tata Group, a strategic partner. During the year, HTL was also disinvested.
12. Government allowed CDMA technology to enter the Indian market.
13. Reliance, MTNL and Tata were issued licences to provide the CDMA based services in the country.
14. TRAI recommended deregulating regulatory intervention in cellular tariffs, which meant that operators need no longer have prior approval of the regulator for implementing tariff plans except under certain conditions.

2002-03

1. International long distance business opened for unrestricted entry.
2. Telephony on internet permitted in April 2002.
3. TRAI finalized the System of Accounting Separation (SAS) providing detailed accounting and financial system to be maintained by telecom service providers.

2003-04

1. Unified Access Service Licences regime for basic and cellular services was introduced in October 2003. This regime enabled service providers to offer fixed and mobile services under one licence. Consequently 27 licences out of 31 licences converted to Unified Access Service Licences.
2. Interconnection Usage Charge regime was introduced with the view of providing termination charge for cellular services and enable introduction of Calling Party Pays regime in voice telephony segment.

3. The Telecommunication Interconnection Usage Charges Regulation 2003 was introduced on 29th October 2003 which covered arrangements among service providers for payment of Interconnection usage charges for Telecommunication Services and covered basic service that includes WLL (M) services, Cellular Mobile services, and Long Distance services (STD/ISD) throughout the territory of India.
4. The Universal Service Obligation fund was introduced as a mechanism for transparent cross subsidization of universal access in telecom sector. The fund was to be collected through a 5 per cent levy on the adjusted gross revenue of all telecom operators.
5. Broadcasting was notified as Telecommunication services under Section 2(i) (k) of TRAI Act.

2004-05

1. In budget 2004-05 it is proposed to lift the ceiling from the existing 49 per cent to 74 per cent as an incentive to the cellular operators to fall in line with the new unified licensing norm.
2. 'Last Mile' linkages were permitted in April 2004 within the local area for ISP's for establishing their own last mile to their customers.
3. Indoor use of low power equipments in 2.4 GHz band was de-licensed from August 2004.
4. Broadband Policy was announced on 14th October 2004. In this policy, broadband had been defined as an "always-on" data connection supporting interactive services including internet access with minimum download speed of 256 kbps per subscriber.
5. The Telecommunications (Broadcasting and Cable Services) Interconnection Regulation 2004 was introduced on 10th December 2004.

6. BSNL and MTNL launched broadband services on 14th January 2005.
7. TRAI announced the reduction of Access Deficit Charge (ADC) by 41 per cent on ISD calls and by 61 per cent on STD calls which were applicable from 1st February 2005.

2005-06

1. Budget 2005-2006 cleared a hike in FDI ceiling to 74 per cent from the earlier limit of 49 per cent. Hundred per cent FDI was permitted in the area of telecom equipment manufacturing and provision of IT enabled services.
2. Annual licence fee for National Long Distance (NLD) as well as International Long Distance (ILD) licences was reduced to 6 per cent of Adjusted Gross Revenue (AGR) with effect from 1st January 2006.
3. BSNL and MTNL launched the 'One-India Plan' with effect from 1st March 2006 which enable the customers of BSNL and MTNL to call from one end of India to other at the cost of Rs. 1 per minute, any time of the day to phone.
4. TRAI fixed Ceiling Tariff for International Bandwidth, Ceiling Tariff for higher capacities reduced by about 70 per cent and for lower capacity by 35 per cent.
5. Regulation on Quality of Service of Basic and Cellular Mobile Telephone Services 2005 introduced on 1st July 2005.
6. BSNL announced 33 per cent reduction in call charges for all the countries for international calls.
7. Quality of Service (Code of Practice for Metering and Billing Accuracy) Regulation 2006 was introduced on 21st March 2006.

Telecom Services in Rural India

Rural markets in India constitute a wide and untapped market for many products and services which are being marketed for the urban masses. There is a demand for telecommunication services in these areas. Hitherto, the government was trying to reach the villages through various initiates, but the rural tele-density is very poor and can be improved only through the introduction of modern and suitable technology along with participation from the private operators. According to NCAER Rural Infrastructure Report (2007), the telecommunication services are surging across rural India, as middle class and upper classes are growing in most villages but the tele-density levels are very low at 2.00 per 100 residents compared with the average of 8.59 overall and 25.90 in Indian cities. Table1.1 gives the details of the urban rural divide in telecom services in India.

Table 1.1 Rural Urban Divide in Telecom Services

Particulars	Rural	Urban
Mobile Phones	0.01mn	75.685mn
Fixed lines	13.9mn	36.988mn
Private Operator share	0.01%	53.54%
PCO's	Approx 20 Lakh	Approx 35 Lakh
VPTs	533,000 villages (as of Sept. 2005)	
VPTs Target	Another 53,800 villages (by 2008)	
Total Number of Phones	Approx 14mn	Approx 112mn
Teledensity	Approx 2%	Approx 31%
Teledensity Targets	15% (by 2007)	43%

The characteristics of the rural areas, low population density and spread out population, difficult topographical and climatic conditions make it difficult to provide telecommunication service of acceptable quality by traditional means at affordable prices. The government made an attempt at providing the Telecom Services in rural India. According to the Government of India's Bharat Nirman Initiative 2005-09, every village in the country to be connected by November 2007. The aim is to provide every village in the country with a Village Panchayat Phone (VPTs)[5].

Telecommunication sector has emerged as a springboard of applications with economy-wide ramifications. There are plenty of anecdotal evidence[6] to show that telecom is improving life chances across the strata of the society tiding over the 'divide'. A whole range of information based industry and applications have come up creating new sources of employment and earning with welfare enhancing consequences for the wealthy and the poor. As a meta-technology, ICT has caused rapid innovations to occur in all other areas of material sciences. As a fabric of information society, ICT has improved access in the fields of education, healthcare, governance and all aspects of business services. It has also improved the abilities of the poor to manage risks and mitigate vulnerabilities through provision of timely information.

Vision 2020 is a vision of information society and knowledge economy built on the edifice of ICT. In India, the aggressive expansion of public sector telecommunications infrastructure in hitherto uncharted territories of geographically remote locations would unleash latent economic energies and market forces, which will erode the very foundation of perceived lack of profitability of rural investment among the private investors. Once this is achieved, Vision 2020 will be a vision of wealthier and more equal society full of creativity, innovation and competition. It is important to encourage private sector also for expanding networks to rural areas to promote higher tele-density in rural parts of the country.

Bharat Sanchar Nigam Limited (BSNL) is a 100 per cent Government of India owned Public Sector Undertaking. It is a technology-oriented company and provides all types of telecom services namely telephone services on fixed line, WLL and mobile, Broadband, Internet, leased circuits and long distance telecom services. The company has also been in the forefront of technology with 100 per cent digital new technology switching network. BSNL has one of the largest base of skilled work force of around 3.20 lakh as on March 31, 2007. The company runs the telecom services all over the country except Delhi and Mumbai, wherein MTNL, another public sector company, operates the services. BSNL is the largest telecom service provider in the country.

Taking into consideration the importance of this sector and the contribution of BSNL to the telecom services, this study has been taken up. Further, BSNL is the market leader in fixed line segment and the company is facing many problems in customer retention and growth dimensions of this segment. Therefore, the scope of the study is limited to fixed line services segment of the company. In order to have an in-depth understanding on the theme and the developments, Review Literature has been taken up.

REVIEW OF LITERATURE

The studies relating to marketing of services particularly in the area of Telecom services are very few. The following is the review of select research works in the area.

Roger G. Noll, Scott J. Wallsten[7], in their work on *Universal Telecommunication Services in India'* focussed on telecom reforms in India, the application of Universal Service and impact on telecom in India, telecom pricing and the role of TRAI. Desai Ashok[8] analysed the *'trends in telecom sector in India* and *the problems and challenges*'. Das, Pinaki and PV Srinivasan[9] in their paper on *welfare implication* of *telecom tariff reform*, highlighted specific advantages of promoting communication among underprivileged sections.

G V Chalam[11] in his work on *'Quality of Services in India Telecom Sector: User's Perception – an assessment'*, revealed that the expectations of the telecom users are high among the subscribers of recent times because of their sense of time vs. money value and awareness of their rights. The study concludes that almost 94% of the subscribers are satisfied with the overall quality of services provided by the telecom department. The basic motto of the telecom department is to provide ultimate services to its customer against the present competition from private sector. In this direction, it is doing its best to acquire and retain its new and old customers. This study also deals with growth, working and types of services provided in macro environment.

Kai Nurmenniemi (2005)[11] in his article *'An open market for cellular station'* focussed on the key challenges faced by the cellular operators and other mobile telecommunication service providers. He opined that in the near feature there will be rising cost of the infrastructure to provide sufficient capacity to advance mobile internet services. As next generation networks are deployed and the number of subscribers rising, more and more base stations need to be provided for coverage and capacity that the market demands. Avinish Bansal (2005)[12] in his article *'3 G Rollout in India'* explained about the adoption of 3G technology in India, Global System for Mobile (GSM) communication technology and the Code Division Multiple Access (CDMA) technology. He opined that the licences should be issued to the cellular operators by the TRAI so as to be in the competitive market. Ashish Kumar Chauhan[13] found that the bandwidth availability and penetration has increased manifold but, when it comes to connecting the remotest of villages, wired connectivity is either not available or not up to the mark. In several cases people have used VSAT to provide connectivity to such places. A VSAT link suffers from high latency, expensive equipment, high power requirement and setup is time consuming.

Rajneesh[14] opined based on his work on *Telecom- IT at the core*, that to manage a growing customer base, the operators have to deal with issues of customer network optimization, and increasing cross-holdings amongst exiting customers. Regularity changes have to be brought in to facilitate the service providers to use IT. Most Telecom service providers recognized business intelligence tools as a strategic IT investment and looked for enterprise BI suites that would serve the needs of several different types of users. Entire enterprises software portfolio, including BI, CRM and related applications, made up a market of the size. As far as telecom service providers are concerned, it was imperative to understand the reasons behind consumer churn and prevent it form happening or at least content it.

Dilip Modi[15] identified that the technological trends have enabled cellular players to connect across circles which make for optimal routing calls and pricing the services right. In his opinion, having unified the access side in the first phase, it is also necessary to unify the long distance. This continues the road map for convergence and unification of the defined objectives of our telecom policy. It would lead to competition in the long distance crating benefits also on the access side. Anup Jayaram[16] in his article Worthless or Gutless discussed the disputes between the TRAI and the cellular services providers, regarding the limited mobility issue, Interconnect issues and the problems and solutions regarding the issue.

Eggleston[17] examined how basic telecommunication infrastructure can create a "Digital Provide" by making market efficient through information dissemination to isolated and information deprived locals and improve the living standards of the world's poor, which in turn accelerates the growth.

Gupta[18] estimates that one per cent growth in telecommunication services generates three per cent growth in the economy. He mentioned that increase in purchasing power (Contributed by Increased telecom services) also increase the demand of such services. Chatterjee[19] pointed out that income patterns decide the disposable income levels i.e., purchasing power for telecommunication services and in turn the growth of services. Thujhunwala[20] mentioned that in developed countries 90% of the households can afford monthly expenditure of US $ 30 on telecommunication services, while only 5 to 6% of the households can afford telecommunication services in developing countries such as India.

Jain.P. and Sreedhar, V [21] suggested to improve rural tele-density by reducing the cost of access loop for providing telecom services using technologies, such as wireless local loop. Souter[22] opined that it is also imperative to improve the economic activity of the rural areas using telecommunication related services so that the rural population has enough disposable income to purchase telecom services. Arun Mehtha[23] observed that allowing private parties in telecom sector is killing a goose that if left alone, should soon start to lay golden eggs. D.Chennappa[24]in his study on *Emerging scenario and future convergence of Telecommunications sector in India*, some reflections 'explained about the investment in telecom sector in the five years plans, the fixed line services providers in India with subscriber base, and various developments in telecom sector in India.

Anup Jayaram[26] in his article '*The Hungry Giant*' observed that the BSNL has an ambitious plan to become the biggest mobile operator in the country. BSNL is also planning to reach out to inaccessible areas with CDMA handsets. S.M. Jhaswal[27] in his article '*Telecom growth in India*' has emphasized that the telecom sector is one of the fastest growing sectors of the Indian economy. The achievement in the telecom sector is a result of several policy initiatives taken by the government. The government has taken many proactive measures to facilitate the expansion and growth of the telecom network.

Pranab Sen[28] in his article, *'Telecommunication in India—Iperatives and prospects* examined the role of telecom in the economic reforms process and the steps that have been taken to ensure that this infrastructure is made available to that extent that is required. He opined that while the National Telecom Policy (NTP) is undoubtedly a bold step, it does not go far enough. In particular, the NTP continues to propagate a central decision making approach, at variance with the emerging needs. T. H. Chowdary[29] in his article *'Telecom de-monopolization policy'*, focussed on the de-monopolization of telecom sector. Rajini Gupta[30] states that the telecom liberalization has many regulatory and legal implications.

Anindita Sen Gupta, Sanjeev Kumar Sharma and P. Sudhakar Rao,[31] in their research report on *'strategic management of organizations: a case study of Bharat Sanchar Nigam Limited'* highlighted the importance of strategic management in Bharat Sanchar Nigam Limited. They have made SWOT analysis of the company and identified the key success factors. They suggested, introduction of innovative products based on convergent technology in order to acquire dominant market position, costumer orientation strategy, extensive use of Information Technology, shortening of the purchase – decision cycle, BSNL- MTNL merger, diversification strategy, overhauling the human recourse management strategy, restructuring of organization on business type model, revenue maximization strategies such as implementation of CDR base building, plugging of leakage of revenue, etc for strengthening of BSNL.

Bagachi. P[32] in his paper on *'Telecommunications reform and the state in India: The contradiction of private control and government competition'* focussed on the emerging competitive scenario in India and the critical challenges to public sector organizations.

Subhash Bhatnagar[33] in his paper on *'Enhancing telecom access in Rural India: some options'* presented the current status of Information and Communication Technology (ICT) in rural India, in terms of access to telephony, Internet and other electronic media. Manas Bhattacharya[34], presented a background paper on *'Telecom sector in India-Vision, 2020'*. The author critically reviewed the telecom reforms, competition scenario technological changes, policy changes and other trends in telecom sector. The author opined that once fixed line market is matured, mobile will cross over fixed line market. India is still much below the crossover point even by the standard of the low-income countries. A mobile revolution is in the offing in India. The next points of crossover will be between data and voice, and between mobile and fixed line Internet. This is going to take some time because this is yet to occur even in high-income countries. The process of technical consolidation and system integration of different competing standards in a single platform will by it self take sometime. The process of commercial consolidation will start there after. Telecom will be the springboard of future expansion of IT heralding in an information society. ICT will spread among the masses and will spur innovation, entrepreneurship and growth.

COMMITIEES ON TELECOM SERVICES

Government of India has appointed different committees to study and suggest measures for the development of telecommunications sector in India on referred matters. The key findings and suggestions of the reports of the Athreya Committee, Murthy Committee and D.K.Gupta Committee are presented hereunder.

The Athreya Committee

A high level committee on Re-organization of Telecom Department headed by Dr. M. B. Athreya was constituted in December 1990. The Committee was setup to recommend the most appropriate organizational structure for the management of telecom services in the country. The Committee submitted its report to the Ministry of

Communications in 1991. The Committee recommended the following measures :

- The present duality of structure, i.e. Part – DOT and Part – MTNL should be ended.
- Value added services be thrown open to competition by public or private enterprises, co-operatives etc.
- Small entrepreneurs may be encouraged to installation, cabling closed user networks and subscriber premises work, for greater efficiency and employment generation.
- The "Policy and Regulation" tier should be separate from the "Operations" tier in any future structure.
- There should be greater, real decentralization, delegation, autonomy and flexibility for the field units so that they can be more responsive to consumer requirement and market opportunities.
- Need for professional management in technical and other areas including marketing, home and resource development, material, projects and financial management.
- Need for massive effort to upgrade staff knowledge, skills and attitudes for absorbing new technology and providing better customer service.
- The Telecom Commission should focus more on its regulatory and strategic roles and distance itself from field operations.
- The Telecom Commission should be expanded by edition of three part-time external members to represent consumer, Industry and labour.
- DOT field organizations, including Delhi and Bombay–the areas under MTNL, should be restructured into Six Corporations., India Telecom Operating Corporation as holding company; Four Zonal telecom operating corporations with Headuarters

at Delhi, Bombay, Kolkata and Madras and one long-distance connector corporation.

- All the above Corporations may begin as 100% PSEs. In due course, based on the government policy, part of the equity may be sold to employees, public and financial institutions. Alternate models of corporate structure such as 51% Government majority PSEs, 26% Government controlled PSEs or joint sector may be considered by the Government at appropriate time.

Murthy Committee

DOT has appointed the Murthy Committee in 1993 to work out a blue print of sublicensing private operators invest in expanding the telephone network at the level of SDCA's, the smallest unit of administration with in DOT (DOT,1993).

The Committee recommended private entry with some conditions. It favoured the entry of private operators as sub contractors for DOT Networks and strongly opined that private operators shall not be allowed to compete with DOT. Private operators shall be allowed in areas where DOT could not serve adequately.

D.K. Gupta Committee

In December 1994, the DOT constituted a Committee to study and make recommendations regarding restructuring of the Headquarters of the DOT under the chairmanship of D.K. Gupta. The terms of reference of the Committee inter alia were; Restructuring the administrative, technical and financial set-up at the Headquarters of the DOT in the context of the 1994 National Telecom Policy and the guidelines for the entry of private sector into basic services, and identifying the critical areas which should receive proper focus.

The Committee submitted its report in 1995. The Committee recommended splitting the DOT into three separate entities with the proposed creation of a new market-

–oriented India Telecom and Telecom Regularity Authority of India. India Telecom will be responsible for development, operation and maintenance of telecom services and for providing inter-connections to private operators of the basic and value added services while the telecom commission would be responsible for policy formulation and resource mobilization. An Independent body TRAI, to be set up, would oversee licensing, tariff, etc., to ensure level playing ground to the private operators.

The review of literature drives to the conclusion that there is no research work under taken on marketing of fixed line services and particularly for BSNL. The study, therefore, attempts to fill the literature gap and also suggest measures for the development of the company.

Need for the Study

BSNL is the market leader in fixed line business in the country with 84 per cent market share. The performance of this segment became a cause of concern to the company. The subscriber growth rate is negative for the last few years. The number of fixed line subscribers decreased by 4.36 per cent in 2005-06, 16.84 per cent in 2006-07 and 21.31 per cent in 2007-08 (up to January 2008). The numbers are evident to infer that things are not seem to be hunky dory as far as the fixed line business is concerned. Over the last three years, more than a million fixed line connections were surrendered by subscribers. On the other hand, private fixed line operators like Bharati, Tata Tele services and Reliance Infocom have added close to a million lines. It clearly establishes the fact that BSNL has lost business because many people are opting for a private fixed line connection.

It is true that the one of serious problems of the fixed line segment is the booming mobile market and the preference of the consumers to shift to mobile. The tariffs for mobile connecting have fallen dramatically making it far more accessible for the common man. The perception of fixed line for masses and mobile phone for classes has changed drastically in the recent past. Already, in the US, the growing mobile base has started to change the contours of the telecom market. According to a study by telecom solutions provider CIT-Pri Metrica, the threat posed by the wireless industry is potentially staggering. Nearly half of the US fixed line users are prepared to shift to a shared wireless phone service. But in countries like South Korea, with the advent of broadband services, earnings of the fixed service providers have actually gone up. Not surprisingly, the highest demand for bandwidth in Seoul is at 2.00p.m.when housewives start surfing the Internet on their home PCs. If operators in India play it right, the same could be replicated here[35].

Though BSNL is the major player in the Telecommunication Sector, it is facing severe competition from private sector. The monopoly situation enjoyed over the years and the most favourable market conditions of demand exceeding supply in almost all parts of the country lead the company to become insensitive to the customers specific needs and services. Value added services including customer services became the weakest part of the company against which the competitors are acting seriously to encourage switchovers in their favour. For the growth and development of the company market orientation is imperative. There is a need to re-engineer the service processes in order to cater to the requirements of the market. The company should learn how to offer value added services to the customers effectively than the competitors. The present study is a modest attempt to study the marketing operations of the company and service expectations of the customers in relation to fixed line services. The finding of the study will be useful to the management to identify problems and initiate suitable measures, for further development of the company.

Hypotheses : The study presupposes that managerial problems in marketing are one of the serious problems that stand in the way of progress of BSNL.

Objectives : The specific objectives of the study are:

- To study the market structure and competition scenario of telecom sector in India.
- To analyse the marketing operations of BSNL including product mix, pricing, distribution, internal marketing and external marketing.
- To study the opinion of employees on various internal marketing measures of the company.
- To study the opinion of the consumers on the service expectations and performance.
- To suggest suitable measures wherever necessary for the development of the company.

Methodology

To pursue the above mentioned objectives, data from primary and secondary sources are necessary. The secondary data has been collected from the Central Office of the BSNL, Ministry of Communications, Government of India and other related Offices and Websites.

The primary data has been collected through opinion surveys. Two surveys are conducted – one for employees and the other for fixed line customers of BSNL. Two questionnaires were designed separately, for each survey. Since the universe is large, a sample survey was taken up. A sample of 300 employees and a sample of 450 customers were selected using quota sampling. Personal interviews and telephone interview techniques have been adopted for the purpose of primary data collection.

Area of the Study

Andhra Pradesh State is selected for a detailed study. Two districts from each of the three regions i.e., Andhra, Rayalaseema and Telangana were selected based on the number of landline connections of the company. The districts selected for the study are : (*i*) Visakhapatnam (*ii*) Krishna (*iii*) Chittoor (*iv*) Kurnool (*v*) Hyderabad and (*vi*) Warangal. From each district, 50 employees and 75 customers were interviewed for the purpose of the study. Appropriate statistical techniques were used for tabulation, analysis and interpretation of data.

REFERENCES

1. Vishal Sethi, Telecom Sector in India – Law, Policy and Procedure, JBA publishers New Delhi 2006, p. 1.
2. www.bsnl.comp.1.
3. G.Raghuram, Rekha Jain, and Sebastian Morris. Project Report on Interconnection Issues in Telecom Sector, Indian Institute of Management, Ahmedabad, 24th August, 2001, p. 4.
4. Rakesh Kumar Sharma and R.K. Yadav, Reforms in India Telecom Sector (http/..//www.indianmba.com/Faculty_Column/FC701/fc701.html. dated 11/13/2008)
5. Government of India, Bharat Nirman-2005-09, New Delhi, 2006, p. 3
6. www.indiamba
7. ROGER G. NOLL, SCOTT J. WALLSTEN; Universal Telecommunication Service in India. India Policy Form, 2005-2006.
8. Desai, Ashok 2004. "India Telecommunications" Trends and Portents. "*Working Paper. National Council of Applied Economic Research*, New Delhi.
9. Das, Pinaki and P V Srinivasan. 1999. "Welfare Implications of Telecom Tariff Reform. "Economic and Political Weekly, 34: 672-75.
10. G. V. Chalam: Quality of Services in India Telecom Sector, Users' Perception—An Assessment, *the ICFAI journal of Managerial Economics*, the ICFAI University Press May, 2005.
11. Kai Nurmenniemi, "An Open Market for Cellular Base Station" Electronic for You: Vol. 37, No. 9, September, 2005.
12. *Avinish Bansal " 3G* rollout in India" Electronics for You, Vol. 37, November 2005.
13. Ashish Kumar Chouhan, "Wireless Franchise" *PC Quest*, May, 2005.
14. Rajaneesh DC, "Telecom I.T. at the Core", *Data Quest*, August 15th 2004, Vol. XXII, No. 15, pp. 60-62.

15. Dilip Modi, "Road Blocks Ahead – Inter- Circle Connectivity is threatening a Truly Unified Licensing Regime", *Business India*, August 30, September 12, 2004.
16. Anup Jayaram "Worthless or Gutless", *Business World* Mumbai 3rd February 2003.
17. Eggleston, K. R. Jen Sen, R. Zeckhanser " Information and Communication Technologies, Markets and Economic Development", *Department of Economics Working Paper*, Tufts University, 2002.
18. Gupta N.K, The Business of Telecommunication, Tata McGraw Hill Publishing Co. Ltd. New Delhi, 2000.
19. Chatterjee .S.C.S. Thachenkary and T. L. Katz, Modelling the Economic Impacts of Broad Band Residential Services Computer and Networks and ISDN Systems 30 (14), 1998.
20. Thunjhunwala. A. "Unleashing Telecom and Internet in India", India Telecom Conference, Asia / Pacific Research Centre, Stanford University, March 3rd 2003.
21. Jain P. and Sreedhar. V. "Analysis of Competition and Market structure of Basic Telecommunication Services in India", Communication and Strategies, 52(4),2003.
22. S Souher D: 'The Role of Information and Communication technologies in Democratic Development", *Info Journal of Policy Regulation and Strategy for Telecommunication Information and Media,* 1(15) October, 1999, pp. 405-417.
23. Arun Mehata: "Telecom" Alternative Economic Survey 2000-2001; Alternative Survey Group, New Delhi, 2001.
24. D. Chennappa: 'Emerging Scenario and Future Convergence of telecommunication Sector in India: Some Reflections', *Institute of Public Enterprise*, Vol. 28, January—March, April - June, 2005, No. 1 & 2, Hyderabad, 2005.
25. K. Ashwatappa, Essential of Business Environment, 7th Edition, Himalaya Public house, Mumbai, 2004.
26. Anup Jayaram, "The Hungry Against", *Business World*, Mumbai 20th September, 2004.
27. Dr. S. M Jhawal, Telecom Growth in India – New Institutions, *Employment News*, Vol. XXX, No. 10, 4-10 June, New Delhi, 2005 pp. 1-40.
28. Pranab Sen, Telecommunication in India Imperatives and Prospects, Economic and Political Weekly, Vol. XIX, No. 44, October 29th 1994.

29. T.H.Chowdary, Telecom Demonopolisation Policy or Force? *Economic and Political Weekly*, February 5th, 2000.

30. Rajini Gupta, Telecommunications Liberalization: Critical Role of Legal and Regulatory regime, *Economic and Political Weekly*, April 27th, 2002.

31. http.//sanjeevkumarsharma tripod/strategy_bsnl.html.

32. Bagachi. P. Telecommunication's reform and the State in India: The Contradiction of Private Control and Government Competition, Centre for the Advanced Study of India, University of Pennsyllvania, Philadelphia PA 2000.

33. Subhash Bhatnagar, Enhancing Telecom Access in Rural India: Some Options, *Paper Presented at India Telecom Conference, Asia Pacific Research Centre Standard University*, November, 2000.

34. Manas Bhattacharya, Telecom Sector in India Vision 2020 Background *Paper Submitted to the Committee on India: Vision 2020, India:* Vision 2020, Planning Commission, Govt of India, New Delhi, 2003.

35. Voice and data, 2006-07 New Delhi http:/www.cybermedia.co.in/press/pressrelease48.html.p.6.

TELECOM SECTOR IN INDIA

Indian Telecom Sector has been one of the biggest success stories of market-oriented reform, and India is now amongst[3] the fastest growing telecom markets in the world. Supportive government policies coupled with private sector participation have fuelled the unprecedented expansion of this sector.

A. Growth of Telecommunications

Communication is the fastest growing sector of Indian Economy. The data presented in Table 2.1 shows the share of communication in GDP which was 1.6 per cent in 1999-2000 increased to 4.00 per cent in 2005-2006. The growth of this sector varied between 19.5 per cent and 26.9 per cent and the contribution of this sector to the GDP varied between 7.66 per cent and 19.58 per cent since the turn of this millennium.

Table 2.1 Growth of communication sector

Year	Share of communications in GDP in %	Growth Sector in %
1999-2000	1.6	—
2000-2001	1.9	26.9
2001-2002	2.2	19.5
2002-2003	2.6	25.6
2003-2004	3.1	25.4
2004-2005	3.5	22.8
2005-2006	4.0	23.9

Sources: Central Statistical Organisation (2007), National Accounts Statistics 2007, Ministry of Statistics and programme Implementation, New Delhi.

In India, there are 18.68 million telecom subscribers in 1998 out of which 17.8 million are fixed line subscribers and 0.88 million are mobile subscribers (Table 2.2). In other words, the fixed line subscribers account for 95.29 per cent of the total telecom subscribers in the year. The total number of telecom subscribers increased to 307.86 million in 2007 recording an increase of more than 16 times during the decade. The share of fixed line segment reduced significantly to reach 15.36 per cent in 2007. The mobile segment claimed the dominant share in the growth of telecom sector during the 1998 to 2007. The share of mobile segment increased from less than one per cent to 84.64 per cent during the period.

Table 2.2. Telecom Subscribers in India (in million)

Year	Fixed	Mobile	Total	Growth(%)
1998	17.80	0.88	18.68	25.54
1999	21.59	1.20	22.79	22.00
2000	26.51	1.88	28.39	24.57
2001	32.44	3.58	36.02	26.88
2002	41.48	13.00	54.48	51.25
2003	42.58	33.58	76.16	39.79
2004	45.00	50.00	95.00	24.74
2005	49.00	76.00	125.00	31.58
2006	40.43	149.50	189.93	51.94
2007	47.29	260.57	307.86	62.09

Source: Department of Telecommunications (2006) and Telecommunications Regulatory Authority of India (various issues)

The telecommunication services are provided by both public sector and private sector companies in India in both fixed line and mobile segments. The data shown in Table 2.3 reveals public sector companies are holding 91 per cent of the ownership share in fixed line category leaving only

9 per cent share to the private companies. In the case of wireless segment, private sector dominance is well established with 81 per cent ownership share as compared to 19 per cent ownership share of the public sector.

Table 2.3. Telecommunications Services according to Ownership (as on May 31, 2007)

(In%)

Type of ownership	Wire-line	Wireless
Public	91	19
Private	9	81
Total	**100**	**100**

Source: Annual Report 2006-07, Telecom Regulatory Authority of India, New Delhi.

The subscriber base of the public sector companies which was 17.80 million in 1998 increased to 71.40 million in 2007 recording an increase of 301.12 per cent (Figure 2.1)

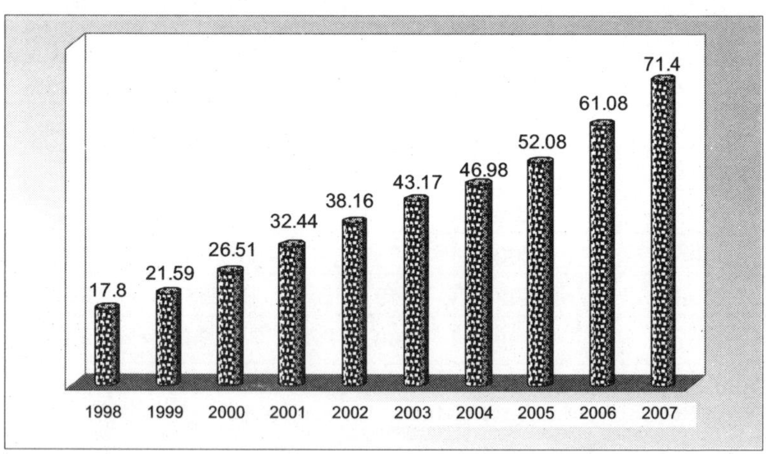

Fig. 2.1. PSU Operators' Subscriber Base during 1998 to 2007 (in millions)

Source: Telecom Regulatory Authority of India Annual Report 2006-07 Government of India 2007, p. 59.

The private sector subscriber base which was 0.88 million in 1998 increased to 134.46 million in 2007 recording a phenomenal growth during the period (Figure 2.2).

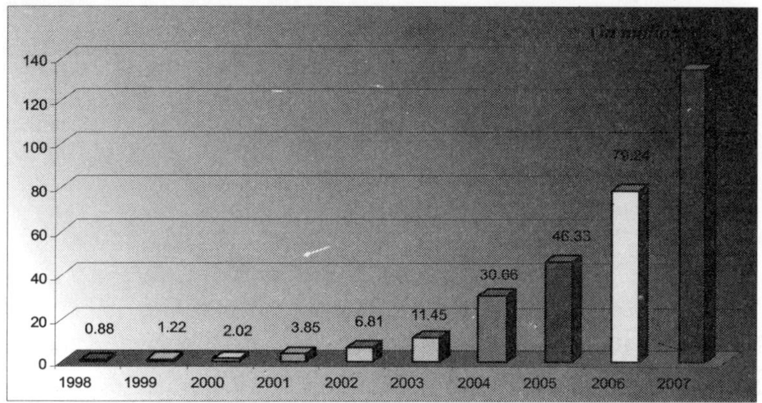

Fig. 2.2. Private Operator's Subscriber Base during 1998 to 2007.

Source: Telecom Regulatory Authority of India Annual Report 2006-07 Government of India 2007 p. 59.

Teledensity

Teledensity, the major indicator of telecom growth in a country, is on the increase year by year during 1997-1998 to 2006-2007. The data shown in Figure 2.3 (see on next page) indicate the growth of teledensity in the country. The teledensity which was 1.90 in 1997-1998 increased to 18.23 in 2006-2007. The Figure further shows the gap between rural and urban teledensity in the country. In urban areas the teledensity has increased from 5.80 to 45.00 during the period. In rural areas the teledensity which was 0.4. in 1997-1998 increased to 2.00 in 2006-2007. In 2006-07 the teledensity in urban areas was 45 where as it was only 2 in rural areas of the country.

B. The Players in Telecom Market

As mentioned already, the telecommunications is presently operated by public sector as well as private sector companies. The public sector companies are:

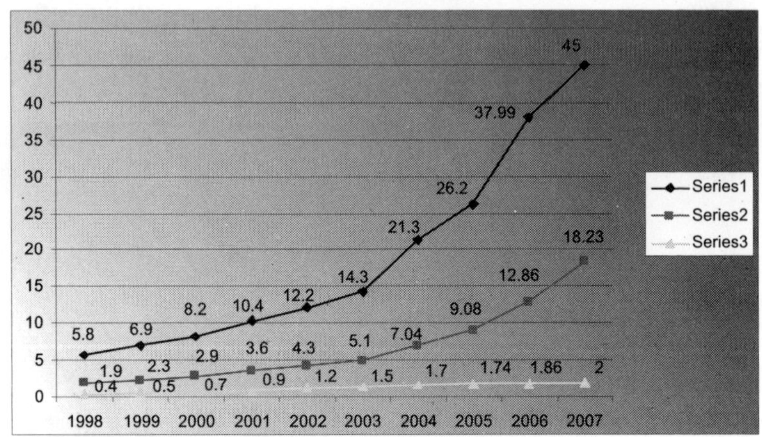

Fig. 2.3. Rural and Urban tele-density during 1998 to 2007

Source: Telecom Regulatory Authority of India Annual Report 2006-07 Government of India 2007 p. 59.

- Bharat Sanachar Nigam Limited (BSNL)
- Maharastra Telecom Nigam Limited (MTNL)

The private sector companies are:

- Bharti Airtel
- Reliance Telecom Limited
- Vodafone
- TATA Teleservices Limited
- Idea Mobile Communication
- Aircel
- Spice Communication
- BPL Mobile
- HPCL Infotel Limited
- Shyam Telelink Limited

The details of Companies operating in fixed line and mobile segments with licenced service areas and number of circles are shone hereunder.

Fixed line

Service providers	Licensed service areas	No. of Circles
BSNL	All India (expect Delhi & Mumbai)	21
MTNL	Delhi, Mumbai	2
Reliance	All India	23
Bharti	All India	23

Source: Service Providers

Mobile Operators

Service Providers	Licensed service areas	No. of Circles
BSNL	All India (expect Delhi & Mumbai)	21
Bharti	All India	23
Reliance	All India	23
Airtel	All India	23
Huch	All India (except MP)	22
Tata Tele-services	All India (except Assam, NE, J&K)	20
IDEA	13 (Delhi, Mumbai, Maharashtra, Gujarat, Andhra Pradesh, Kerala, Haryana, UP-W, UP-E, Rajasthan, Madhya Pradesh, Himachal Pradesh, Bihar)	13
BPL	Mumbai	1
MTNL	Delhi, Mumbai	2
Spce Communi-cations	Karnataka, Punjab	2
HPCL	Punjab	1
Shyam Telelink	Rajasthan,	1

Source: DOT and Service Providers

C. Development of Telecommunication under Five Year Plans

The development of telecommunication of India has been given focus in the successive Five Year Plans. The initiatives during the plan periods are briefly presented in the following paragraphs.

First Five Year Plan: At the beginning of The First Five Year Plan, the telecommunication network in India is very limited. There are only 1.68 lakh telephone connections in 1951. The plan provided for the extension of telecommunication services to many parts of the country. An amount of Rs.50 crores was allotted to increase the local exchange capacity by 0.116 million and to increase the direct exchange lines by 0.053 million. About 1,00,000 telephones have been installed during the plan period. The trunk telephone service was provided by public call offices and trunk exchanges were connected to the trunk network by physical circuits and carrier systems worked on open-wire routes and underground cables.

Second Five Year Plan: The Second Five Year Plan provided an outlay of Rs. 76 crores for post, telegraph and telephone services. However, an amount of Rs. 63 crores was expended during the plan period. The targets set for the plan period were to increase the local exchange capacity by 0.174 million, 0.159 million direct exchange lines and 4.60 lakh telephone connections.[1]

In the Second Five Year Plan, provision has been made for substantial increase in the number of public call offices and trunk exchanges in the country and for the expansion of the net-work of open-wire trunks and carriers. Adequate provision was also made for the laying of long distance underground Trunk cables.

For the rapid development of the telephone service it was found necessary that telephone equipment should be manufactured within the country. The production targets envisaged for the second plan are 40,000 exchange lines and 60,000 telephone instruments per annum. For extending and strengthening contacts with other countries India needed a well-developed system of overseas communications. The objective of overseas Communications Service was to establish direct wireless telegraph, telephone and radio-photo services with all important countries. Before the first plan, India had direct radio services with six countries, namely U.K., U.S.A, Australia, China, Afghanistan and Japan. The plan provides for direct radiotelegraph, radio-telephone and radio-photo circuits with 25 more countries. Further the plan provides for a high-grade privacy system on radio-telephone circuits, special facilities for news transmissions for the press, larger coverage for press broadcasts undertaken for the Ministry of External Affairs and a number of 'leased circuit' channels for the benefit of aviation companies and business houses.[2]

Third Five Year Plan : In the Third Five Year Plan, an allocation of Rs.77.6 crores was provided for communications. A number of development programs were taken up during the plan period. The allocated amount was expended totally to increase local exchange capacity by 0.359 million, direct exchange line by 0.319 million.[3]

Fourth Five Year Plan : An outlay of Rs.520 crores was provided for the development of telecommunication in the Fourth Five Year Plan. The allocation was more than seven times to the Third Five Year Plan provision. During the plan period the local exchange capacity was increased by 0.444 million lines and direct exchange lines increased by 0.430 million.[4]

Fifth Five Year Plan : In the Fifth Five Year Plan, an outlay of Rs.1129.45 crores was provided to enable creation of additional exchange capacity of 8.42 lakh lines. Adequate funds have been set apart for expanding the telegraph system and opening of about 45 Telex exchanges with 10,000 lines capacity. During the plan period 7,70,000 direct exchange lines were added. Besides, 11,970 telegraph offices and 8825 long distance public call offices were opened during the plan.[5]

Sixth Five Year Plan: During the Sixth Five Year Plan, the communication services, particularly the postal and telecommunication services, were extended to all parts of the country with a view to sub-serve a balanced and sustained growth in the key sectors of development. Special attention was given to the development of communication facilities in rural areas including backward, tribal and hilly areas in order to correct the persisting imbalances in the communications net work.

While significant progress in telecommunications has been made, the supply capabilities have not been able to keep pace with growing demand resulting in mounting backlog. The focus of the telecommunication Plan was to reduce the backlog for telephone demand and to relieve the heavy congestion in the network over a ten year time-frame. Technological updating of telecommunication services was also envisaged by way of introducing modern techniques through SPC electronic Local Exchanges, SPC electronic TAXs, SPC Electronic Telexes, Digital Trunk Exchanges, Digital Microwave Systems, Satellite Communication, etc.

The telecommunication Plan envisages an addition of 14 lakh direct exchange connections to the existing 20.14 lakh working connections. About 18,300 telex connections are provided during the Plan period. The requirement of the rural areas including the backward, hilly and tribal areas were met by opening 20,000 long distance public call offices. About 20,000 telegraph offices were established during the Plan period and a large majority of them located in rural areas. A provision of Rs.85 crores has been made in the Plan for the Overseas Communications Service.[6]

Seventh Five Year Plan: In the Seventh Plan, the development of the Communications Sector was characterized by a five-pronged strategy: balanced growth in net-work, rapid modernization, a quantum jump in technology, increased productivity and innovations in organizations and management. The specific objectives of the plan are: to improve or replace worn-out equipment and make a jump in digital electronic and optic fiber; to prescribe precise time frames for the introduction of new services and network expansions; to integrate services with the eventual target of providing Integrated Services Digital Network (ISDN); to advise on application of new technologies in fields of hardware and software in India's future network plans; to extend telecommunication to rural areas; to provide new services to help promote growth in the business and industrial sectors; to provide facilities for training and strengthening of R&D facilities; and to introduce effective telecom organisation and management to be able to operate its systems and plans for the future.

The total outlay for the Department of Telecommunications during the Seventh Plan was Rs. 4530.00 crores. A provision of Rs. 933 crores has been made for long distance transmission systems. A provision of Rs. 606 crores has been made for open wire Telegraphs, Telex, Rural Tele-Communication and Non-Voice services. A provision of Rs. 335 crores has been made for the development programmes of the Indian Telephone Industries. A provision of Rs. 146.55 crores was made for the development schemes of the Overseas Communication Services.

The Seventh Plan of the Department of Telecommunications was principally aimed at reducing the long waiting period for a telephone connection. Therefore, almost 60% of the investment on the telecom services was made on providing additional switching capacity in the local telephone system. Consequently, 16.98 lakh direct exchange lines (DELs) were provided during the Plan against a target of 16 lakh lines. The waiting list, however, did not come down but increased from 8.43 lakhs to 12.87 lakhs. Targets were achieved in most of the other components except in the trunk automatic exchange capacity, telex capacity and optical fibre cables, where substantial shortfalls occurred.[7]

Eighth Five Year Plan: The Eighth Plan of telecommunication services was framed on the long-term objective of a gradual building up of the telephone density to 6/7 telephones for every 100 persons. The waiting period for the telephone connection was very long not only in the metropolitan cities but also in smaller towns which have shown a sharp increase in demand. Hence, the Plan aimed at reducing the waiting period to less than two years in general and also to provide the telephones practically on demand in rural and tribal areas, by installing additional switching capacity of 93 lakh (110 lakh including replacements) lines in order to provide 75 lakh new telephone connections. In addition to the availability of telephones, accessibility, connectivity and reliability have been the primary goals. The target of 110 lakh gross additions of direct exchange lines over a five year period was set.

The two basic thrust areas of the Eighth Plan were rapid expansion of telecom network and its transformation into a modern and efficient system. Provision of an additional 75 lakh Direct Exchange Lines (DELs) and installation of 3.09 lakh Village Public Telephones (VPTs) were among the major targets fixed for the Eighth Plan. With the announcement of the National Telecom Policy in 1994, it was estimated that 100 lakh DELs will be required to be provided during the Eighth Plan to make available telephone on demand by 1997 and cover all the villages by public telephony by March 1997. The private sector was envisaged to play an important role in achieving this objective.

The performance of the Government sector in achieving the targets has been quite encouraging. Against the target of creating an additional net switching capacity of 93 lakh lines, the achievement has been 109.58 lakh lines i.e. 17.8% more than the target. Similarly, in the case of providing new connections, about 87.33 lakh DELs have been provided against the target of 75 lakh DELs, the achievement being about 16.4% more than the target.

Rural connectivity was one of the major objectives of the Eighth Plan. According to the original Plan target, 3.09 lakh villages were to be covered by March 1997. The value-added services witnessed a healthy growth during the Eighth Plan. For Radio Paging and Cellular Mobile Telephone services private operators were given licences through a system of tendering. Licences have also been issued to 36 companies for operation of Public Mobile Radio Trunked Services (PMRTS) in 80 cities. For the operation of E-Mail, Voice/ Audiotex and 64 Kbps CUG domestic Data VSAT service using INSAT satellite system thirteen licences have been issued. These services have become operational on a commercial basis in many areas of the country. Cellular Mobile Telephone Services have started in four metropolitan cities with two operators in each city. In other telecom circles, 33 licences for 18 circles have been issued to 13 companies. Out of 33 licensees, 22 have started their services in more than 50 cities/ towns with a customer base of more than one lakh.

The basic telecom services network has expanded from one lakh connections at the time of independence to 178 lakh Direct Exchange Lines (DELs) in 1998. It has witnessed a consistently high growth of 16-17 per cent per annum during the decade i.e. 1987-97. The growth was further accelerated to more than 20 per cent during the Eighth Plan. During 1997-98, the growth rate was still higher at 22.4 per cent. However, the growth in the waiting list has been equally impressive growing from 12.87 lakh in 1987-88 to 27.06 lakh in 1997-98. During the plan period, the waiting list on the average has been about 26.5 lakh. Viewed in the context of requirement and population size of the country, the rapid expansion seems moderate as reflected in the low telephone density of 1.84 (March, 1998) against the world average of 12.

The telecom sector has witnessed some fundamental structural and institutional reforms. Telecom equipment manufacturing was completely deregulated in 1991. Value added services (including cellular services) were thrown open to private sector participation in 1992. Basic services were opened to private participation in 1994 by dividing the country into 21 Telecom Circles and allowing one private operator per Circle to compete with DOT. An independent Telecom Regulatory Authority of India was set up in 1997. A new Policy for Internet Service Providers (ISPs) was announced in 1998 allowing independent service providers to enter the sector ending the earlier monopoly of VSNL.[8]

Ninth Five Year Plan: The major objectives envisaged for the Ninth Plan are: Universal coverage or telephone on demand; Universal and easy accessibility; World standard services to the consumers at affordable prices; Demand-based provision of existing value-added services and introduction of new services; and Exports of telecom equipment and services as a major thrust area. Thus the focus of the plan was to achieve global competency for the Indian telecom sector.

There is a large element of latent demand, which has led to ever increasing waiting list along with sustained high growth of network expansion and provision of new connections. As on 31.3.1997, the telecom network had 145.33 lakh Direct Exchange Lines (DELs), with a waiting list of 28.87 lakh. The demand at the beginning of the first year of the Ninth Plan is estimated to be 174 lakh DELs. It is projected to grow to 360-380 lakh DELs by the terminal year i.e. 2001-2002 and 818 lakh DELs by 2007. Thus, 186-237 lakh additional DELs would have to be provided by the Government and the private sector during the Ninth Plan to achieve the objective of providing telephone on demand in Ninth Plan and 437 lakh additional DELs during the Tenth Plan. The Department of Telecommunication, including MTNL, is expected to provide 185 lakh new connections and the remaining 52 lakh DELs are envisaged to be the private sector's contribution. Similarly, Govt. sector is envisaged to provide 285 lakh DELs in the Tenth Plan, the private sector expected to contribute the remaining 152 lakh DELs.

Rural connectivity was one of the major thrust areas during the Ninth Plan. Out of about 6 lakh villages, 3.01 lakh villages have been provided with telephone facilities by the end of 31.03.98. The remaining villages would be covered by the year 2002 through the joint efforts of the Department and the private operators.

The other major targets envisaged for the Department of Telecommunication for the Ninth Plan are:

1. One Public Call Office (PCO) for every 500 population in urban areas;
2. Provision of adequate number of PCOs in public institutions like hospitals, shopping centres, educational institutions etc.
3. STD PCO for every 10 kms. on the national highway;
4. STD facility to all exchanges by the year 2000;
5. Digital connectivity to all exchanges upto SDCC level;
6. Packet Switched Public Data Network (PSPDN) to cover all District Headquarters (DHQs).

The Centre for Development of Telematics (C-DOT) is the main public sector agency engaged in the research and development activities in the telecom sector. The focus of its activities is on finding comprehensive solutions appropriate to the telecom network requirements of the country. The C-DOT has been a leader in the development of rural switching systems i.e. Rural Auto Exchanges (RAX). During the Eighth Plan, it has developed low capacity rugged digital switching systems. These are ideal for rural conditions as they are capable of operating in non-air-conditioned environment with simple maintenance procedures and operational back-up. For urban and semi-urban applications, the C-DOT has developed a family of digital switching systems ranging from 1500 lines to 40,000 lines. In the area of transmission, its main achievements have been the development of low capacity digital radio technologies for interconnecting rural and urban exchanges, satellite system for digital multiplexers and optical communication systems. During the Ninth Plan, the C-DOT plans to enhance its 256p RAX, both in technology and in features, so as to make it most contemporary. The major projects envisaged during the Ninth Plan in the area of switching include:

1. Developing a large switch with a capacity of providing connectivity to 1,00,000 subscribers and associated trunks and Busy Hour Call Access (BHCA) of 1.5 million;
2. Providing necessary support functions for deployment of intelligent network services in the field, including service switching functionality in the local exchanges and toll exchanges;
3. Undertaking a project to design and develop Service Control Points (SCP), Service Management Systems (SMS) and Service Creation Environment (SCE) to make service provisioning very fast and to offer services as desired by the customers. The system shall facilitate the service provider to be different from network provider/operator; and
4. Developing ATM technology-based Broad Band ISDN (B-ISDN) family of switching systems.

In the area of transmission, the major projects envisaged during the Ninth Plan include:

1. Undertaking extensive work on optical switching systems relating to Optical Line Terminating Equipment, Synchronous Digital Optical Network and Photonic Amplifiers;
2. Developing personal wireless communication systems based on different technologies;
3. Developing high speed optical network; and
4. Developing high speed satellite systems for cell transportation.

The overall implementation of the programmes in the telecom sector was looked after by the Department of Telecommunications (DOT). This includes overall policy formulation including licensing. DOT would also oversee the overall coordination between private and Govt. sector including the public sector companies. The Telecom Regulatory Authority of India (TRAI) looks after the various functions pertaining to regulation including ensuring compliance of terms and conditions of the licences, protecting interests of consumers, revenue sharing arrangement between operators, disputes between licensor and licensee etc.

During the Ninth Plan period, a record growth rate of telecom services was achieved in the country. The network (equipped capacity) grew at an average rate of about 22 per cent. Growth of both cellular mobile phones and fixed line phones has been equally impressive. While private sector concentrated in cellular mobile phones segment, the growth in the Government sector was primarily due to fixed line connections. Against the target of providing 237 lakh Direct Exchange Lines (DELs), about 240.55 lakh additional DELs have been provided during the Ninth Plan. The cellular network has grown from a small base of 3.40 lakh connections to 64.31 lakh connections by the end of the Plan. As a result of this growth, the tele-density has nearly tripled from 1.57 at the beginning of the Ninth Plan to 4.4 as on March 31, 2002.[9]

Tenth Five Year Plan: The focus of Tenth Plan was to provide world class telecommunication facilities at reasonable rates. Provision of telecom services in rural areas was another thrust area to attain the goal of accelerated economic development and social change. The New Telecom Policy (NTP) announced in 1999 modified the NTP 1994 to take into account the far-reaching technological developments taking place in the telecom sector globally and to implement the Government's resolve to make India a global IT superpower. NTP 1999 also seeks to solve problems arising out of the implementation of NTP 1994.

The Tenth plan policies and programmes were guided by the basic goal of creating a world- class telecom infrastructure in order to meet the requirements of IT based sector and needs of a modernising economy on the least cost basis. Ensuring value for money to the consumers and easy and affordable access to basic telecom services to everyone and everywhere were the other goals to be pursued in Tenth Plan. The major objectives envisaged for the Tenth Five Year Plan are:

1. Affordable and effective communication facilities to all citizens;
2. Provision of universal service to all un-covered areas, including rural areas;
3. Building a modern and efficient telecommunications infrastructure to meet the convergence of telecom, IT and the media;
4. Transformation of the telecommunications Sector to a greater competitive environment providing equal opportunities and level playing field for all the players;
5. Strengthening R&D efforts in the country;
6. Achieving efficiency and transparency in spectrum management; and
7. Protecting the defence and security interests of the country and enabling Indian telecom companies to become truly global players.

An outlay of Rs. 86984.00 crore including the budgetary support of Rs. 1500 crore has been provided for the Telecommunications sector in the Tenth Plan. The telecom sector has shown tremendous growth during the Tenth Plan period. It has also undergone a substantial change in terms of mobile versus fixed phones and public versus private participation. The Tenth Plan had envisaged a teledensity of 9.91 per cent by March 2007. In order to achieve this target, about 65.0 million additional connections were needed to be provided during the Tenth Plan. However, during 2002-07, the total telephone connections increased by 161.86 million as on 31 March 2007, thereby achieving a teledensity of 18.31 per cent by March 2007 and exceeding the Tenth Plan target by 149 per cent. With the opening of the telecom sector to the private operators, their share in the number of subscribers has significantly increased.

Recognizing that the telecom sector is one of the prime movers of the economy, the regulatory and policy initiatives taken by the government during the Tenth Plan have been directed towards establishing a world-class telecommunications infrastructure in the country. This has led to a positive result in the sector and major objectives envisaged in the Tenth Plan were achieved to a great extent. Affordable and effective communication services could be offered as the tariff declined substantially due to intense competition among the operators.

During the Tenth Plan period, the Internet subscribers grew from 3.64 million in 2002-03 to 9.21 million in 2006-07. The broadband subscribers base stood at only 2.28 million connections (2006-07) from 1.8 lakh connections in 2004-05. One of the factors for such a low broadband subscriber base could be the pricing structure.

The number of telephones has increased from 44.97 million as on 31st march 2002 to 206.83 million as on 31st March 2007, exhibiting a CAGR of around 35.68 per cent. The number of mobile phone/wireless subscribers increased from 6.68 million as on 31 march 2002 to 166.05 million as on 31st march 2007, exhibiting a CAGR of 90.15 per cent. The number of Internet subscribers grew at 23 per cent, while the broadband subscribers grew from a meagre 0.18 million during the year 2004-05 to 2.28 million during the year 2006-07.

Teledensity in the country increased steadily from 4.29 per cent in 2002 to 18.31per cent in 2007. However, there is a wide gap between urban teledensity (45 per cent) and rural teledensity (2 per cent). In fact, the rural telephony has not kept pace with the impressive growth in the urban connectivity.

Apart from the 14.77 million fixed and wireless in local loop (WLL) connections provided in the rural areas, 564610 VPTs have also been provided. Thus, 90 per cent of the villages in India have been covered by the VPTs. In addition, more than 2 lakh public call offices (PCOs) are also providing community access in the rural areas. Mobile Gramin Sanchar Sewak Schme- a mobile PCO service – is also being provided at the doorstep of villagers. There are, 2772 GSSs covering 12043 villages. Further, in order to provide internet services, Sanchar Dhabas (Internet kiosks) have been provided in more than 3500 block head quarters out of the total 6337 blocks in the country.

The telecom network in the rural areas also expanded during the Tenth Plan (2002-07). The number of phones in the rural area has increased from 9.01 million in March 2002 to 22.66 million by March 2007. The bulk of the investment in rural telecom has been made by the public sector operator, viz., BSNL. The private operators have provided only 12665 VPTs by the end of March 2006.

Some of the major policy initiatives introduced in the telecom sector during the Tenth Plan period for giving a boost to the sector are as follows:

- National long distance (NLD) service was opened to operator's w.e.f. 13 Augusts 2002.
- National Frequency Allocation Policy 2002 was evolved.
- The monopoly of Videsh Sanchar Nigam Limted (VSNL) in international long distance (ILD) terminated on 31st March 2002.
- National Internet Backbone covering all states has been commissioned.
- Instruction issued to all state Governments to provide expeditious approval for right of way.
- Guidelines for Unified Access Service Licence regime were issued on 11 November 2003.

- Calling Party Pays (CPP) regime was implemented w.e.f. may 20003, under which fixed line telephone users were to pay airtime charges apart from normal charges if the call was made to a cellular phone.
- Indian Telegraph Act was amended for establishment of USOF. Non-Lapsable USOF was created in April 2002.
- Interconnection Usage Charge regime was introduced.
- Several directive/regulatory measures have been issued by TRAI regarding different telecom services, their tariffs, quality and Internet services, which have contributed positively towards the growth of telecommunication sector.
- Internet service provider (ISPs) allowed setting up submarine cable landing stations for international gateways for internet.
- Radio frequency (RF) spectrum management has been modernized and automated to efficiently address dynamic needs of the liberalized user.
- Broadband policy was announced on 14th October 2004.
- ISPs have been permitted to use underground copper cables for establishing last mile linkages.
- FDI ceiling has been raised to 74 per cent for various telecom services.
- The operation of automated spectrum management was commenced in January 2005.
- Access service provider can provide Internet telephony, Internet services, and broadband services. They can use the network of NLD/ILD service.
- Prior experience in telecom sector is no more a prerequisite for grant of telecom service licences.
- Annual licence fee for NLD, ILD, Infrastructure Providers, VSAT Commercial, and ISP has been

reduced to 6 per cent of Adjusted Gross Revenue (AGR) with effect from 1st January 2006.

- Internet Protocol based Virtual Private Network service is permitted to ISPs.
- Delicensing has been done of 2.40-2.4835 GHz Frequency band for indoor and outdoor are and 5.15 – 5.13 GHZ frequency band for indoor use.[10]

Eleventh Five Year Plan : The broad objectives for the telecom sector during the Eleventh Plan period (2007-12) are; to reach a telecom subscriber base of 600 million; to provide 200 million rural telephone connections by 2012, that is to reach a rural teledensity of 25 per cent; to provide telephone connection on demand across the country at an affordable price; to reach a target of 20 million broadband connections and 40 million internet connections by 2010 as envisaged in Broad-band Policy 2004; to provide broadband connection on demand across the country by 2012; to provide Third Generation (3G) services in all cities/towns with more than 1 lakh population; to facilitate introduction of mobile TV; to provide broadband connectivity to every secondary school (SS), health centre, GP on demand in two years; to make India a hub for telecom equipment manufacturing by facilitating establishment of telecom specific SEZs.

Network Expansion and Rural Telephony: The following are the measures taken for the purpose:

- One telephone per three rural households by 2007 (about 50 million rural connections).
- One phone per two rural households by 2010 (about 100 million rural connections).
- 200 million rural connections by 2012 (i.e. a rural teledensity of 25 per cent).
- For rural telephony network expansion the strategies will be to provide individual access: (i) through market forces for viable areas and (ii) USOF for non-viable areas.

- For providing public access in rural areas, USOF will be provided for (*i*) VPTs; and (*ii*) Rural Community Phones (RCPs).
- For rural telephony the infrastructure will be shared at least amongst three service providers.
- To support for development of general telecom infrastructure in rural areas, initially pilot projects would be undertaken for the same.

Broadband Coverage: Broadband coverage for all secondary and higher secondary schools and for all public health care centres is stipulated by 2007.Broadband coverage for all GPs is stipulated by 2010.Linkage is to be provided between block headquarters and nearest exchange for completing state-wide areas networks (SWANs) connectivity.

Manufacturing and R&D: The plan provides for making India a hub for telecom manufacturing by facilitating more and more telecom specific SEZs. It provides platform for export promotion of telephone equipment and services by setting up export promotion Council. It also provides for promoting R&D in key and emerging technologies appropriate for the country as well as in the area of telecom network security.

The DOT has proposed to take up the following programmes/initiatives during the Eleventh Five Year Plan period:

- Identify and make available adequate spectrum for both expansion of network and introduction of new value-added services.
- Setting up of Telecom Testing and Security Certification Centre (TETC).
- Setting up of Centre for Communication Security Research and Monitoring
- Setting up of NGN Laboratory.
- Undersea cabling between Mainland and Andaman& Nicobar (A&N) Islands.

- Modernization of Radio Spectrum Monitoring Capabilities.
- Promote induction of new technologies at Indian.
- Setting up of Telecom Export Promotion Forum/Council for promotion of export of telecom services.

The public sector investment in the telecommunication sector (through BSNL and MNTL) would be mainly funded through IEBR to the tune of Rs. 80753.00 crore at 2006-07 price and Rs. 89581.56 crore at current price (including Rs.337.47 crore at C-DOT as internal resources) over the Eleventh Plan Period. It is assumed that the private investment in this sector will also grow substantially. The total investment in the telecommunication sector during the Eleventh Plan period is projected at about Rs. 2,31,000 crore.

The overall focus of the Eleventh Five Year Plan, in respect of telecom, would be on evolving a strategy for the development of world-class infrastructure for supporting accelerated growth of all sectors, bridging the digital divide, an optimum utilization of spectrum, focus on policy recommendation for promotion of private sector investment including FDI, and to take suitable initiatives for improving the performance of telecom equipment manufacturing sector.

- Availability of local content and applications is an important constituent for overall growth of internet and broadband services. For achieving these goals the major steps are proposed to be undertaken include: (i) facilitation for creation of multimedia and video content in the country; (ii) devising proper incentive for development of regional and local language content; and (iii) thrust to the development of content and application for e-governance, e-education, e-health.
- Effective promotion and diversified use of shared rural broadband infrastructure to provide new opportunities, augment income, promote overall development in the areas of Tele-education, Tele-medicine, and E-governance.

- Online retail in a broadband environment may be promoted. The role of other facilitators such as electricity authorities, Department of IT of various state governments, department of local self-governments, Panchayats, Department of Agriculture, Department of Health and Family Welfare, Department of Education, needs to be properly co-ordinated, so that these department/organization/ agencies can carry forward the advantages of broadband services to users particularly in rural areas.[11]

D. Organisation Setup and Regulatory Mechanism

Department of telecommunication which is popularly known as DOT, is the principal government body that takes care of policy, licensing and co-ordination matters relating to telegrams, telephones, wireless, data, facsimile and telematic services and other like forms of communications.

The DOT takes care of International cooperation in matters connected with telecommunications including matters relating to all international bodies dealing with telecommunications such as International Telecommunication Union (ITU), its Radio Regulation Board (RRB), Radio Communication Sector (ITU-R), Telecommunication Standardization Sector (ITU-T), Development Sector (ITU-D), International Telecommunication Satellite Organization (INTELSAT), International Mobile Satellite Organization (INMARSAT), Asia Pacific Telecommunication (APT). It also looks after the Promotion of standardization, research and development in telecommunications, Promotion of private investment in Telecommunications and financial assistance for the furtherance of research and study in telecommunications technology and for building up adequately trained manpower for telecom programme, including assistance to institutions, assistance to scientific institutions and to universities for advanced scientific study and research; and grant of scholarships to students in educational institutions and other forms of financial aid to individuals including those going abroad for studies in the field of telecommunications.

The department is responsible for the administration of laws with respect of any of the matters specified in Indian Telegraphy Act 1985, The Indian Wireless Telegraphs Act 1933 and The Telecom Regulatory Authority of India Act 1997.[12]

The Department Telecommunications has nine units working for different purposes relating to telecommunications. They include:

PUBLIC SECTOR UNITS

Bharat Sanchar Nigam Limited (BSNL): Bharat Sanchar Nigam Ltd, formed in October, 2000, is World's 7th largest Telecommunications Company providing comprehensive range of telecom services in India: Wireline, CDMA mobile, GSM Mobile, Internet, Broadband, Carrier service, MPLS-VPN, VSAT, VoIP services, IN Services etc. Within a span of five years it has become one of the largest public sector units in India.

BSNL has installed Quality Telecom Network in the country and now focusing on improving it, expanding the network, introducing new telecom services with ICT applications in villages and wining customer's confidence. It has about 47.3 million line basic telephone capacity, 4 million WLL capacity, 20.1 Million GSM Capacity, more than 37382 fixed exchanges, 18000 BTS, 287 Satellite Stations, 480196 Rkm of OFC Cable, 63730 Rkm of Microwave Network connecting 602 Districts, 7330 cities/towns and 5.5 lakh villages by the end of 2007-08 BSNL is a 100 per cent Government of India owned PSU with an authorized capital of Rs. 17,500 crore a paid up capital of Rs. 12,500 crore, a net worth of Rs.80,099 crore (estimated) and a staff strength of about 3.39 lakh.

BSNL is the only service provider, making focussed efforts and planned initiatives to bridge the Rural-Urban Digital

Divide ICT sector. In fact, there is no telecom operator in the country to beat its reach with its wide network giving services in every nook and corner of country and operates across India except Delhi and Mumbai. BSNL serves its customers with its wide bouquet of telecom services.

BSNL is *numero uno* operator of India in all services in its license area. The company offers vide ranging and most transparent tariff schemes designed to suite every customer.[13]

Indian Telephone Industries Limited (ITI): ITI Limited is India's pioneering venture in the field of telecommunications. Born in 1948, this premier PSU has contributed to 50 per cent of the present national telecom network. The objective of the company is to establish leadership in manufacturing and supply of new technology telecom products and also to retain status of top turnkey solution provider.

With state-of-the-art manufacturing facilities spread across six locations and a countrywide network of marketing/ service outlets, the Company offers a complete range of telecom products and total solutions covering the whole spectrum of Switching, Transmission, Access and Subscriber Premises equipment. In tune with the technology trend, it has embarked on manufacture of mobile infrastructure equipment based on GSM (Global System for Mobile) technology. ITI has also acquired the technology for manufacture of broadband infra equipment, NGN (New Generation Network) equipment based on IP technology and SDH (Synchronous Digital Hierarchy) products. The company has a dedicated Network Systems Unit for carrying out installation and commissioning of equipment as well as for undertaking turnkey jobs and providing value-added services. The successful completion of the mammoth strategic communication network ASCON for the Indian Army underlines ITI's ability in standing up to the challenge of enhancing the reach of communication and information seamlessly over diverse media. The Company continues to hold the *numero uno* position as India's top telecom turnkey solutions provider.

ITI joined the league of world class vendors of GSM technology with the inauguration of mobile equipment manufacturing facilities at its Mankapur and Rae Bareli Plants which opened a new era of indigenous mobile equipment production in the country. These two lines will augment the capacity to more than nine million lines for catering to both domestic as well as export markets.

By deploying its rich telecom expertise and vast infrastructure, the Company is consolidating its diversification into ICT (Information and Communication Technologies) space to hone its competitive edge in the convergence market. Network Management Systems, Encryption and Networking Solutions for Internet Connectivity are some of the major initiatives by the Company.[14]

Mahanagar Telephone Nigam Limited (MTNL): MTNL was set up on 1st April, 1986 by the Government of India to upgrade the quality of telecom services, expand the telecom network, and introduce new services and to raise revenue for telecom development needs of India's key metros Delhi and Mumbai. In the past 20 years, the company has taken rapid strides to emerge as India's leading and one of Asia's largest telecom operating companies. Besides having a strong financial base, MTNL has achieved a customer base of 5.92 million by the end of 2006. The company has also been in the forefront of technology induction by converting 100 per cent of its telephone exchange network into the state-of-the-art digital mode. The Government of India currently holds 56.25 per cents take in the company.[15]

Telecommunication Consultants India Limited (TCIL): Telecommunications Consultants India Limited (TCIL) is a leading ISO-9001:2000 certified public sector undertaking. Backed by the vast network of DoT / BSNL/ MTNL, in terms of trained and experienced manpower, research and development and training facilities, TCIL has made rapid strides. TCIL offers total telecom solutions for projects. TCIL works in almost 45 Countries mainly in Middle East Africa, South-East Africa, South-East Asia and Europe. The Organisational Structure is formed with the objectives of providing globally world-class technology and Indian expertise in all fields of Telecommunications and to provide total Quality management and excellence in project execution.[16]

OTHER UNITS

Wireless Planning and Coordination (WPC): This wing of the Ministry of Communications, created in 1952, is the National Radio Regulatory Authority responsible for Frequency Spectrum Management, including licensing and caters for the needs of all wireless users (Government and Private) in the country. It exercises the statutory functions of the Central Government and issues licences to establish, maintain and operate wireless stations. WPC is divided into major sections like Licensing and Regulation (LR), New Technology Group (NTG) and Standing Advisory Committee on Radio Frequency Allocation (SACFA). SACFA makes recommendations on major frequency allocation issues, formulation of the frequency allocation plan, making recommendations on the various issues related to International Telecom Union (ITU), to sort out problems referred to the committee by various wireless users, Sitting clearance of all wireless installations in the country etc.[17]

Telecommunication Engineering Centre (TEC): This is a technical body representing the interest of Department of Telecom, Government of India. It specifies common standards with regard to Telecom network equipment, services and interoperability. The TEC issues interface approvals and service approvals, formulates of standards and fundamental technical plans, interact with multilateral agencies like APT, ESTI and ITU etc. for standardization. The centre develops expertise to imbibe the latest technologies and results of R&D, Provides technical support to DOT and technical advice to TRAI and TDSAT, and Coordinates with C-DOT on the technological developments in the telecom sector for policy planning by DOT.[18]

Controller of Communication Accounts (CCA): The offices of CCA (DoT Cells) were created on 01.10.2000 due to the corporatisation of the Department of Telecom Operation and the Department of Telecom Services. These units were created, co-terminus to the territorial/ancillary telecom circle headquarters to ensure government presence for settlement of retirement/pensionary benefits like; pension, commutation of pension, DCRG etc. of the BSNL employees. With the expansion of the range of functions delegated to these DoT Cells, beyond the mere settlement of pension and terminal benefits, the nomenclature of the DoT Cells was changed to the office of Controller of Communications Accounts. There are 26 CCA offices located across the length and breadth of the country. The function performed by CCA office include statutory function, revenue function (collection of spectrum charges and disbursement of USO fund of India) and administrative function.[19]

Telecom Enforcement, Resource and Monitoring (TERM) Cells: With the increasing number of telecom operators in the country, the Government felt the need for presence of Telegraph Authority in the field at all the Licence Service Areas and Large Telecom Districts of the country, in order to ensure that service providers adhere to the licence conditions and for taking care of telecom network security issues. With the growth of private telecom and internet services, an increase in illegal/clandestine telecom operations was also observed. To address these issues, the Government created initially four Vigilance Telecom Monitoring cells (VTM) in Nov.2004 at Delhi, Mumbai, Hyderabad and Chennai. Nine more VTM Cells were created during the 2006 for the circles of Punjab, Rajasthan, Gujarat, Kerala, Karnataka, Maharashtra, Tamil Nadu, West Bengal and UP (E) and fifteen VTM Cells were subsequently added in Jan

2007 for Andhra Pradesh, Bihar, Madhya Pradesh, Haryana, UP (West), Andaman & Nicobar, Assam, Chhattisgarh, Jammu and Kashmir, Jharkhand, Himachal Pradesh, North East-I, North East-II, Orissa and Uttaranchal. Six more VTM Cells were added in March, 2007 for Kolkata, Ahmedabad, Bangalore, Pune, Jaipur and Lucknow, taking the total number of VTM Cells to 34. Since formation of Vigilance and Telecom Monitoring (VTM) Cells in the DOT, the role and functions of VTM Cells have increased manifold. With a view to reflect the entire gamut of functions assigned to the Cells and to distinguish their role *vis-à-vis* staff-vigilance activities, the name of VTM Cells has been changed to Telecom Enforcement, Resource and Monitoring (TERM) Cells in August 2008. The key functions of VTM cells are vigilance, monitoring and security functions.

Vigilance Functions: The vigilance functions include Inspection of premises of Telecom and Internet Service Providers, Curbing illegal activities in telecom services, control over clandestine / illegal operation of telecom networks by vested interests having no license, to file FIR against culprits, pursue the cases, issue notices indicating violation of conditions of various Acts in force from time to time, analysis of call/subscription/traffic data of various licensees, technical arrangement for the lawful interception/monitoring of all communications passing through the licensee's network, to ascertain that the licensee is providing the services within permitted area, and co-ordination with all service providers.

Monitoring Functions: Monitoring functions include such activities as coordination with various network operators, Monitoring of network parameters, checking of the compliance by the licensee in respect of the licence conditions and any directions issued by the licensor in public interest, to ensure optimum call completion ratio of inter operator calls, matters related to national security, disaster management taking over of network in the events of natural calamities or the other emergency situations, grievance redresses of subscribers in respect of deficiency by various operators, customer document verification with the objective to ascertain whether the mobile service operators are following the DoT guidelines for Customer verification before providing connections, and perform such other functions as may be entrusted to it from time to time by the DOT in overall interest of the country and consumers.

Security Functions: These functions include technical interface between security agencies and telecom service providers, service testing of various licensed service providers in the licence area and checking roll-out obligation as per licence condition, registration of OSPs and telemarketers in licence service areas[20].

Center for Development of Telematics (C-Dot): This center is the telecom technology development centre of the Government of India. It was established in 1984 as an autonomous body. It was vested with full authority and total flexibility to develop state-of-the-art telecommunication technology to meet the needs of the Indian telecommunication network. The key objective was to build a centre for excellence in the are a of telecom technology. While the initial mandate of C-DOT was to design and develop digital exchanges and facilitate their large scale manufacture by the Indian industry, the development of transmission equipment was also added to its scope of work in 1989. The center works on telecom technology products and services; provides solutions for current and future requirements of telecommunication and converged networks including those required for rural applications; provides market orientation to R&D activities and sustain C-DOT as a centre of excellence; builds partnerships and joint alliances with industry, solution providers, Telcos and other development organisations to offer cost effective solutions; builds partnerships and joint alliances with industry, solution providers, Telcos and other development organisations to offer cost effective solutions.[21]

Telecom Commission: The Telecom Commission was set up by the Government of India in 1989 with administrative and financial powers of the Government of India to deal with various aspects of Telecommunications. The Commission consists of a Chairman, four full time members, who are ex-officio Secretary to the Government of India in the Department of Telecommunications and four part time members who are the Secretaries to the Government of India of the concerned departments.

The Telecom Commission and the Department of Telecommunications are responsible for policy formulation, licensing, wireless spectrum management, administrative monitoring of PSUs, research and development and standardization/validation of equipment etc. The multi-pronged strategies followed by the Telecom Commission have not only transformed the very structure of this sector but have motivated all the partners to contribute in accelerating the growth of the sector.

Telecom Regulatory Authority of India (TRAI)

The TRAI came into existence as per the provisions of TRAI Act 1997. TRAI is responsible to make recommendations, either suo-motu or on a request from the licensor (Central Government or telecom authority), on the following matters, namely:

- Need and timing for introduction of new service provider;
- Terms and conditions of license to a service provider;
- Revocation of licence for non-compliance of terms and conditions of licence;
- Measures to facilitate competition and promote efficiency in the operation of telecommunication services so as to facilitate growth in such services;
- Technological improvements in the services provided by the service providers;
- Type of equipment to be used by the service providers after inspection of equipment used in the network;

- Measures for the development of telecommunication technology and any other matter relatable to telecommunication industry in general; and
- Efficient management of available spectrum.

The Functions of TRAI are as following

- Ensure compliance of terms and conditions of licence;
- Notwithstanding anything contained in the terms and conditions of the licence granted before the commencement of the telecom regulatory authority (amendment) Ordinance, 2000, fix the terms and conditions of inter-connectivity between the service providers;
- Ensure technical compatibility and effective inter-connection between different service providers;
- Regulate arrangement amongst service providers of sharing their revenue derived from providing telecommunication services;
- Lay down the standards of quality of service to be provided by the service providers and ensure the quality of service and conduct the periodical survey of such service provided by the service provider so as to protect interest of the consumers of telecommunication services;
- Lay down and ensure the time period for providing local and long distance circuits of telecommunication between different service providers;
- Maintain register of interconnect agreements and of all such other matters as may be provided in the regulations;
- Keep register maintained under clause (viii) open for inspection to any member of public on payment of such fee and compliance of such other requirement as may be provided in the regulations;

- Ensure effective compliance of universal service obligations;
- Levy fees and other charges at such rates and in respect of such services as may be determined by regulations;
- Perform such other functions including such administrative and financial functions as may be entrusted to it by the Central Government or as may be necessary to carry out the provisions of this Act:

The mission to of the TRAI is to create and nurture conditions for the growth of telecommunications including broadcasting and cable services in the country. The prime objective is to keep the pace of development to enable India to play a leading role in the emerging global information society. TRAI is carrying activities with goals and objectives focussed towards providing a regulatory regime that facilitates achievement of the objectives of the New Telecom Policy (NTP) 1999. The goals and objectives of TRAI are as follows:

- Increasing teledensity and access to telecommunications in the country at affordable prices;
- Making available telecommunication services which in terms of range, price and quality are comparable to the best in the world;
- Providing a fair and transparent policy environment which promotes a level playing field and facilitates fair competition;
- Establishing an interconnection regime that allows fair, transparent, prompt and equitable interconnection;
- Re-balancing tariffs so that the objectives of affordability and operator viability are met in a consistent manner;
- Protecting the interest of consumers and addressing general consumer concerns relating to availability, pricing and quality of service and other matters;

- Monitoring the quality of service provided by the various operators;
- Providing a mechanism for funding of net cost areas/ public telephones so that Universal Service Obligations are discharged by telecom operators for spread of telecom facilities in remote and rural areas;
- Preparing the grounds for smooth transition to an era of convergence of services and technologies;
- Promoting the growth of coverage of radio in India through commercial and non-commercial channels;
- Increasing consumer choice in reception of TV channels and choosing the operator who would provide television and other related services;

TRAI is mandated to lay down the parameters of quality of service to be provided by the various service providers and to ensure the quality of service. Accordingly, in July, 2000, TRAI had issued a Regulation on Quality of Service for Basic and Cellular Services. In this regulation, TRAI had prescribed the QoS parameters to be achieved.

TRAI reviewed the quality of service parameters and a revised Regulation on Quality of Service for Basic and Cellular Mobile Services was introduced in 2005. Through this regulation, TRAI has prescribed some new parameters for extensive monitoring of the cellular mobile network conditions and also to monitor responsiveness of the customer help lines of all operators. The Regulation includes network related parameters and also parameters on customer perception of service to be assessed through customer satisfaction survey. The Authority also decided that the parameters for basic service using wireless should be the same as that of cellular mobile service. TRAI has notified a Regulation on Quality of Service of Dial-up and Leased Line Internet Access Service in 2001 fixing benchmarks for Internet Dial-up Access. ISPs are required to comply with the benchmarks as per this regulation.

TRAI holds half yearly meetings with the registered consumer organizations for better understanding of the problems of consumers across the country, as provided in the Regulation. TRAI also invites consumers to seminars, workshops and conferences on telecommunication issues to acquaint the consumer organizations about various developments in the telecom sector. Such exposures help them build their capacity and develop consumer advocacy skills. One important development resulting from the various consultations TRAI had with the NGOs/Consumer Advocacy Groups and telecom service providers, was finalization of a common charter for adoption by all Telecom service providers. The common charter is a written voluntary declaration by the service providers about the various dimensions of service. It is an open invitation to the consumers to demand quality of service. The charter would be reviewed and upgraded at regular intervals to match the changing expectations of the consumers.

TRAI had issued the Quality of Service (Code of Practice for Metering and Billing Accuracy) Regulation 2006 to (i) bring uniformity and transparency in the procedures being followed by service providers with regard to metering and billing; (ii) prescribe standards relating to accuracy of measurement, reliability of billing; (iii) measure the accuracy of billing provided by the Service Providers from time to time and to compare them with the norms so as to assess the level of performance; (iv) minimize the incidences of billing complaints; and (v) to protect the interest of consumers of telecommunication services. The regulation mandates the service providers to arrange audit of their metering and billing system on an annual basis through any one of the auditors notified by TRAI and to furnish to TRAI an audit certificate thereof not later than 30th June of every year. The regulation also provides that the service providers have to take corrective action on the inadequacies, if any, pointed out by the auditing agency in the certificate and to file with TRAI an Action Taken Report thereon not later than 30th

September of every financial year. The authority notified the panel of auditors to take-up the auditing process.[22]

E. National Telecom Policy 1994

The focus of the Telecom Policy 1994 was *telecommunication for all and telecommunication within the reach of all.* This means ensuring the availability of telephone on demand as early as possible. Another objective was to achieve universal service covering all villages as early as possible and provision of access to all people for certain basic telecom services at affordable and reasonable prices. The quality of telecom services should be of world standard. Removal of consumer complaints, dispute resolution and public interface was received special attention.

The policy set certain targets of performance in Telecommunications. They include:

- Telephone should be available on demand by 1997.
- All villages should be covered by 1997.
- In the urban areas a PCO should be provided for every 500 persons by 1997.
- All value-added services available internationally should be introduced in India to raise the telecom services in India to international standard well within the VIII Plan period, preferably by 1996.

Additional resources are provided for meeting the targets over and above the provisions made under VIII plan with the objective of meeting the telecom needs of the country, the sector of manufacture of telecom equipment has been progressively relicensed. Substantial capacity has already been created for the manufacture of the necessary hardware within the country.

In order to achieve standards comparable to the international facilities, the sub-sector of value-added services was opened up to private investment in July 1992 for the following services:

- Electronic Mail
- Voice Mail
- Data Services
- Audio Text Services
- Video Text Services
- Video Conferencing
- Radio Paging
- Cellular Mobile Telephone

With a view to supplement the effort of the Department of Telecommunications in providing telecommunication services to the people, companies registered in India were allowed to participate in the expansion of the telecommunication network in the area of basic telephone services also. These companies were required to maintain a balance in their coverage between urban and rural areas. Their condition of operation includes agreed tariff and revenue sharing arrangements.

Implementation of NTP 1994

In order to implement the above policy, suitable arrangements have been made (a) to protect and promote the interests of the consumers and (b) to ensure fair competition. As against the NTP 1994 target of provision of 1 PCO per 500 urban population and coverage of all 6 lac villages, DoT has achieved an urban PCO penetration of 1 PCO per 522 and has been able to provide telephone coverage to only 3.1 lakh villages. As regards provision of total telephone lines in the country, DoT has provided 8.73 million telephone lines against the eighth plan target of 7.5 million lines.

NTP 1994 recognized that the required resources for achieving these targets would not be available only out of Government sources and concluded that private investment and involvement of the private sector was required to bridge the resource gap. The Government invited private sector participation in a phased manner from the early nineties, initially for value added services such as Paging Services and Cellular Mobile Telephone Services (CMTS) and thereafter for Fixed Telephone Services (FTS). After a competitive bidding process, licenses were awarded to 8 CMTS operators in the four metros, 14 CMTS operators in 18 state circles, 6 BTS operators in 6 state circles and to paging operators in 27 cities and 18 state circles. VSAT services were liberalised for providing data services to closed user groups. Licences were issued to 14 operators in the private sector out of which only nine licencees are operational. The Government has announced the policy for Internet Service Provision (ISP) by private operators and has commenced licensing of the same. The Government has also announced opening up of Global Mobile Personal Communications by Satellite (GMPCS) and has issued one provisional license. Issue of licenses to other prospective GMPCS operators was also considered.

The Government recognised that the result of the privatisation has not been entirely satisfactory. While there has been a rapid rollout of cellular mobile networks in the metros and states with currently over one million subscribers, most of the projects are facing problems. The main reason, according to the cellular and basic operators, has been the fact that the actual revenues realised by these projects have been far short of the projections and the operators are unable to arrange financing for their projects and therefore unable to complete their projects. Basic telecom services by private operators have only just commenced in a limited way in two of the six circles where licenses were awarded. As a result, some of the targets as envisaged in the objectives of the NTP 1994 have remained unfulfilled. The private sector entry has been slower than what was envisaged in the NTP 1994.

The government views the above developments with concern as it would adversely affect the further development of the sector and recognises the need to take a fresh look at the policy framework for this sector[23]. Accordingly, the government has announced New Telecom Policy in 1999.

F. New Telecom Policy 1999

The Government of India (Government) recognizes that provision of world class telecommunications infrastructure and information is the key to rapid economic and social development of the country. It is critical not only for the development of the Information Technology industry, but also has widespread ramifications on the entire economy of the country. It is also anticipated that going forward, a major part of the GDP of the country would be contributed by this sector.

In addition to some of the objectives of NTP 1994 not being fulfilled, there have also been far reaching developments in the telecom, IT, consumer electronics and media industries world-wide. Convergence of both markets and technologies is a reality that is forcing realignment of the industry. At one level, telephone and broadcasting industries are entering each other's markets, while at another level, technology is blurring the difference between different conduit systems such as wireline and wireless. As in the case of most countries, separate licences have been issued in our country for basic, cellular, ISP, satellite and cable TV operators each with separate industry structure, terms of entry and varying requirement to create infrastructure. However, this convergence allows operators to use their facilities to deliver some services reserved for other operators, necessitating a relook into the existing policy framework. The new telecom policy framework is also required to facilitate India's vision of becoming an IT superpower and develop a world class telecom infrastructure in the country.

The Objectives of the NTP 1999 :

The following are the objectives of the New Telecom Policy 1999.

- Access to telecommunications is of utmost importance for achievement of the country's social and economic goals. Availability of affordable and effective communications for the citizens is at the core of the vision and goal of the telecom policy.

- Strive to provide a balance between the provision of universal service to all uncovered areas, including the rural areas, and the provision of high- level services capable of meeting the needs of the country's economy;
- Encourage development of telecommunication facilities in remote, hilly and tribal areas of the country;
- Create a modern and efficient telecommunications infrastructure taking into account the convergence of IT, media, telecom and consumer electronics and thereby propel India into becoming an IT superpower;
- Convert PCO's, wherever justified, into Public Teleinfo centres having multimedia capability like ISDN services, remote database access, government and community information systems etc.;
- Transform in a time bound manner, the telecommunications sector to a greater competitive environment in both urban and rural areas providing equal opportunities and level playing field for all players;
- Strengthen research and development efforts in the country and provide an impetus to build world-class manufacturing capabilities;
- Achieve efficiency and transparency in spectrum management;
- Protect the defence and security interests of the country;
- Enable Indian Telecom Companies to become truly global players.

Specific Targets of NTP 1999

In line with the above objectives, the specific targets that the NTP 1999 seeks to achieve would be:

- Make available telephone on demand by the year 2002 and sustain it thereafter so as to achieve a teledensity of 7 by the year 2005 and 15 by the year 2010.
- Encourage development of telecom in rural areas making it more affordable by suitable tariff structure and making rural communication mandatory for all fixed service providers.
- Increase rural teledensity from the current level of 0.4 to 4 by the year 2010 and provide reliable transmission media in all rural areas.
- Achieve telecom coverage of all villages in the country and provide reliable media to all exchanges by the year 2002.
- Provide Internet access to all district head quarters by the year 2000.
- Provide high speed data and multimedia capability using technologies including ISDN to all towns with a population greater than 2 lakh by the year 2002.

New Policy Framework

The New Policy Framework must focus on creating an environment, which enables continued attraction of investment in the sector and allows creation of communication infrastructure by leveraging on technological development. Towards this end, the New Policy Framework would look at the telecom service sector as:

- Cellular mobile service providers, and Cable Service Providers, collectively referred to as 'Access Providers'
- Radio Paging Service Providers
- Public Mobile Radio Trunking Service Providers
- National Long Distance Operators
- International Long Distance Operators
- Other Service Providers

- Global Mobile Personal Communication by Satellite (GMPCS) Service Providers
- V-SAT based Service Providers

Restructuring of DoT

World-wide, the incumbent, usually the Government owned operator plays a major role in the development of the telecom sector. In India, DoT is responsible for the impressive growth in number of lines from 58.1 lakh on April 1, 1992 to 191 lakh in December 1998, showing a CAGR of 20 per cent. DoT is expected to continue to play an important, and indeed, dominant role in the development of the sector. Currently, the licensing, policy making and the service provision functions are under a single authority. The Government has decided to separate the policy and licensing functions of DoT from the service provision functions as a precursor to corporatisation. The corporatisation of DoT shall be done keeping in mind the interests of all stakeholders by the year 2001.

All the future relationship (competition, resource raising etc.) of MTNL / VSNL with the corporatized DoT would be based on best commercial principles.

The synergy of MTNL, VSNL and the corporatized DoT would be utilised to open up new vistas for operations in other countries.

Spectrum Management

With the proliferation of new technologies and the growing demand for telecommunication services, the demand on spectrum has increased manifold. It is, therefore, essential that spectrum be utilized efficiently, economically, rationally and optimally. There is a need for a transparent process of allocation of frequency spectrum for use by a service and making it available to various users under specific conditions.

The National Frequency Allocation Plan (NFAP) was last established in 1981, and has been modified from time to time since. With the proliferation of new technologies it is essential to revise the NFAP in its entirety so that it could become the basis for development, manufacturing and spectrum utilization activities in the country amongst all users. The NFAP is reviewed and the revised NFAP-2000 was be made public, detailing information regarding allocation of frequency bands for various services, without including security information. NFAP shall be reviewed no later than every two years and shall be in line with radio regulations of International Telecommunication Union.

Relocation of Existing Spectrum and Compensation

Considering the growing need of spectrum for communication services, there is a need to make adequate spectrum available. Appropriate frequency bands have historically been assigned to defence and others and efforts would be made towards relocating them so as to have optimal utilisation of spectrum. Compensation for relocation may be provided out of spectrum fee and revenue share levied by Government. There is a need to review the spectrum allocations in a planned manner so that required frequency bands are available to the service providers.

There is a need to have a transparent process of allocation of frequency spectrum which is effective and efficient. This would be examined further in the light of ITU guidelines. For the present, the following course of action shall be adopted to make the process transparent and efficient.

- Spectrum usage fee shall be charged.
- Setting up an empowered Inter-Ministerial Group to be called as Wireless Planning Coordination Committee (WPCC) as part of the Ministry of Communications for periodical review of spectrum availability and broad allocation policy.
- Massive computerisation in the WPC Wing will be started during the next three months' time so as to achieve the objective of making all operations completely computerised by the end of year 2000.

Universal Service Obligation (USO)

The Government is committed to provide access to all people for basic telecom services at affordable and reasonable prices. The Government seeks to achieve the following universal service objectives:

- Provide voice and low speed data service to the balance 2.9 lakh uncovered villages in the country by the year 2002.
- Achieve Internet access to all district head quarters by the year 2000.
- Achieve telephone on demand in urban and rural areas by 2002.

The resources for meeting the USO would be raised through a 'universal access levy' which would be a percentage of the revenue earned by all the operators under various licences. The percentage of revenue share towards universal access levy would be decided by the Government in consultation with TRAI. The implementation of the USO obligation for rural / remote areas would be undertaken by all fixed service providers who shall be reimbursed from the funds from the universal access levy. Other service providers shall also be encouraged to participate in USO provision subject to technical feasibility and shall be reimbursed from the funds from the universal access levy.

Role of Regulator

The Telecom Regulatory Authority of India (TRAI) was formed in January 1997 with a view to provide an effective regulatory framework and adequate safeguards to ensure fair competition and protection of consumer interests. The Government is committed to a strong and independent regulator with comprehensive powers and clear authority to effectively perform its functions.

Towards this objective the following approach will be adopted:

- Section 13 of the TRAI Act gives adequate powers to TRAI to issue directions to service providers. Further, under Section 14 of the Act, the TRAI has full adjudicatory powers to resolve disputes between service providers. To ensure a level playing field, it will be clarified that the TRAI has the powers to issue directions under Section 13 to Government (in its role as service provider) and further to adjudicate under Section 14 of the Act, all disputes arising between Government (in its role as service provider) and any other service provider.
- TRAI will be assigned the arbitration function for resolution of disputes between Government (in its role as licensor) and any licensee.
- The Government will invariably seek TRAI's recommendations on the number and timing of new licences before taking decision on issue of new licences in future.
- The functions of licensor and policy maker would continue to be discharged by Government in its sovereign capacity. In respect of functions where TRAI has been assigned a recommendatory role, it would not be statutorily mandatory for Government to seek TRAI's recommendations.

Standardisation

To enable the establishment of an integrated telecommunication network, common standards with regard to equipment and services would be specified by the Telecom Engineering Centre (TEC). TEC would also continue to grant interconnect and interface approvals for various service providers.

Telecom Equipment Manufacture

With a view to promoting indigenous telecom equipment manufacture for both domestic use and export, the Government would provide the necessary support and encouragement to the sector, including suitable incentives to the service providers utilising indigenous equipment.

Human Resource Development and Training

Human resources are considered more vital than physical resources. Emphasis would be placed on the development of human resources for all fields related to telecommunications and the dispersal of this expertise to the related fields. Such expertise shall also be made available to other countries.

Telecom Research and Development

Recognising that telecommunications is a prime pre-requisite for the development of other technologies, telecommunications research and development (R&D) activities would be encouraged. Government would take steps to ensure that the industry invests adequately in R&D for service provision as well as manufacturing. Indigenous R&D would be actively encouraged with a view to accelerate local industrial growth and hasten transfer of technology. Premier technical institutions would be encouraged to undertake R&D activities on a contribution basis by the telecom service providers and manufacturers so as to develop multi-dimensional R&D activities in telecommunications and information technology.

Disaster Management

International co-operation in the use of terrestrial and satellite telecommunications technologies in the prediction, monitoring and early warning of disasters, especially in the early dissemination of information would be encouraged. Financial commitment to disaster management telephony and the development of appropriate regulatory framework for unhindered use of trans-boundary telecommunications would be put in place.

Remote Area Telephony

Rural Telephony, areas of North East, Jammu and Kashmir and other hilly areas, tribal blocks, etc. may be identified as special thrust areas for accelerated development of telecommunica-tions. The Ministry of Defence shall be assigned a more active role in the development of telecommunications in such remote areas as are identified for accelerated development of telecommunications.

Export of Telecom Equipment and Services

Export of telecom equipment and services would be actively incentivised. Synergies among the various telecom players (manufacturers and service providers would be exploited and used to provide integrated solutions for exports.

Right of Way

Government recognises that expeditious approvals for right-of-way clearances to all service providers are critical for timely implementation of telecom networks. The Central/State Government / Local bodies / Ministry of Surface Transport etc. shall take necessary steps to facilitate the same.[24]

G. Vision for the Future

The Department of Telecommunication is planning to achieve a total of 650 million telephone connections (including 66 million wired and 584 million wireless connections) by the end of 2012. Concurrently, there is also a vision of providing 200 million rural telephone connections, which translates into a rural tele-density of 25 per cent. Broadband connectivity would be made available on demand, without limiting the speed. Each village would have at least one broad-band enabled kiosk. Broad-band connection would be provided to schools, health centers and panchayat offices. It is also envisaged that internet and broad-band subscribers will increase to 40 million and 20 million, respectively, by 2010.

REFERENCES

1. Planning Commission, First Five Year Plan, Press and Publication, Government of India, New Delhi 1951.
2. Planning Commission, Second Five Year Plan, Press and Publication, Government of India, New Delhi 1956.
3. Planning Commission, Third Five Year Plan, Press and Publication, Government of India, New Delhi 1961.
4. Planning Commission, Fourth Five Year Plan, Press and Publication, government of India, New Delhi 1969.
5. Planning Commission, Fifth Five Year Plan, Press and Publication, Government of India, New Delhi 1974
6. Planning Commission, Sixth Five Year Plan, Press and Publication, Government of India, New Delhi 1980.
7. Planning Commission, Seventh Five Year Plan, Press and Publication, Government of India, New Delhi 1986.
8. Planning Commission, Eighth Five Year Plan, Press and Publication, Government of India, New Delhi 1992.
9. Planning Commission, Ninth Five Year Plan, Press and Publication, Government of India, New Delhi 1997.
10. Planning Commission, Tenth Five Year Plan, Press and Publication, Government of India, New Delhi 2002.
11. Planning Commission, Eleventh Five Year Plan, Press and Publication, Government of India, New Delhi 2007.
12. http://www.dot.gov.in
13. http://www.bsnl.co.in
14. http://www.itiltd-india.com/
15. http://www.mtnl.net.in/
16. http://tcil-india.com/new/index.htm
17. http://www.wpc.dot.gov.in/
18. http://www.tec.gov.in/
19. http://www.dot.gov.in/cca/cca.htm
20. http://www.dot.gov.in/vtm/vtm.htm
21. http://www.cdot.com/
22. http://www.trai.gov.in/dthguidelines.aspP
23. http://www.trai.gov.in/telecomPolicy_ntp94.asp
24. http://www.trai.gov.in/telecomPolicy_ntp99.asp

CHAPTER 3

BSNL—ORGANISATION SYSTEM AND PERFORMANCE PERSPECTIVES

In pursuance of the New Telecom Policy 1999, the Government of India has decided to corporatise the service provision functions of Department of Telecommunications (DoT). Accordingly, Bharat Sanchar Nigam Limited (BSNL) was incorporated on 15 September 2000 as a wholly owned Central Government Company under the Companies Act, 1956. The business of providing telecommunication services in the country, hitherto entrusted to the Department of Telecom Services (DTS) and the Department of Telecom Operations (DTO), was transferred to BSNL. However, the functions of policy formulation, licensing, wireless spectrum management, administrative control of Public Sector Undertakings (PSUs), standardisation and validation of equipment and research and development (R&D) were retained by the Government under the responsibility of the Department of Telecommunications (DoT) and the Telecom Commission.

The BSNL has a vision to become the largest telecom service provider in Asia. The mission of the company is to provide world class state-of-art technology telecom services to its customers on demand at competitive prices; to provide world class telecom infrastructure in its area of operation; and to contribute to the growth of the country's economy.

The Objectives of the company are:

- To be the Lead Telecom Services Provider;
- To provide quality and reliable fixed telecom service to the customers and there by increase customers' confidence;

- To provide mobile telephone service of high quality and become no. 1 GSM operator in its area of operation;
- To provide point of interconnection to other service provider as per their requirement promptly;
- To facilitate R & D activity in the country;
- To contribute towards:
  (*a*) National Plan Target of 500 million subscriber base for India by 2010;
  (*b*) Broadband customers base of 20 million in India by 2010 as per Broadband Policy 2004;
  (*c*) Providing telephone connection in villages as per government policy;
  (*d*) Implementation of Triple play as a regular commercial proposition.

BSNL is carrying out the duties and responsibilities relating to establishment, maintenance and working of all types of telecommunication services in the country in accordance with and under the terms and conditions of the licence granted by the Central Government under the Indian Telegraph Act, 1885 and such other directions as may be given by the Central Government from time to time.

BSNL has installed Quality Telecom Network in the country and now focussing on improving it, expanding the network, introducing new telecom services with ICT applications in villages and wining customers' confidence. BSNL is the only service provider, making focused efforts and planned initiatives to bridge the Rural-Urban Digital Divide ICT sector. In fact, there is no telecom operator in the country to beat its reach with its wide network giving services in every nook and corner of the country and operates across India except Delhi and Mumbai. Whether it is inaccessible areas of Siachen glacier and North-eastern region of the country, BSNL serves its customers with its wide bouquet of telecom services. BSNL has set up a world class multi-gigabit, multi-protocol convergent IP infrastructure that provides convergent services like voice, data and video through the same Backbone and Broadband Access Network.

The company has vast experience in Planning, Installation, network integration and Maintenance of Switching and Transmission Networks and also has a world class ISO 9000 certified Telecom Training Institute. The turnover, nationwide coverage, reach, comprehensive range of telecom services and the desire to excel has made BSNL the No. 1 Telecom Company of India.

ORGANISATION STRUCTURE

The Corporate Office of Bharat Sanchar Nigam Limited is located in New Delhi. The administrative as well as the overall functional control of the company is vested with Broad of Directors headed by the Chairman and Managing Director (CMD). There are five directors in the Board looking after the functions such as finance, operations, commercial and marketing, planning and new services and human resource development. The organisation structure of Bharat Sanchar Nigam Limited is presented in Exhibit-3.1.

Exhibit-3.1: Organization structure of BSNL central office

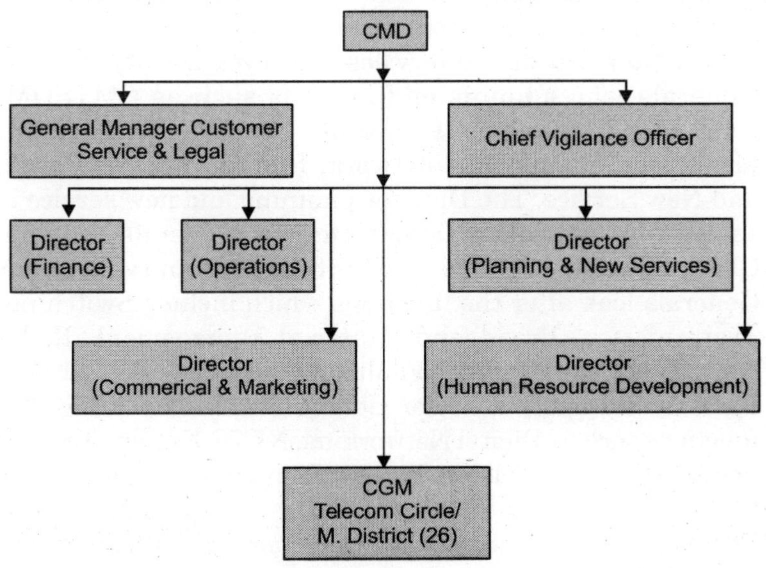

The Director, Finance is assisted by three Senior Deputy Director Generals (DDGs), six Deputy Director Generals (DDGs) and one Chief General Manager (CGM). The functions such as Provident Fund, Financial Planning (FP) and Supply Price of Finance (SPF) are performed by each of the Senior Deputy Director Generals (DDG). The functions such as BBF, EF/TAX, Telecom and Costing, Accountant, and Internal Audit, Telecom Revenue Finance (TRF) are performed by each of the Deputy Director Generals (DDG). The Chief General Manager looks after the activity of NATFM. The Director Operations is assisted by seven Deputy Director Generals, each of them looking after the functions of Customer Service, Mobile Service, PG, Information Technology, Network Management, Management Information System, Transmission Systems, respectively. The Director, Operations is also assisted by seven Chief General Managers performing the functions relating to Eastern Telecom Region, Northern Telecom Region, Southern Telecom Region, Western Telecom Region, National Council of Engineering Service, Telecom and Development, Information Technology respectively. The Director, Commercial and Marketing is assisted by one senior Deputy Director General to look after Broadband services and seven Deputy Director Generals who administer functions such as CMTSOM, Customer Management Telecom Service, Commercial, Marketing, Regular line network, Internal Long Distance, and New Service. The Director planning and new service is assisted by five Senior Deputy Director Generals and nine Chief General Managers. The Senior Deputy Director Generals look after the functions which include Switching, Transmission, Broadband, Material Management, Radio Networking, Transmission Fault, and Customer oriented Task Force. The Deputy Director Generals will take care of the functions such as Digital Networking, NETF, Eastern Telecom Project, Northern Telecom Project, Southern Telecom Project, Western Telecom Project, Quality Assurance and Transmission Switching, Telecom Factory's functions are taken care of by a Chief General Managers. The Director Human Resources Development is responsible for Human Resources Development operations. The Director is assisted by three Senior Deputy Director Generals for Establishment, Recuitement, and Personal and five Deputy Director Generals to look after the operations relating to Administration, Restructuring, Service, Training and WS&I. The Chairman and Managing Director will take assistance from General Manager, Customer Service and legal and Chief Vigilance Officer (CVO) to control operations.

Exhibit: 3.2. List of Telecom Circles/M. Districts

Andaman & Nicobar	Maharashtra
Andhra Pradesh	North East-I
Assam	North East-II
Bihar	Orissa
Chhatisgarh	Panjab
Gujarat	Rajasthan
Haryana	Tamilnadu
Himachal Pradesh	Uttar Pradesh (W)
Jharkhan	Uttar Pradesh (E)
Jammu & Kashmir	Uttaranchal
Karnataka	West Bengal
Kerala	Chennai TD
Madhya Pradesh	Kolkata TD

The BSNL has divided the operational market area into 26 Telecom Circle/M. Districts. Exhibit-3.2 depicts the list of Telecom Circle/M.Districts. Each Telecom Circle / M. District is headed by Chief General Manager who reports the Chairman and Broad of Directors. The Chief General Manager is responsible for all operations of the BSNL in the Telecom Circle/M. District.

Exhibit-3.3 shows the Organisation Chart of a Telecom Circle. Chief General Manager is the Head of telecom circle. He is assisted by two Principal General Managers (PGMs). One PGM takes care of area functions. Another Principal

General Manager is responsible for Circle Office Operations. The Chief General Manager's office consists of General Manager, Finance, PCE (electrical), Civil Engineering (civil), Chief Architect and Deputy General Manager, vigilance. The Principal General Manager (area operations) will be assisted by General Managers to look after the function such as Planning, South region and North region, West region, Central region, Finance. The Principal General Manager (Circle Office) will be assisted by General Managers and General Manager, Telecom District. The General Managers are to look after the functions such as business development, marketing, telegraph traffic, planning new connections and operations, The General Manager Telecom Districts are in charge of various telecom districts in the circles.

Exhibit: 3.3 Organization Structure of a Telecom Circle (A.P)

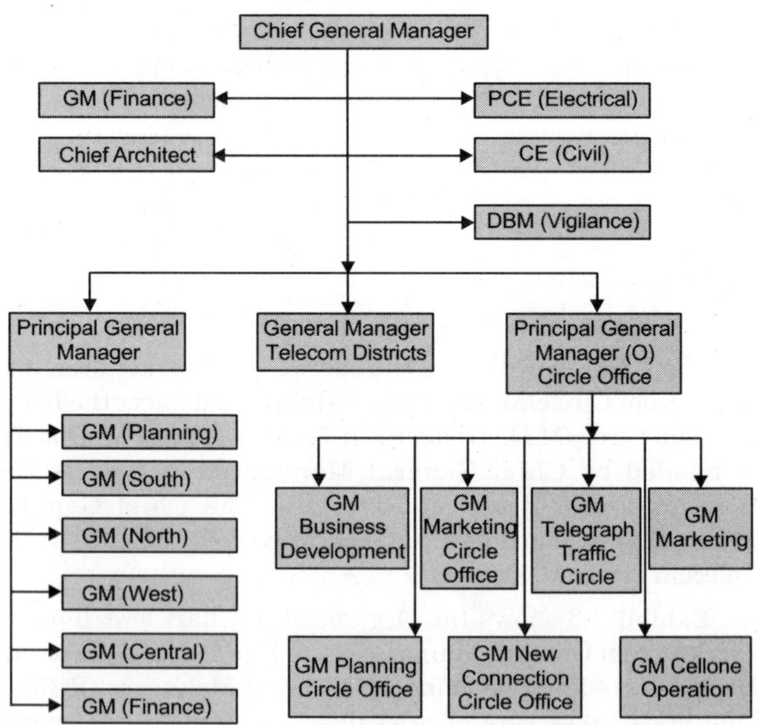

Each Telecom District is headed by the official of the level of a General Manager. The GM of telecom district is assisted by Deputy General Manager, Administration and Planning, Deputy General Manager, Finance and one Deputy General Manager each for north and south regions each. The Deputy General Manager of a region is assisted by Divisional Engineer and Senior Divisional Engineer to look after the telecom operation in that region.

Exhibit: 3.4 Organisation Structure of a Telecom District

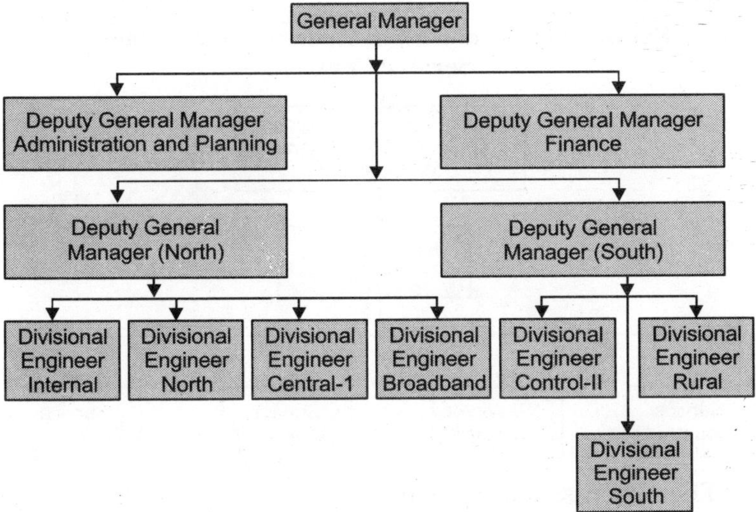

Telephone Exchange is the administrative unit close to the customers. A telephone exchange is headed by Junior Telecom Officer (Exhibit-3.5). The Junior Telecom Officer (JTO) is assisted by Telecom Technical Assistants (TTAs), Phone mechanics (PMs), and Regular Mazdoors (RMs).

Exhibit 3.5 : Organisation Structure of a Telephone Exchange

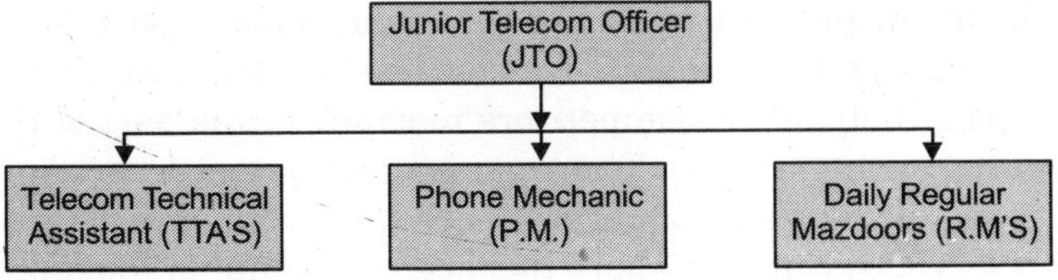

The organisation structure of customer service centre is shown Exhibit 3.6. Customer Service Centres are the most common customer interaction points of the company. Each centre is headed by a Senior Divisional Engineer (SDE) for customer relationship management. The SDE is assisted by a Junior Telecom Officer (JTO). There will be service counters in the Centre, the number of the counters depends upon the customer traffic. Bill collection, receiving complaints, organisation of customer meets are the major responsibilities of the centre.

Exhibit 3.6: Organisation structure of customer Service Centre

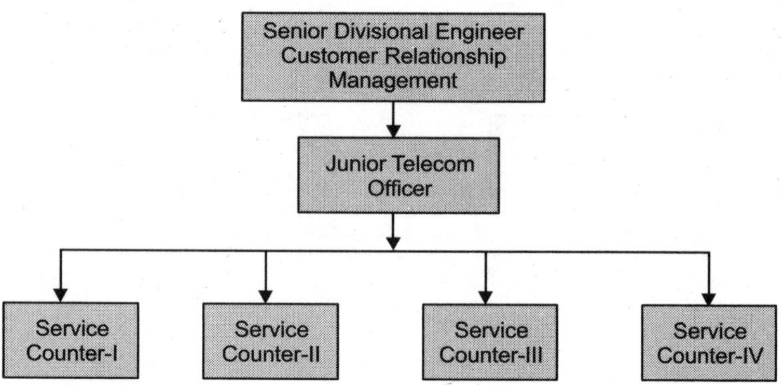

The organisation system of the BSNL handles all the services offered by the company which include fixed line, mobile, Internet and broadband and auxiliary services. BSNL holds the lion share in fixed line segment. The growth rate of the company in the mobile segment is impressive. In broadband services, the company is unable to meet the demand and as a result losing prospective buyers to competing organisations. Inspite of its huge organisation mechanism and loyal customer base it could not make a mark in mobile service segment. The low level performance of the company helped the competitors to capture this part of the highly growing market. The organisation system is certainly responsible for the poor performance of the company in these two services. Further, there has been a decline in fixed line subscriber base year by year. The company lost sizable fixed line subscribers to the competitors.

Taking the above facts into consideration, it is felt that there is need for re-organising the management system of the company. It is suggested therefore to divide BSNL into two autonomous corporate bodies such as 1. BSNL (wire line and Internet and Broadband), and 2. BSNL (mobile). As the nature of the operations, markets and marketing challenges are different for each of the services, the suggested reorganisation may yield desired results. The two Corporations shall be continued under public sector so that the corporate responsibility and social obligations do not stand as issues of conflict. There will be competitive strategic approach to address to current problems and to execute growth plans competitively. The man power may be shared by the three corporations. The employees will have clear orientation and direction in work when they are identified with specific services consistently.

Physical Performance

The capital structure of BSNL consists of authorised share capital and preference share capital. The authorised equity share capital is Rs. 10,000 crores, out of which Rs.5,000 crores is the paid equity share capital. The preference share capital is Rs. 7,500 crores. While promoting the company, the government of India treated the paid up equity capital and preference share capital as investment of the government. The physical performance of BSNL during 2000-01 to 2003-04 is shown in the following figures. The physical performance of the company is analysed by taking the variables such as, Telephone exchanges, equipment capacity of DELs, number of telephone connections, capacity utilisation of DELs, waiting list of prospective customers and Number of Mobile phones.

Figure 3.1 depicts the growth of telephone exchanges during2000-01 to 2003-04. The number of telephone exchanges which was 31,589 in 2000-01 increased to 36,618 in 2003-04, recording an increase of 15.92 per cent. The growth of telephone exchanges over the previous year was highest in 2001-02 with 9.51 per cent while it was only 1.33 per cent growth over the previous year in 2003-04.

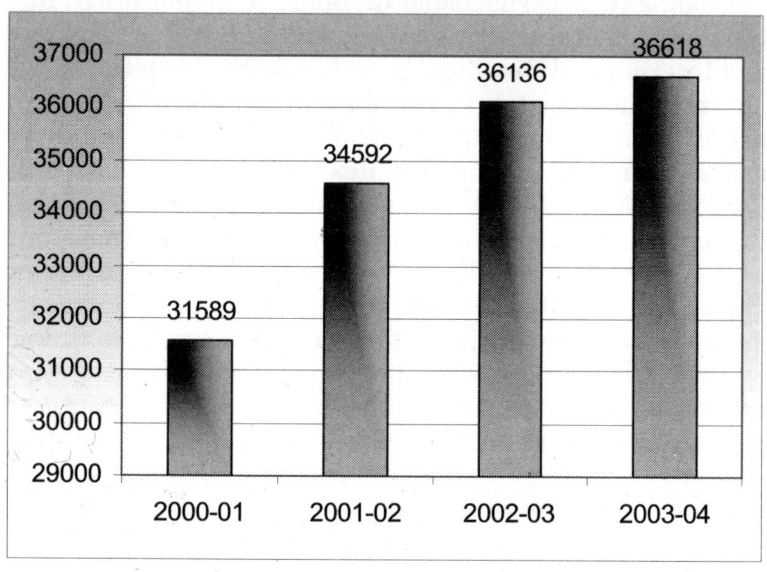

Fig. 3.1. No. of Telephone Exchanges

Source: Bharat Sanchar Nigam Limited, Report No. 5 of 2005 (Commercial).

The growth of the total equipped capacity of Direct Exchanges Lines (DELs) including WLL is shown in Figure 3.2. The equipment capacity has increased from 347.93 lakh lines to 485.60 lakh lines during 2000-01 to 2003-04 recording an increase of 39.57 per cent. The growth in the equipped capacity is consistent during the period.

The data relating to the growth of number of telephone connections (DEL) including WLL is presented in Figure 3.3. The number of telephone connections which was 281.09 lakhs in 2000-01 increased to 363.94 lakhs recording an increase of 29.48 per cent. However, in terms of capacity utilization the trend is on the reverse side.

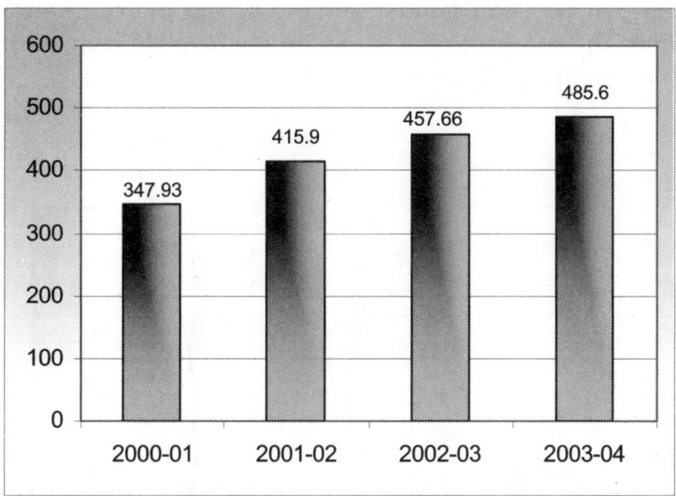

Fig. 3.2. Total Equipment capacity of direct exchange line (DELs) including Wll (in lakh)

Source: Bharat Sanchar Nigam Limited Report No. 5 of 2005 (Commercial).

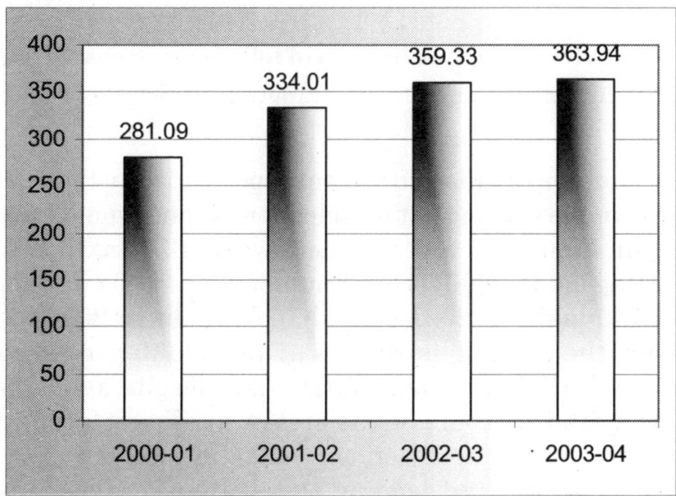

Fig. 3.3. Number of Telephone connections (DELs) including WLL (in Lakh)

Source: Bharat Sanchar Nigam Limited Report No. 5 of 2005 (Commercial)

As can be seen from Figure 3.4, the overall capacity utilization of exchanges went down from 81 per cent in 2000-01 to 75 per cent in 2003-04.

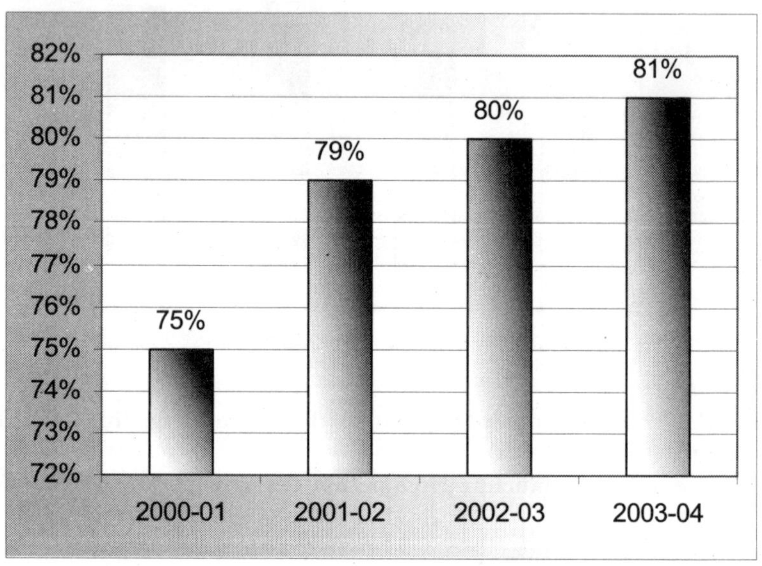

Fig. 3.4. Capacity utilisation of telephone exchanges

Source: Bharat Sanchar Nigam Limited Report No. 5 of 2005 (Commercial)

Despite the availability of equipped capacity there were persons in the waiting list for telephone connection. The data shown in Figure 3.5 reveals, there were 28.71 lakh persons in waiting list in 2000-01. The number of persons in waiting was 16.49 lakhs in 2001-02 and 18.07 lakhs in 2002-03. In 2003-04, the waiting list stands at 18.15 lakh persons. The reasons for the continued waiting list, despite available of occupied capacity could be the presence of large 'technically not feasible' (TNF) areas, enhancement in equipped capacity towards the year-end leading to release of connections in subsequent years, etc.

The growth of cellular mobile connections is shown in Figure 3.6. The company started offering mobile services in

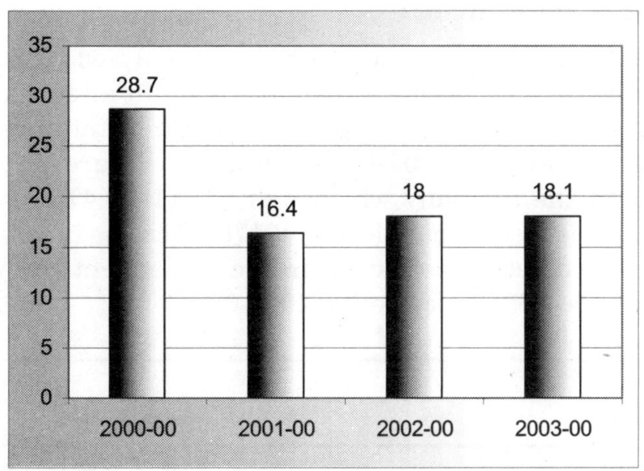

Fig. 3.5. No. of persons on the waiting list (in lakh)

Source: Bharat Sanchar Nigam Limited Report No. 5 of 2005 (Commercial)

2001-02 with a modest beginning of 1.78 lakh mobile telephone connections. In one year a number of connections rose to 22.56 lakhs. In the subsequent year, the number of connections risen to 52.54 lakhs.

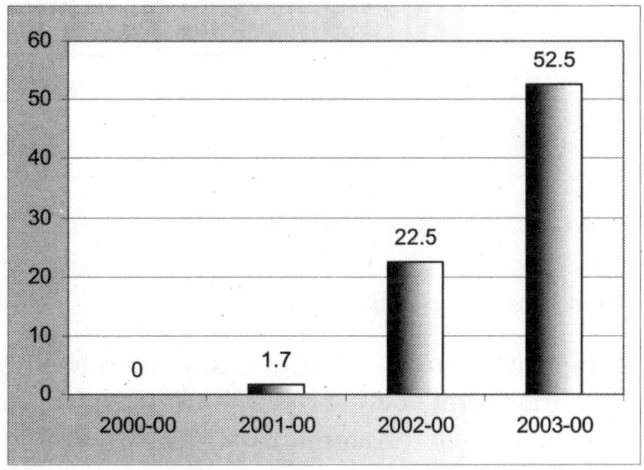

Fig. 3.6. No. of Mobile telephone connections (in lakh)

Source: Bharat Sanchar Nigam Limited Report No. 5 of 2005 (Commercial)

Business Performance

The business performance of BSNL is analysed by taking variables such as income, expenditure, profit after tax, and fixed assets. The data relating to income of the company during 2000-01 to 2007-08 is shown in Figure 3.7. The income of the company which was Rs. 11699.47 crores in 2000-01, reached as high as Rs. 40176.58 crores in 2005-06. There was a decline in income in the subsequent two years to reach Rs. 38053.4 crores in 2007-08.

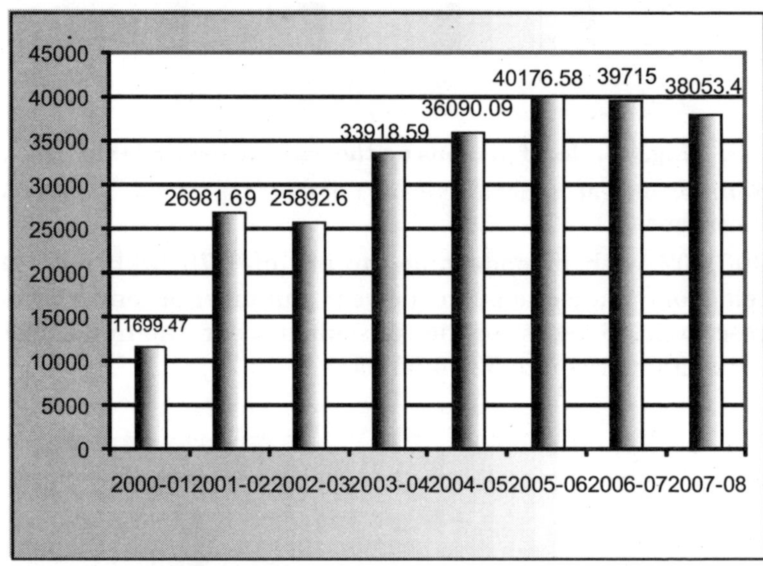

Fig. 3.7. Income of BSNL (in Rs. crores)

Source: Bharat Sanchar Nigam Limited, Annual Reports, www.bsnl.co.in/company/results

The expenditure on the other hand increased year by year except a marginal decline in 2006-07 as shown in Figure 3.8. The expenditure of the company which was Rs. 10,699.42 crores in 2000-01 increased to Rs. 33,636.43 crores in 2007-08 recording an increase of 214.38 per cent.

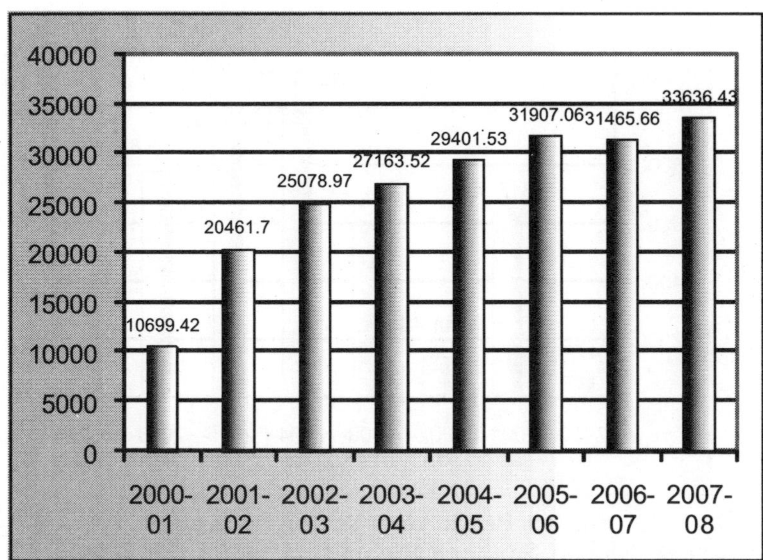

Fig. 3.8. Expenditure of BSNL (in Rs. crores)

Source: Bharat Sanchar Nigam Limited, Annual Reports, www.bsnl.co.in/company/results

The profit after tax of the company is fluctuated in the first four year of the period under study (see fig. 3.9 on next page). The company earned a profit of Rs. 747.05 crores in 2000-01. In the subsequent year the profit after tax zoomed to Rs. 6,312.16 crores. There was a steep decline in profit in 2002-03 as the company earned only Rs. 1,444.44 crores during the year. The company jumped back in the subsequent year and made a profit of Rs. 5,976.52 crores. In 2004-05, the company earned the highest level profit of Rs. 10,183.29 crores. In the subsequent two years there was a decline in profit. The decline was very sharp in the year 2007-08 as the company could make only Rs. 3,009.39 crores of profit after tax.

BSNL has got Fixed Assets in the form of land, buildings, cables, apparatus and plants, etc. The value of fixed assets of the company during 2000-01 to 2007-08 is shown in Figure 3.10 (see fig on next page).

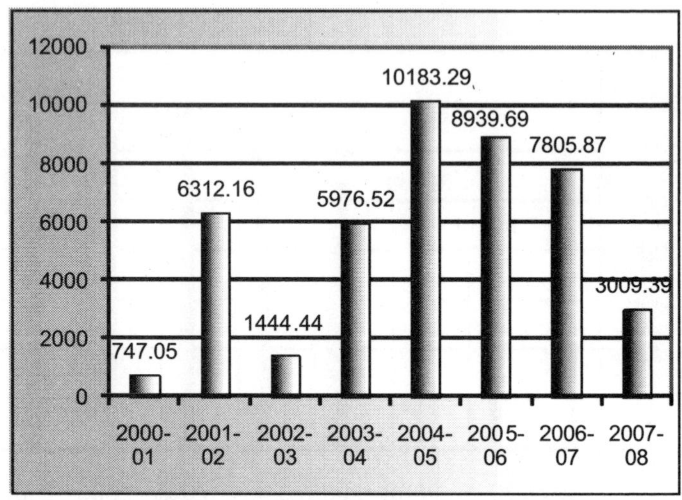

Fig. 3.9. Profit After Tax (in Rs. crores)

Source: Bharat Sanchar Nigam Limited, Annual Reports, www.bsnl.co.in/company/results

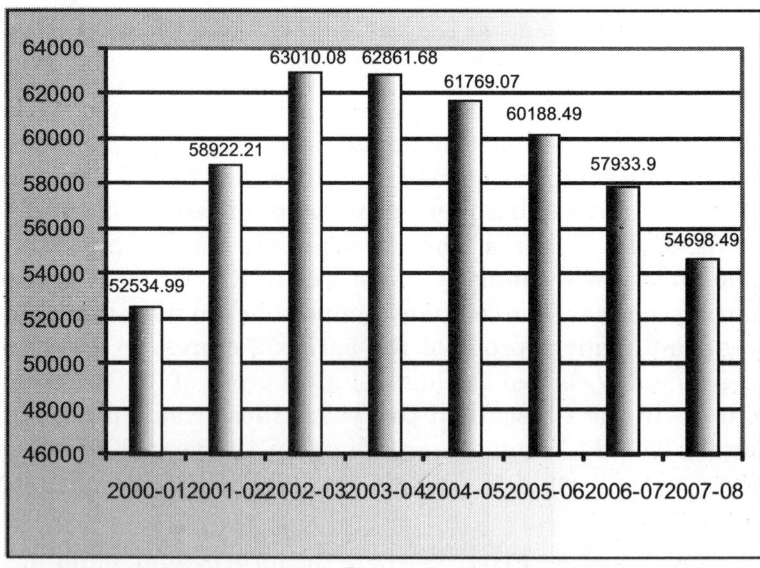

Fig. 3.10. The Value of Fixed Assets of BSNL (in Rs. crores)

Source: Bharat Sanchar Nigam Limited, Annual Reports, www.bsnl.co.in/company/results

The value of fixed assets which was Rs. 52,534.99 crores in 2000-01 increased to Rs. 63,010.08 crores in 2002-03. Since then, the value of the fixed assets has been on the decline. By the end of 2007-08, the value of fixed assets of the company reached to Rs. 54,698.49 crores.

It can be inferred from the data shown in Figure 3.7 to 3.20 that the company's financial performance is not impressive. The expenditure is increasing while income is receding, the profit after tax is highly fluctuated and it was on the decline for the last three years. One of the serious problems identified is the revenue arrears. The company has been facing the problem since its inception as can be seen from Table 3.1. The outstanding arrears which was Rs. 2,946.78 in 2000-01 increased year by year and reached to Rs. 4,086.97 crores in 2003-04. The dues are from Central Government, state governments and private subscribers. In all the years, more than 90 per cent of dues are from private subscribers. The amount as well as the proportion of outstanding bills against private subscribers was persistently increasing every year. Therefore, BSNL should make concerted efforts to recover dues outstanding from the private subscribers. Not only from telephone subscribers, the arrears of revenue has been increasing on renting of telegraph, teleprinter and telephone circuits and telex/intelex connections in the various categories of subscribers. It is necessary therefore, to identify the reasons for low level performance in recovery of arrears and initiate necessary measures for the same.

Table 3.1 Outstanding arrears of BSNL

Year	Arrears (in Rs. Crore)
2000-2001	2946.78
2001-2002	3608.07
2002-2003	3596.86
2003-2004	4086.97

Source: Bharat Sanchar Nigam Limited Report No.5 of 2005 (Commercial)

BSNL has to gear itself to meet competition in various segments – basic services, long distance (LD), and International Long Distance (ILD), and Internet Service Provision (ISP), and Mobile services. With the advent of competition, the private operators have been impacting the strategic matrix by influencing regulatory bodies, adopting intelligent media strategies, and by targeting the creamy layer of customers.

In changing trends, situations, and events, gaining an accurate understanding of BSNL's strengths and limitations will help in better strategic management of organization. Therefore, an attempt is made to develop SWOT analysis of BSNL taking in to consideration the present business environment. Exhibit 3.7 presents the SWOT analysis of the company.

Exhibit 3.7 : SWOT analysis of BSNL

Strengths	Weaknesses
• Extensive reach to all parts of the Country • Time tested telecom service provider • Large customer base • Financial resources • Huge Optical Fibre network and associated bandwidth • Transparency in billing	• Under utilisation of network capabilities • Poor marketing strategy • Public Sector mindset • Poor franchisee network • Aged manpower • Incumbency problem like outdated technologies, unproductive rural assets, social obligations, political interference etc.
Opportunities	**Threats**
• High market growth rate • Increasing potential for broadband services • Un-invaded VSAT market • Exploitation of Public Sector image	• Competition from private operators • Fast changing technology • Manpower churning • Possible entry of Multinational Corporations with state of the art technology • Non-professional management practices

Though BSNL is an eight year old company, it has inherited many strengths and weakness from the Department of Telecommunications. There are six key strengths identified which can be used for the advancement in desired directions. The company has extensive reach to both urban and rural parts of the country. No other company can have the similar reach in the near feature. The company is the time tested telecom service provider. It need not provide evidence to the customers on its capabilities of providing telecom services. The third strength is the largest customer base of the company. The customer base is not only large but also to a greater extent loyal. The company will not find any problems as far as introduction of new services of concerned. Moreover, the cost of new services would be very less compared to the competing companies due to the existence of large customer base. Huge financial resources is yet another strength of the company. This strength facilitates the company to take up new projects and also to strengthen research and development activities. The company has huge optical fibre work and associated bandwidth. In this competency the company stands far ahead of competitors. Another inherited strength is transparency in billing. Very few public sector companies have this kind of competency displayed.

There are six major weakness identified in the company. Underutilisation of network capabilities stands in the forefront of the company's weaknesses. The company could not achieve optimum results because of its inability to exploit the network capabilities. Poor marketing strategy is considered as another weak point. The company allowed the private sector to dominate in the mobile service segment. Instead of adopting the leader strategy the company played the role of a follower. Market aggression is not seen in the company's strategy. The third weakness is the public sector mind set. The spirited motivation is lacking in the top management of the organisation. Job security, generalised policy framework for all public sector companies, etc., have their influence on performance of the employees. Poor franchisee network is considered as another weakness of the company. The company adopted conservative approach in identifying franchisees and developing a strong franchisee network. The company is lagging behind the competing organisations in this respect. Aged manpower is one of the serious problems of the company. The company has stopped recruitment for the last three years. The majority of the employees are said to be non-conversant with the changing technology. Another weakness of the company is incumbency problems like outdated technologies, unproductive rural assets, social obligations, political interference, etc.

The company has many business opportunities in the market environment. The market growth rate particularly in mobile services is very high and company has bright chances to capture the market. High market potential for broadband services is another identified opportunity. The VSAT market is un-invaded so far and this area of business offers great potential. The company can exploit public sector image very well in India to enhance its business opportunity. The majority of the Indians prefer public sector organisations compared to private sector when the value of the offer perceived to be more or less equal.

The threats of the company are competition of private operators, fast changing technology, manpower churning and possible entry of multinational companies with state of the art technology and non-professional management practices.

The biggest challenge before BSNL is to acquire new subscribers and retain the existing ones. Price-based selling does not seem to be going very far now, as it has more or less peaked. Therefore, BSNL will have to look for newer carrots to dangle.

Effective growth of a public enterprise depends on appropriate balance between value and economic aspects of strategy. Value aspects comprise of the socio-political obligations of a public sector entity while economic aspects would be considerations regarding products, markets, costs, revenues as well as technological and organizational capabilities. BSNL is still at the formative stage and is attempting to make over to the next stage i.e. to strike an appropriate balance between value and economic aspects.

BSNL should change its very strategy of acting as follower to that of leader. Instead of reacting to other operators' moves, it should start acting proactively. BSNL should adapt greater standardization and flexibility in systems. Only then new service rollouts will be faster, and ideas will be converted into revenue streams. The overall strategy of BSNL can be of concentrating on the mobile and broadband business in near future and to immediately phase out loss making businesses like telegraph, VSAT communication etc. BSNL can leverage on its pan India reach and economies of scale to achieve overall cost leadership. At the same time capital investments can be made in next generation networks where stress should be on Wi-Max, content based data service and VOIP. Emphasis on organizational restructuring coupled with customer orientation and operational efficiency can help BSNL find place in Asian Telecom market.

THE PRODUCT MIX OF BSNL

Marketing deals with identifying and meeting human and social needs[1]. According to American Marketing Association 'marketing is an organisational function and a set of processes for creating, communicating, and delivering value to customers and for managing customer relationships in ways that benefit the organisation and its stake holders'[2]. The objective of any firm is to satisfy its customer needs profitably, and in this the marketing role is to find out what the needs are, whether they are being met, and how to meet them better. Therefore, services marketing is a managerial process which ensures the efficient serving of the customers' needs[3]. A key ingredient of the marketing management process is insightful, creative marketing strategies and plans that can guide marketing activities. Developing the right marketing strategy over time requires a blend of discipline and flexibility. Firms must stick to a strategy but must also find new ways to constantly improve it[4]. Marketing strategy also requires a clear understanding of how marketing works[5]. Successful marketing thus requires companies to have capabilities such as understanding customer value, creating customer value, delivering customer value, capturing customer value, and sustaining customer value[6].

Service Marketing Mix

Service characteristics add too many challenges in the market place over goods marketing. The traditional marketing mix that was developed, keeping in view the goals of marketing, may also be adopted to services marketing. But the service organisations cannot satisfy themselves with the use of the traditional marketing mix as they are to stay at sub-optimal performance in marketing[7]. Merely adopting marketing labels cannot resolve problems associated with the marketing of services. The four P's of traditional marketing mix (product, price, place and promotion) are controllable variable. It is believed that an effective combination of these four components will make an organisation have a competitive edge in getting preference by the target market. Marketing researchers have well identified the limitations and insufficiencies of the traditional marketing mix if applied to services also[8]. Booms and Bitner suggested in 1981, a seven P's marketing mix model to service firms. The seven P's were later supported by McGrath and other marketing specialists. The marketing mix for service organisations are product, physical evidence, price, place, people, promotion and process.

The Product Mix

The service offering i.e. the service product is the basis for marketing activity. According to Philip Kotler, product is anything that can be offered to a market for attention, acquisition, use or consumption that might satisfy a want or a need[9]. A service product refers to an activity or activities that a marketer offers to perform which results in the satisfaction of a need or want of a predominant target customer. It is the offering of a firm in the form of activities (intangible) that satisfy needs. The totals range of services that a service firm offers to a veriety of customers can be broken into subsets labelled as individual service products. The most important issue in the service product understands what benefits and satisfaction the customer is seeking from the service. According to Rama Mohana Rao, K[10], a service product is a package of a service or service elements executed in proper order in keeping with the needs and wants of the consumer, with an attention to maximise consumer satisfaction.

BSNL is the largest telecom operator in India and is known for Basic Telephony Services for over 100 years. Presently the Plain old, Countrywide telephone service is being provided through 32,000 electronic exchanges, 326 Digital Trunk Automatic Exchanges (TAX), Digitalized Public Switched Telephone Network (PSTN) all interlinked by over 2.4 lakh km of Optical Fiber Cable, with a host of Phone Plus value additions to Customers. BSNL's telephony network expands throughout the vast expanses of the country reaching to the remotest part of the country.

The product mix of BSNL is presented in Exhibit 4.1. BSNL offers products under four product line (PL) categories. They are Fixed line services (PL-I), Mobile services (PL-II), Internet and Broadband services (PL-III) and Auxiliary services (PL-IV). The details of services offered under each product line are presented here under.

Product Line 1 : Fixed Line Services

This product line can be broadly categorised into two types. They are permanent connection and temporary and casual connection.

Permanent Connection: Permanent connections are offered in the following categories to suit the needs and wants of different telecom subscribers.

A. Tatkal Scheme (Highest Priority): New telephone connection under this scheme will be provided within 15 days after the payment of the entire deposit amount. The applicant has to pay a non-interest bearing deposit of Rs 30,000/- per connection. An applicant desirous of applying under TATKAL Scheme has to register by paying an initial deposit equivalent to registration fee for Non-OYT at the time of submitting application. The remaining amount will be collected only if the telephone connection is feasible to be provided within two weeks. If the telephone connection is not feasible, the initial deposit will be refunded within two weeks.

Exhibit – 4.1 Product Mix of BSNL

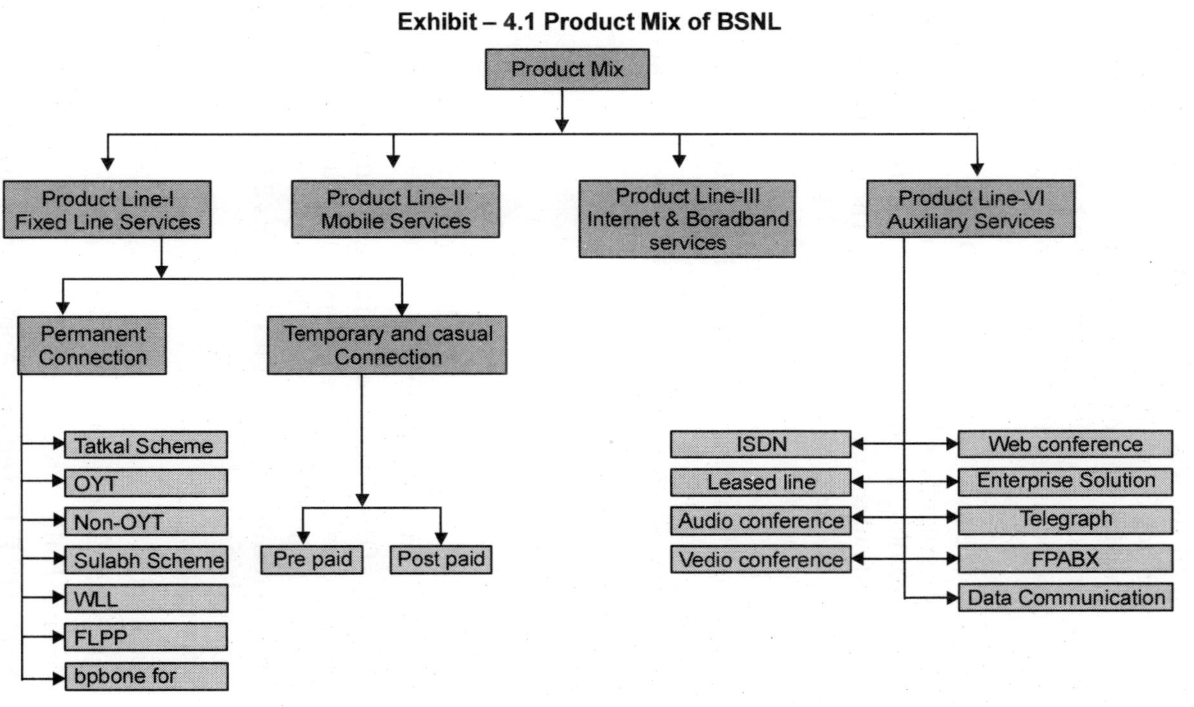

Normal rental will be charged for a telephone connection provided under this scheme. Third party transfer of this connection will not be permitted during the first 3 years. But normal transfer/shift of telephone will be permitted as per the normal-rules applicable to other telephones. The telephone provided under the scheme can be surrendered at any time.

B. Own Your Telephone (OYT) Category: Applications are registered under OYT on payment of initial deposit of Rs. 8000/-, Rs. 10,000/- or Rs. 15,000/- depending upon the capacity of the exchange system. The deposits carry an interest for the period from the date of payment to the date of installation of telephone at the rate payable by the State Bank of India on Fixed Deposit for one year. Deposit amount may vary from time to time. Under the OYT category, there are two schemes; OYT general and OYT special. OYT general is open to all. But OYT special is offered only to the following categories:

- Government Departments
- Statutory Bodies
- Foreign Exchange Earners
- Public and Joint Sector Undertakings (Government interest is more than 50%)
- Retired Officials (and Officials on voluntary retirement after 20 years of service) of Public and Joint Sector Undertakings, whose basic pay (for one year prior to retirement) is not less than Rs 2,000/- p.m.(old pay scale as on July 1976)
- LPG Dealers
- Private hotels
- Schools and Colleges
- Cinema Halls

C. NON-OYT Category: Applications are registered under NON-OYT, on payment of initial deposit of Rs 500/-

or Rs 2,000/- depending upon the type (rural or urban) and capacity of the exchange system. The deposits carry an interest for the period from the date of payment to the date of installation of telephone at the rate payable by the State Bank of India on Fixed Deposit for one year. Under Non-OYT category there are five schemes offered. The following are the details:

(*a*) **NON-OYT General Scheme:** This scheme is open to all.

(*b*) **NON-OYT Special Scheme:** The following types of applicants are eligible for registration under this category:

- Doctors holding recognized degree or diploma in any approved system of Medicine or Surgery and registered with Medical Council.
- Advocates on the role of bar Council
- Judicial Officers
- Qualified Nurses and Midwives.
- Blind persons supported by a "Visually Blind" Certificate issued by CMO/MS Ophthalmic Surgeon of a District Level Government Hospital are also eligible for registration under this category. As a welfare measure 50% concession in rent and advance rental deposit is allowed to the blind person registered under this category.
- Newspapers, journals and magazines registered with Registrar of newspapers
- Registered News agencies.
- Accredited press correspondents and press photographers.
- Public Institutions (run by public funds and for the benefit of public), Govt. schools and colleges, but not private schools and colleges. Political Parties recognized by the Election commission, Social

Organizations and Mission Orphanages, Leper Houses, Public Hospitals, Registered Trade Unions, Co-op. Societies, Sports and cultural organizations.

- Small Scale Industries
- Eminent Public men
- Legal Aid Committees
- Naturopaths, Physiotherapists and Occupational Therapists
- War widows and Disabled soldiers (No Registration and installation and half the normal rent) 100% exemption in rentals to Gallantry Award winners in three Defence Services and awardees of Presidents' Police Medal for Gallantry
- Defence Personnel, Ex-Serviceman
- Independent Student Hostels recognized by Central/ State Government.

(*c*) **NON-OYT Swatantrata Senani Scheme(SWS) :** Freedom Fighters and Spouse of Freedom Fighters are eligible for this scheme. Under this scheme no installation or registration fee will be charged and only half the normal rental will be charged.

(*d*) **NON-OYT SS Scheme:** The following types of applicants are eligible for registration under this category:

- Foreign Missions and Embassies.
- U N Organizations.
- MPs, MLAs and Municipal Councillors.
- Distinguished Persons
- Retired employees of all Courts
- Retired Senior Officers of State and Central Government whose monthly basic pay is Rs 3,700/- and above as per pay scales before implementation of fifth pay commission Rs. 12,000/- w.e.f. 13.8.1998 for

one year prior to retirement. In the case of DoT and Department of Posts officers the pay limit is Rs. 3,000/- and above (old scale) and Rs. 10,000/- w.e.f. 13.8.1998 for one year prior to retirement (Retiring officers will not get SS Category if they have already one Telephone in same station).

- Presidents, Vice Presidents, Chairman of Standing Committee of Districts, Block and Gram Panchayats and Members of Zilla Parishads.

(*e*) **Non-OYT-G-SE-DoT:** The service employees of DoT and BSNL are eligible for registration and Non-OYT-G-SE-DoT category. The registrants under this category will be given priority for installation at par with registrants under non-OYT-SWS Category. The facility is allowed only once during the entire service span of the employees.

D. Sulabh Scheme: BSNL has a tariff plan, for those customers who use their bfone for incoming call only. The phone has only incoming call facility and out going calls may be made through these telephones through India Telephone Card (ITC) or normally after depositing annual rental. This plan is called "SULABH PLAN".

E. Permanent Telephone Connection— 2nd concessional bfone for internet use: In order to promote use of internet on the fixed line, BSNL has decided to introduce this service with the following conditions:

- The internet usage charges will be payable separately by the customer to the concerned ISP. In places where CLI based Internet facility is available, the additional charges@Rs.0.10/- per minutes shall be payable.
- This scheme is considered only where surplus capacity is available.
- Only existing customers of BSNL can avail of the second telephone exclusively for Internet.

- The scheme is available to only individual customers and not for commercial users like Internet Dhabas, Internet Cafes etc. The 2nd bfone for internet shall be installed at residential premises only and application for 2nd bfone connection should be in name of individual only.
- In case 2nd bfone is installed at official/ commercial premises the same shall be disconnected immediately.
- No telephone instrument will be provided for this connection.
- No installation charges will be taken for providing this second connection.
- The first connection against which the second connection is being taken should have the required ARD/Security as per the existing policy. The ARD for the new connection shall be Rs 1000/-
- No volume or any other discounts will be applicable on the connections provided under this scheme.
- Conversion of existing second wire line connection under this scheme is permitted.

Temporary Connections

Temporary Connections are provided for short period for emergency requirements of purely temporary nature. Temporary connections are to be provided for a maximum period of 3 months at a time in the case of private individuals and 6 months at a time in the case of Government Offices. The charges for the entire period along with security deposit, installation charges and rentals will be collected in advance. No waiting list is maintained for this category.

Casual Connections

Casual connections are provided to applicants for social/ religious functions, marriages, and exhibitions etc., for a period not exceeding 30 days.

Phone Plus Service

BSNL offers a host of phone plus services, converting the old basic telephones to a sophisticated tool which can be used for a variety of applications.

All the Phone facilities are available free of cost with effect from January 22nd, 2003. The following are the details of free services offered to the fixed line subscribers:

- **Call Waiting:** This facility lets the customer receive incoming calls even when the telephone is busy. The user will get a short duration pip-pip tone when busy talking, indicating that another call is waiting, provided this facility is activated. One can talk to any one of the callers keeping the other waiting. Complete secrecy of communication between the two callers is maintained.
- **Abbreviated Dialing:** A customer may be calling a few people very frequently. It is possible to programme these numbers as abbreviated codes of 1 or 2 digits. A maximum of 20 numbers can be programmed for abbreviated dialling. It is ideal for STD/ISD.
- **Hot Line:** Customers may want to be connected directly to a pre-determined number as soon as the hand set is lifted even without dialing. At the same time the customers may want to have the flexibility to dial any other number of their choice. It is possible to have this facility in the digital exchanges by the delayed hotline feature. The number of the customer choice can be programmed by the exchange staff at the customer request. After doing so if the customer lifts the telephone and do not dial within 5 seconds, he/she will be automatically connected to the programmed number. However, if the customer starts dialling with in 5 seconds, he she can make an outgoing call as usual.
- **Call Transfer (Call Forward):** This facility is useful for mobile persons who may not want to miss incoming

calls. Using this facility Calls can be forwarded to another telephone number designated by the customer.

- **Automatic Wake-Up/Reminder Call Service:** When a customer wants to be given reminder at a specific time, the customer has to call the exchange and leave the time to be reminded. The facility allows initiating a call automatically by the exchange at a fixed time specified by the user of the telephone.
- **Number /Call Hunting Service:** If a customer has more than one telephone line, this facility is very helpful for the caller. If the called line is engaged, the caller does not have to disconnect and dial other line(s). This facility automatically transfers the incoming call to whichever line is free.
- **Calling Line Identification Presentation (CLIP):** The subscriber has to buy separately the CLIP display device from market. Using this facility one can see the number of the calling party before lifting the telephone. This facility is very useful to trace malicious caller. However, the CLIP instrument shall be procured and installed by the users themselves.
- **Calling line Identification (CLI) Announcement Service:** The customer shall have top dial 164 and listen to the number of the phone line that have been used to make the call. This facility is useful when in doubt about the phone number.
- **Phone Bell Check:** This facility is to adjust the volume of bell of the phone and to check the functionality of the bell.
- **Electronic Locking for STD/ISD:** This facility offers 100% protection against improper use. Customers can lock their telephone electronically. Here, the customer only knows the secret code. He/she can lock/allow Local, STD or ISD calls in many way viz.

all calls allowed, only local calls allowed, only STD and Local calls allowed, all outgoing calls barred etc.

- **Call Conferencing:** With this service telephonic conference can be set up within three or more parties. This service is available subject to technical feasibility.

Wireless in Local Loop (WLL) Mobile Telephone Connections

BSNL WLL-M is a communication system that connects customers to the BSNL Landline network using radio frequency signals instead of conventional copper wires, for the full or part connection between the subscriber and the exchange. This comes with superior voice quality and high speed data capabilities. CDMA is popular with more than 100 million subscribers worldwide, and the number keeps on increasing exponentially. In this case, subscriber can carry a small handset of CDMA technology. There is no antenna or any other equipment is required at subscriber's premises.

BSNL WLL service is the most reliable and affordable service providing both fixed line telephony and Mobile telephony services. It offers a host of value added services at virtually no cost to subscribers. Customer may get the handset by paying a premium of about Rs. 20/- per month only for the comprehensive policy taken for the cost of handset.

Product Line-II : BSNL Mobile Services

The mobile services are offered in two categories. They are post paid and pre paid.

Post-paid: BSNL Mobile offers a host of value added services and unmatched features which are not found in any other Cellular service. BSNL Mobile is the only Cellular service which is available in all major cities and covers all major highways. BSNL Mobile gives all India roaming facility (including Delhi and Mumbai) and international roaming facility to more than 300 networks across the world. A BSNL Mobile subscriber will enjoy benefits like:

1. No security Deposit for the existing BSNL subscriber
2. No security deposit or monthly rental for national roaming facility in Plan-325 and 525
3. Free Voice Mail recording and receiving facility
4. Free CLIP
5. Free Call waiting and Call holding facility
6. Missed call alerts by SMS at free of cost!

BSNL Mobile Post paid service offers 10 plans to the customers'. The following are the plans:

- Plan -99
- Plan 225
- Plan 299 - One India
- Plan 325
- Plan 490
- Plan 525
- Plan 550 - Free incoming calls while roaming
- Plan 725 and
- Plan -999

Besides the plans, the company offers Optional Services (SMS,VMS,E-mail etc.) Domestic SMS , International SMS, CLIP, GPRS, WAP, MMS, Voice Mail, Corpaorate and Non Copoarte VPN, Corpaorate and Non Corpoarte VPN, Zonal corpaorate and Non Corpoarte VPN/CUG, Unlimited and concessional VPN packages between BSNL fixed and BSNL cellular service, and International roaming tariff.

A host of **value added services** are also available at economical charges including, Voice Mail Service, Short Message Service (SMS), Group Messaging, National and International Roaming, Call forwarding, Corporate Virtual

Private Network, Call conferencing, Friend and Family Talk, Call waiting and Call holding facility.

Wireless Application Protocol (WAP): By using this service WAP enabled websites can be surfed.

Unified Messaging Services: This service provides for integrating mobile phone with the Internet to access e-mails, faxes, voice mail etc on mobile phone.

BSNL MOBILE – Prepaid

BSNL Mobile prepaid service offers value added services and features that are not found in any other Cellular service. All India roaming facility is also available on BSNL mobile prepaid service. Initial activation charges for Prepaid Mobile is only Rs. 200/- and free talk value of Rs. 50/- is given to all subscribers. BSNL Mobile Pre paid cards are available in the denominations of Rs. 70,150, 300, Rs. 500, Rs. 1000 and Rs. 2000. The validity period of which are 7,15, 30, 45, 120 and 180 days respectively. Moreover, on any later date if customers want to convert BSNL Mobile pre-paid scheme to post paid scheme it can be done without paying any additional activation charge.

BSNL Mobile Prepaid service offers five plans which includes BSNL Mobile Prepaid, Prepaid Anant (Lifetime prepaid), Own Your Vanity Prepaid worth Rs. 3000/-, See Card Options, and Optional Services (SMS, VMS etc).

The value added services available for the service at very economical charges includes Voice Mail Service, Short Message Service (SMS), All India Roaming, Call Forwarding (within same Service Area), Call Conferencing, Call Waiting and Call holding facility, Wireless Application Protocol (WAP) and Unified Messaging Services.

Product Line III : Internet and Broadband Services

Inter Net: BSNL is India's no. 1 Internet service provider with more than 17 lakh subscribers, providing Internet service throughout the country (except in New Delhi and

Mumbai) under the brand name of "Sancharnet". Sancharnet provides free all India roaming and enables it's users to access their accounts, using the same access code (172233) and user ID from any where in the Country. In order to make Internet available throughout the length and breadth of the Country, Internet Dhabas are being commissioned at all the Block Headquarters. BSNL has also started DIAS and Account free internet access (CLI based) facility on few select cities.

Broadband Service: Broadband service is based on DSL technology (on the same copper cable that is used for connecting telephone). This provides high speed Internet connectivity upto 8Mbps. This is always - on internet access service with speed ranging from 256Kbps to 8 Mbps.

Wi-Fi: Wi-Fi Services have been introduced for providing high speed internet access at convenient public locations which are called as Hot Spots. Hot Spot Type-A is applicable for public utility services like Airports, Railway Stations, Universities and their campus etc.

Sancharnet Card: BSNL has also launched "SANCHARNET CARD". The Sancharnet Card" is a prepaid Internet Access Card with following features for customers:

- Self-register for internet access with your choice of userid
- Renew your existing Sancharnet Account
- Wide Range of Internet Access Packages
- Sancharnet Cards are available in the following cities

Web Co-location Services: BSNL provides Internet services to the customers located in about 450 locations. Web Co-location is an easy and cost effective solution to house a company's powerful infrastructure without losing the administrative control on the equipments. Web Co-location eliminates much of the Infrastructure costs as well as the maintenance cost of such equipments apart from avoiding the last mile problems. Web Co-location enables customer's equipment/ Servers to be treated as a part and parcel of the

ISP network enjoying all the facilities as the ISP servers. Web Co-location provides the infrastructure at a nominal value keeping the customer comfortable and focussed in maintaining the Applications /Services of the company. Apart from enjoying the bandwidth and facilities, the customer retains control over his equipment, software and operating system.

Web Hosting Services: Web hosting is a service that allows users to post Web pages to the Internet. It allows users to publish their own information resources to any Internet user interested in accessing them. It is a business that provides the technologies and services needed for web sites to be viewed on the web.

The Web Hosting Services of BSNL has been launched and are being hosted presently through web servers located at New Delhi and Bangalore. By hosting their pages through the Web servers of BSNL, the customer can save lot of access time.

BSNL's IP Backbone using MPLS Technology: Keeping pace with the technological trend to provide latest and varied value added services to its customers, BSNL harnesses IP Infrastructure based on MPLS Technology to offer world class IP VPN services. MPLS is an acronym for "Multi Protocol Label Switching". MPLS VPN is a technology that allows a Service Provider like BSNL to have complete control over parameters that are critical to offering its customers service guarantees with regard to bandwidth throughputs, latencies and availability. The technology enables secure Virtual Private Networks (VPN) to be built and allows scalability that will make it possible for BSNL to offer assured growth to its customers without having to make significant investments. BSNL is geared to provide Bandwidth on demand, Video Conferencing, Voice Over IP (VoIP) and a host of other value added services that could revolutionize the way a corporate business works.

MPLS based VPNs reduce customer networking complexity, costs and totally do away with the requirement of in-house technical work force. Rather than setting up and managing individual point-to-point circuits between each office using pair of Leased Lines, MPLS VPN customers need to provide only one connection from their office router to a service provider edge router.

BSNL has tied up with various Networking solution providers to provide end-to-end solution to its valued customers, including Customer End (CE) routers and other networking components.

Product Line IV : Auxiliary Services

BSNL is providing many auxiliary services, besides the three core services. The auxiliary services include ISDN, Leased line, Audio conference, Video conference, Web conference, Enterprise solution, EPABX and Data communication.

The following are the details of each of the auxiliary services.

ISDN: ISDN has emerged as a powerful tool worldwide for provisioning of different services like voice, data and image transmission over the telephone line through the telephone network. ISDN is being viewed as the logical extension of the digitalization of telecommunication network and most developed countries are in different stages of implementing ISDN. An ISDN subscriber can establish two simultaneous independent calls (except when the terminal equipment is such that it occupies two 'B' channels for one call itself like in video conferencing etc.) on existing pair of wires of the telephone line (Basic rate ISDN) where as only one call is possible at present on the analog line /telephone connection. The two simultaneous calls in ISDN can be of any type like speech, data, image etc. The call setup time for a call between two ISDN subscribers is very short, of the order of 1 to 2 seconds. The ISDN subscriber will have full connectivity, nationally, to other analog telephone subscribers.

Services Offered by ISDN include Normal Telephone and Fax (G3),Digital Telephone-with a facility to identify the calling subscriber number and other facilities.,G4 Fax,Data Transmission at 64 Kbps with ISDN controller card, Video Conferencing at 128 Kbps,Video Conferencing at 384 Kbps (Possible with 3 ISDN lines),*ATM (Asynchronous Transfer Mode) or PVC (Permanent Virtual Circuit).*

Leased Line: To transmit data between computer and electronic information devices, BSNL provides data communication services to its subscribers. It offers a choice of high, medium and low speed leased data circuits as well as dial-up lines. Bandwidth is available on demand in most of the cities. Managed leased Line Network (MLLN) offers flexibility of providing circuits with speeds of n x 64 Kbps up to 2 Mbps. useful for internet leased lines and international principle Leased Lines (IPLCs).

For dedicated point to point speech, private wire, teleprinter and data circuits are given on lease basis. Leased circuits are provided to subscribers for internal communication between their offices/factories at various sites within a city/town or different cities/town on point to point basis, or on a network basis interconnecting the various sites.

Managed Leased Line Service (MLLN): The MLLN is a Managed Leased Line Network system which is proposed to provide Leased line connectivity. The State-of-the-art technology equipment of MLLN is designed mainly for having effective control, monitor on the leased line so that the down time is very much minimized.

FLPP (Fixed Line Pre-Paid) Service: This service enables a subscriber to make calls from a prepaid account linked to his telephone number. Unlike the prepaid card 'ITC' service, where the authentication is done every time through a 16-digit PIN, the authentication of FLPP is linked to his telephone line and the user is not required to dial the Account number/ PIN for authentication making it simpler to use.

There can be four types of FLPP accounts namely; PCO FLPP Account; PCO Local FLPP Account; General FLPP Prepaid Account; and General FLPP Prepaid + Post paid Account.

India Telephone Card (ITC) Service: This prepaid card enables the customers to make local, STD or ISD calls even from a STD/ISD barred telephone. The calls are charged to the secret number specified in the card and not to the telephone connection being used. Equipped with this card, the customer can enjoy the freedom of making calls anywhere, anytime, from any telephone. India Telephone cards are available on sale at all the Customers Service Centers of BSNL and through its franchises appointed in different cities. ITC card purchased in one city can be used in any other city where this service is available.

Voice Virtual Private Network (Voice VPN): The Voice VPN service enables the subscribers to establish a private network using public network resources. The subscriber's lines are connected to different fixed line network switches. Restrictions on outgoing and incoming calls can also be imposed in this network.

Audio Conferencing: Audio Conferencing service allows multiple participants to converse with each other regardless of their location through the normal fixed line telephone or cellular phone. An audio conference subscriber can add two or more participants in a particular conference. The customers can schedule their audio conferences through the Web or through IVR. The service is available to existing BSNL subscribers only. Any conference scheduled can have both Dial-in and Dial-out participants. Conference can be scheduled one time or standing. A standing conference is always on. The authorized participants have just to dial in a particular telephone number followed by a password to enter into a conference.

Video Conferencing: Video Conferencing service allows multiple participants to converse with each other regardless of their location through the video end-points or Personal computers. It involves Video and Audio communication. It's about connecting people. A video conference subscriber can add two or more video participants in a particular conference.

The customers can schedule their video conferences through the Web. The video conferencing service can be availed by any user through IP or ISDN interface. The service is available to existing BSNL subscribers only.

BSNL Web Conferencing: BSNL Web Conferencing Service is made available on the desktop of the customer and enables the customers to conduct virtual meetings with partners, suppliers, employers etc. It has the innovative feature such as Persistent meeting rooms, which simulates physical room environment wherein authorized users can enter their designated rooms the way they do in physical meetings. The users can access the rich features, apart from multi-point, multi-media (Audio, Video and Data) conferencing service, BSNL web Conferencing service provides data conferencing tools to enhance collaboration among users such as sharing of Power Point Presentation, Whiteboard, Documents, and Chat facility amongst the conference participants, which will significantly aid in increasing the effectiveness of business meetings.

Enterprise Solutions

Fleet Management Solution: The fleet management solution is an innovative on-line tracking system powered by BSNL to manage fleets comprising of trucks, car carriers, trailers, tankers, containers or vehicles moving hazardous and specialty explosive chemicals etc. The e-TracK vehicle tracking system uses vehicle-mounted, microprocessor-controlled device which sends periodic messages from the vehicle to a network command centre through SMS/GPRS. The received data is authenticated and forwarded to an application server which provides tracking information through an internet. Customers are provided a user name and password to access the fleet information on line. The user also has options to receive tracking information via e-mail, fax or SMS besides the facility of calling the customer support team on a toll-free telephone line.

I-NET: I-net is available at 102 cities in the country grouped on the basis of business activity and demand. The services available on I-Net include Permanent Virtual Circuits, Reverse Charging, Closed User Group, Fast Select, Charging Information Indication, Call Redirection/Call Transfer, Hunt Group, Network User Identification, Flow Control Parameter Negotiation, and Restriction List.

Permanent Virtual Circuits: The Permanent Virtual Circuit initiates a permanent link between two subscribers of the Network. The Permanent Virtual Circuit replaces an end-to-end Leased line without the need for call set-up procedure. The circuits are very useful for Corporate Houses wishing to link two or more major offices. It is like a HOTLINE linking the offices across the country.

Reverse Charging: In Reverse Charged calls, the call is billed on the CALLED subscriber. This enables Information Bureaus, Computing Bureaus etc. to exclude communication costs as a part of their services to the customers. i.e. the customer is able to access the service without having to pay for it. It is akin to a TOLL FREE number for the CALLING subscriber.

Closed User Group: A group of users may form themselves into a CUG, creating a Pseudo "Private" sub-networking, utilizing the facilities of the network. This service enables the subscribers belonging to the same CUG to make communications with each other preventing access from or to the world outside the group. An organization with CUG would be like a giant EPABX exchange over the whole country.

Fast Select: To send even one packet of data, a Data Terminal must exchange at least 3 packets to establish and later release the logical connection. This overhead is avoided by Fast Select facility, whereby the Terminal may send up to 128 packets of data in the CALL REQUEST/INCOMING CALL packet. This is useful in applications like Credit Card Verification Systems leading to enormous savings in the communications cost.

Telegraph : Telegram is a common man's communication need. The first telegraph message was transmitted live on Morse through electrical signals between Calcutta and Diamond Harbour on 5th November 1850. The Telegraph services were opened to public during February 1855. To implement modern technology in the telegraph network a National Message Switching Network Plan was prepared in 1986.

The growth of Telegraph services has been affected owing to the impact of other non-voice services and improvement in density of telephones, nevertheless the service has social relevance and historical importance. All the cities (300) and towns (4689) as per 1991 census and a large number of villages have access to Public Telegraph Services through Telegraph Offices.

Telegraph services are being provided through Telegraph offices, Telecom Centers and Bureau FAX centers. A number of new types of telegraph services such as Store and forward message switching system, electronic key-board concentrator, electronic teleprinters and formatted terminals have been introduced.

Express Money Transfer Service: This service aims at delivering money within few hours after rendering at the counter of a telegraph office was introduced in A.P. Telecom Circle on experimental basis. This service is being made available at many of the stations in Tamilnadu, Kerala, Karnataka, Maharashtra and metro cities of Delhi and Calcutta.

Apart from the facility of booking of telegrams, following services are also offered in some Telegraph Offices:

- FAX Service is available at many selected telegraph offices for national and international outgoing and incoming messages.
- A new class of telegram called "Fax Telegram" is available for public.

- Booking of telegrams on phone.
- Delivery of telegram over Phone if the same is specified in the address of the telegram.
- Delivery of telegrams through Fax, if the telegrams contain fax number in the address.

EPABX: BSNL permits telephone subscribers to use their own PABX/EPABX connected to the BSNL network under certain commercial/technical conditions. The type of Subscriber owned EPABX should be approved by BSNL. External extensions outside subscriber's premises will be permitted only on the specific approval of the concerned authority and charged as per departmental tariff. In cases where external extensions from subscriber owned EPABX are provided within the premises of the subscribers using their own cables and wires without crossing any public road, no charge will be levied. Subscriber is free to use the existing internal wiring of the internal extensions left at the premises after the closure of the PABX. External extensions from subscriber owned PABX may be provided by the department and charged. Underground cables and lines may continue to be maintained by the department since the same may be required for provision of various telecom services the subscriber may require. In cases where BSNL feels that the existing cables/overhead wires are not be used/likely to be used by the company the same can be made over to the user after recovering the depreciated value of assets. Where subscribers themselves provide and maintain external extensions from the EPABX, applicable licence fee would be charged if the extensions are crossing a public road. Cases where PBX/PABX facilities are surrendered before the expiry of the guarantee period will be regulated as per Company rules.

Free Voice and Data EPABX

To meet the aspirations of the Customers, BSNL has brought out a scheme to provide bundled telecommunication services through the provision of Voice and Data EPABX systems at customer location connected to the telecom backbone on BSNLs nationwide telecom network.

The scheme provides for free deployment of state of the art EPABX systems capable of providing both voice and data connectivity at the customer premises wherein the supply, installation, operation and maintenance of the entire system would be done by BSNL through its appointed and empanelled vendor(s). The voice and data connectivity to the said systems shall be provided by BSNL at the applicable rates. BSNL has tied up with various Telecom Solution Providers to provide end-to-end solution to its valued customers.

The BSNL will permit interested parties to have a group EPABX on shared basis in large multistoried building/office/department/commercial/industrial establishment and residential premises. Junctions for the EPABX will be provided on out of turn basis under NO-OYT general category subject to some general conditions:

Data Communications

HVNET, the High Speed Satellite based VSAT network of Department of Telecom Services, provides high speed data transfers (up to 64 Kbps) and voice communication service covering the entire country. The network consists of a HUB station located near Thane (40 kms from Mumbai) and number of VSATs/Personal Earth Stations (PES) located throughout the country. The VSAT communicates to the HUB through the THAICOM III Satellite. All VSATs are connected in STAR topology and VSAT to VSAT communication is through the HUB at Mumbai.

The VSAT, which is required to be installed at subscribers premises consists of three units, namely an outdoor unit, an indoor unit and Inter Facility Link (IFL) cable interconnecting the two units. The outdoor unit contains the antenna assembly & associated RF equipments. The antenna is of 2.4 meter diameter parabolic type and can be installed easily in any open space and required a floor area of about 4 Mt. X 4Mt. The RF equipment includes an up converter, down converter, solid state power amplifier which together comprise the ODU and low noise amplifier which are installed on the antenna.

Services on HVNET: The following are the services provided on HVNET:

- Data communication at speeds up to 64kbps.
- Support of X.28 and X.25 protocols for data communication.
- Voice facility on the VSAT with connection to public telephone network(PSTN of BSNL).
- Access to BSNL's RABMN network and Inet Phase I and II networks.
- Access to International data networks through GPSS of VSNL.
- Shell account access to subscribers of the Internet.

RABMN: Remote Area Business Message Network (RABMN) provides instant data communication between computers and data terminals. This is a satellite based network that provides communication to any remote part of India. The network consists of the Master Earth Station along with the Packet Switch located at Sikandarabad (U.P) and customer terminals known as micro earth stations or VSATs (Very Small Aperture Terminals) located at customer premises. VSATs are linked to the Master Earth Station through the satellite. Customers can connect their data terminals to the VSATs and transmit data.

INMARSAT: Subscriber dialled INMARSAT services from shore to ship, ship to shore and ship to ship in Indian region are operational in the BSNL Network. Subscriber dialled INMARSAT calls are also accessible to STD/ISD, PCOs where these have been made available to ISD subscribers.

The product mix of BSNL is very large and management of the product mix offers many challenges. The pace of change in telecom technology in the international scenario, affect the product mix of the company. New product development, infrastructure upgradation, manpower building and skill development, policy restrictions, social obligations and priorities, etc. are all the critical issues need to be addressed all the time. BSNL is so far lagging behind to provide innovative leadership in introducing new products and in improving the service package of the existing products. The company moves are rather reactive to the advances of the competing private companies. BSNL should develop expertise in leading innovations to protect its leadership position or to catch the position. It is necessary to have state of the art technology as well as the motivated human resource towards the achievement of such goal.

REFERENCES

1. Philip Kotler and Kevin Lane Keller, '*Marketing Management*", 12e, Pearson Education, New Delhi, 2006, p. 5.
2. *Ibid.*, p. 6.
3. Ronald T. Rust, Antony J. Zoharik and Timothy I. Keming Ham, '*Services Marketing*', Addition Wesley Longman, New Delhi, 1999, p. 15.
4. Keith H. Hammonds, '*Michael Porter's Big Ideas*', *Fast Company*, March 2001, pp. 150-154.
5. http://www.h&m.com, and Eric Sylvers, 'Cut-Rate Swedish Retailer Enters the Italian Market', *New York Times*, August 27, 2003, p. W1.
6. Philip Kotler, and Kevin Lane Keller, '*Marketing Management*", 12e, Pearson Education, New Delhi, 2006, p. 39.
7. Rama Mohana Rao, K., '*Service Marketing*', Pearson Education, New Delhi, 2005, p. 62-63.
8. *Ibid.*
9. Philip Kotler, '*Marketing Management – Analysis, Planning, Implementation and Control*', Prentice Hall of India Pvt. Ltd., New Delhi, 1987, p. 463.
10. Rama Mohana Rao, K., '*Service Marketing*', Pearson Education, New Delhi, 2005, p. 123.

PRICING POLICY

Pricing is an essential and one of the most important decision areas of marketing. It is a major determinant of the market demand. Either a buyer or a seller may propose a price, but it does not become one until accepted by the other.[1] Price affects the firms competitive position and its share of the market. As a result, price has considerable influence on the revenue of the business. "Price is the mechanism for translating into quantitative terms the perceived value of the product to the consumer. Price is one of the main considerations for the consumer for making the final choice".[2] Pricing plays a dominant role in the determination of the present as well as the future revenues of a concern. "Prices not only determine what can be obtained for goods or services which are already produced or being served, but also influence plans for future production and future marketing" .[3]

Telecom sector was under public sector monopoly until it is opened up to the private sector. The pricing policy reflected government policy and it was an administered one. The entry of TRAI and the emergence of competitive environment brought in several changes. The following is the brief description of the Telecom pricing:

Historical Perspectives of Telecom Tariffs

Telephone service was introduced in 1882 at Calcutta and Bombay with annual rental of Rs. 150 per connection within three miles of exchange. In the year 1920 telephone rental was fixed at Rs. 150 per annum uniformly for all connections upto three miles from the exchange. In October 1922, higher rates of annual rental were introduced for bigger exchanges at Rs. 175 upto 100 lines, Rs. 200 upto 200 lines, Rs. 225 upto 500 lines. In 1934, rentals were re-grouped according to small exchanges and important exchanges. The annual rates of rental for small exchanges were prescribed depending upon the distance of connection that is, Rs. 168 within one mile, Rs. 180 within 2 miles, and Rs. 192 with in three miles.

Telecommunications Tariff Structure Involves the Following:

1. An installation charge
2. Rental charge
3. A call charge — volume charge depends on duration in the case of local call and for long distance call, it depends on both duration and distance.

Tariff Policy

Prior to 1960, there was no tariff policy. As such, the charges were not based on any cost study. The main guiding factor was the need of balancing the budget. Subsidized rates were provided to the certain categories like press, hospitals etc. The First Tariff Revision Committee was constituted in 1956 and the Committee submitted its report in 1958. Tariff revision came into effect in 1960. The Committee considered all relevant issues for the growth of telecom service, such as commercial character, past financial working of the department, capital structure, reserve funds, anticipated trend of revenue and the future needs of departmental expenditure. Since then, many committees have been constituted for both tariff revision as well as for recommending progressive structure of DOT, embracing all facets of telephone service and incorporating many features.

To begin with, only annual rental was being charged uniformly to all the customers. Later, differentiated annual rental were charged depending upon number of connection of each exchange servicing the areas. In the subsequent change, surcharge was introduced in addition to annual rental. This was prevailing upto 1960.

The surcharge on rental of telephones was abolished and merged with basic rates in 1952. Rental for measured rate system was revised from 16-1-1966 and prescribed in two rates for the four metro cities and for other exchanges. In measured rate system, the deposit of one year's advance rental was introduced from January 1968. Measured rate system was introduced in systems having 300 lines of equipped capacity and measured rate rental was prescribed separately for system of less than 10000 lines. From June 1979, two more rates were introduced for systems of (1) 30,000 to 1 lakh lines (2) 1 lakh lines and above. Advance deposit scheme requiring a deposit at the time of application for new telephone connections was introduced from 1975. The minimum rate of 15 paise prevailing from 16th January 1966 was revised to 20 paise from 10-8-1971, 25 paise from 15-5-1974, 30 paise from March 1976, 40 paise from July 1981, and 60 paise from December 1986.

Quarterly rental was introduced from April 1960 as also free calls of 150 for each connection. Free calls were increased to 250 in 1971, 350 in 1974 and again reverted to 250 in 1976 and this limit was retained upto 1981. In 1982, free call limit was further reduced to 200. In December 1982, free call limit was increased to 275. Local call tariff was fixed at 60p and 80p for two call slabs (276 to 2000 and more than 2000 calls respectively). In 1988, local call tariff was increased to 80p for first slab of calls (276-2000) Rs. 1 for second slab (2000-5000) and Rs. 1.25 for third slab (greater than 5000). In April, 1990 the number of free calls was reduced to 150 from 275. Lowest call rate of 0.80 p was charged to first slab of 151-1000 calls, and Rs. 1.10 paise for the second slab in excess of 1000. Rental was Rs. 250 and Rs. 330 for 30,000 to 1 lakh lines exchange and above 1 lakh lines respectively.

In 1993, rental was increased from Rs. 330 to Rs. 360 for are exchange capacity of one lakh lines to three lakh lines.

For exchange capacity of above three lakh lines, rental was increased to Rs. 380.

Trunk Call: In laying down the trunk call charges from May 1922, the principle adopted was to charge trunk call for every 12(1/2) miles or part thereof at the rate of three annas upto 100 miles (16annas =Rs 1) and at two annas for further distance of 12 (1/2) mile or part thereof. The trunkcall rates were revised several times along with telephone charges. As per 1999 tariff revision, inland trunk tariff is merged with STD tariff, but Rs. 5 is charged extra towards trunkcall booking.

Subscriber Trunk Dialling (STD): STD was introduced from 20th November 1960. STD is also termed as (1) NSD (National subscriber dialling), and (2) DLD (Domestic long distance call service). Periodicity of STD pulse rate was fixed from December 1962 in seven different slab distances. From 16th January 1966, the distance slab for STD was revised and concessions were introduced for night tele-traffic and holiday traffic. Day time pulse rate was fixed at 36 seconds for 20-50 kms; 18 seconds upto 100 kms; 12 seconds upto 200 kms; 6 seconds upto 500 kms; 4 seconds upto 900 kms; and 2 seconds for distance above 900 kms. The STD charges were revised in 1972, 1976, 1982, and 1993.

A drastic change has been effected in STD tariff structure revision in 1999. Seven distance slabs were reduced to five. As regards to periodicity of pulse rate, about 25 per cent increase has been affected. In other words, long distance call tariff has been reduced by about 25 per cent.

Telex Service: Automatic telex service was introduced in 1953 between Bombay and Ahmedbad with line rental of Rs. 12 per month upto four miles radial distance. Teleprinter rental was fixed at Rs. 1000 per annum. Local telex call was charged at nine annas for three minutes duration. Telex tariff for all places in India was revised from 1962. Annual rental for telex connection within local areas was Rs. 800. Annual rental for each km beyond local area was Rs.75 local call charges for unit duration three minutes was 40 p. long distance pulse rate for slab distance of 200 kms was 60 seconds, 600 kms - 30 seconds, 1000 km - two second and above 1000 kms - 12 seconds. The tariff of Telex service was revised in 1964, 1966, 1969, 1976, 1983, 1986 and 1994 before 1999 Tariff revision.

Telecom Tariff Order 1999

TRAI began the Tariff rebalancing with second consultation paper in September 1998 and specified the tariffs in *the first Telecom Tariff Order, March 1999 ((TTO, 99).*

Objectives of Tariff Policy

The modern approach to telecom tariff recognizes the existence of several objectives or criteria, that is, multi dimensional. The broad objectives can be clarified as: financial, economic and social. Social objective is to ensure that price structure takes into account policy and institutional objectives that involves provision of services at special tariffs to target groups, areas etc.

For fixed services, the TTO, 99 was the first step in the process of tariff rebalancing. The tariffs were specified in terms of standard packages that all providers were obliged to offer. However, there was provision for both fixed and cellular service providers to offer alternative packages in terms of monthly rentals and per minute charges. The TTO 99 envisaged an increase in monthly rentals and a decrease in National Long Distance and ILD tariffs to bring them near costs in three phases over a three year period. The phasing would help to cushion the impact of changes. The TTO 99 categorized the users as rural and urban (based on classification as per census) and further within each category, the users were divided into low, general and commercial. The rentals for the different categories varied and also depended on the exchange capacity to which the subscriber was connected.

The categorization into low and general user was based on the usage in terms of metered call units (MCUs). For both the urban and rural users, low users were those who made less than or equal to 500 MCUs per month, while general users were those who belonged to neither commercial nor low user categories. The definition of commercial user was left to be decided in the future after a due process of consultation. For the time being, commercial users were those who opted for a rental under the commercial category. For rural subscribers, if MCUs were less than or equal to 500, then the per call unit charge would be Rs 0.80, additional MCUs would have a charge of Rs 1 per unit, while for urban areas, the corresponding charges were Rs 1 and Rs 1.20 paise respectively. The per minute charge did not vary within the specific sub categories (low, general, or commercial). The rural and urban subscribers got 75 and 60 free MCUs per month.

For the long distance and international calls, the TTO 99 specified a pulse rate and charge on different distance slabs. These were expected to reduce over the three-year period. The minimum and maximum charges for a one minute long distance call for rural subscriber at pulse charge of Rs 0.80 per minute would be Rs 0.80 (for a call within 50 kms) and Rs 20.00 (for a call distance of greater than 1000 kms). These were expected to be Rs 0.80 and Rs 14.40 respectively by 31st March 2002. For the urban subscriber the corresponding rates would be Rs 1.00 and Rs 25.00, expected to go to Rs 1.00 and Rs 18.00 respectively over the three-year period. The above elements were a part of the standard package which all service providers were required to provide. For cellular services, the TTO specified "cost based" rentals (Rs 600 per month) and air time tariffs (Rs 6 per min).

Interconnections: Interconnection regulation had been in terms of interconnection charges (set up charges) and revenue share (usage charges). The basic framework was laid down in TRAI's consultation paper on Telecom Pricing (September 9, 1998) and TTO 99. Key aspects of the framework were: Interconnection prices were based on costs and usage charges were based on a percentage of revenue share. For interconnections between fixed services providers, the provision for the local calls was on the basis of bill and keep, for national long distance (NLD) calls the revenue share proportion was 40:60 for the originating and terminating service provider respectively. For international long distance (ILD) services, revenue share proportion was 45:55 between the originating and terminating network, in this case the DOT.

For interconnection between fixed and mobile services, the *receiving party pays* principle was followed, with no revenue share. The called party would pay the airtime. For calls between the mobile to fixed services, the originator would pay the airtime + PSTN charges (as applicable). The PSTN charges were to be passed on to the fixed service provider in toto for the long distance and the international component. The TRAI proposed a shift to the *calling party pays* regime in September 1998 but shifted the implementation to August 1999, as the implications of the National Telecom Policy 1999 (NTP 99) that was likely to be announced in March 1999 also needed to be factored in. The NTP 99 changed the annual licence fee to a one time entry fee and an annual revenue share. This had implications on the cost based tariffs. TRAI subsequently reviewed the tariffs and reduced the cap on rentals (from Rs 600 to Rs 450) and airtime (from Rs 6.00 per min to Rs 4.0 in metros and Rs 4.50 in circles). The revenue share for NLD and ILD continued as before.

For fixed to mobile local calls, TRAI specified a charge of Rs 2.40 for the first minute and Rs 1.20 for each successive minute. Along with it, the revenue share was mandated as 33:67% between the fixed and mobile operator specified as a mobile terminating charge. Due to MTNL and others filing a case in the High Court requesting for a stay on the CPP regime on the grounds that this would lead to (*i*) increased costs due to network upgradation, bill collection, and bad debts and (*ii*) TRAI had no jurisdiction to issue or to make regulations to regulate arrangements amongst service providers. The courts held that TRAI did not have powers to alter the terms and conditions of the licence (through specifying the revenue sharing regulation).

The TRAI Amended the Ordinance in January 2000. This changed the composition and powers of TRAI, specifically giving TRAI the power to fix interconnectivity terms, and setting up the Telecom Dispute Settlement Appellate Tribunal (TDSAT). In addition to the scope of the disputes in the earlier act, the tribunal would also be the appeal mechanism for decisions of the TRAI. The decisions of the tribunal could be appealed against only in the Supreme Court.

The second phase of the rebalancing was to be effective from July 2000. During the review process the service providing arm of the erstwhile DOT, called Department of Telecom Services (DTS), (now BSNL) mentioned that due to tariff rebalancing, (the long distance calls becoming cheaper), it had earned lower revenues by Rs 2000-2200 crores during 1999-2000. The flexibility of the alternative tariff package had been utilized to the extent of not charging rent for subscribers making 200 MCUs. This had led a further loss of Rs 1000-1200 crores.

However, in TRAI's assessment, due to the delays in implementation of the second round of rebalancing, declining cost of telecom equipment and overall revenue increase due to lower priced STD/ISD calls, the effects of the rebalancing in the first phase had not been very severe. As it expected the DTS to bring about efficiency changes to further reduce its costs, TRAI decided to go ahead with the second round of rebalancing which'would be applicable until 31st March 2002. The longer time frame would enable elasticity of demand to manifest itself, and give greater time to the incumbent to make structural adjustments.

The STD rates were expected to decline by nearly 11.5%, while the rentals were not expected to significantly change during this period. While the original plan had envisaged an increase in rentals for the general subscriber category, the TRAI decided not to implement it, as it felt that the total "loss" on this account would be about Rs 200-220 crores. This amount, as a percentage of total revenues of DTS was very small and could be made up by greater number of STD/ISD calls and improved efficiency of the incumbent. It felt that not increasing the rental would help in the increase of teledensity. Since the TRAI was in the process of working out the cost based tariffs on the basis of "forward looking" costs and a different methodology, both of which were going to be a part of a further consultation process, it deferred an increase in rentals. The revised tariffs were to be effective from 1st October 2000.

In August 2000, the National Long Distance Competition policy that would allow private operators to offer long distance services was announced and it was expected that this would bring down long distance prices. A revision in the cellular air time to Rs 3 per min was also affected.

Competition in telecom services driven by regulatory initiatives and technological advancement continued to push the prices down. This trend was more visible in mobile and long distance services. The competitive pressures also made the service providers to be more innovative in their tariff offerings. Products like "2 years validity prepaid coupons" and "Life Time Validity" schemes have made telecom services more affordable and also led to large-scale subscriber acquisitions. The National Long Distance (NLD) tariff has further declined subsequent to the implementation of new ADC/IUC regime effective from 1st March 20 March 2006. Another development in the NLD segment is the launch of "One India" tariff plan by BSNL and other similar plans by other operators. This plan permits the subscribers to make long distance calls anywhere in the country at a flat rate of Rs. 1/- per minute for a fixed monthly rental of Rs. 299. The tariff for International Long Distance (ILD) service has also come down with the reduced ADC. The ILD tariffs of Rs. 7.20 per minute (to US, UK and Canada) and Rs. 9.60

per min (to South East Asia, Rest of Europe) that were initially offered as promotional tariffs have since become the standard ILD rates.

The ceiling tariff for International Private Leased Circuits (IPLC) of El Capacity (2 Mpbs) has been fixed at Rs.13 lakhs per year in comparison to the prevailing listed price of Rs. 20.2 lakhs, indicating a reduction of about 35 per cent. The ceiling tariff for higher capacities, i.e., DS3 and STM1 streams for IPLC has been fixed at Rs. 104 lakhs per year and Rs. 299 lakhs per year, respectively, in comparison to prevailing lised price of Rs. 361 lakhs and Rs. 1000 lakhs, respectively, indicating reduction of 71 per cent and 70 per cent in their respective tariff.

The ceiling tariffs for Domestic Leased Circuit (DLC) for different capacities were revised during the year indicating a reduction by 3 to 70 per cent in comparison to the existing market rates. The key users of the service in India are Internet Service Providers, Informational Technology (IT) and IT-Enabled Service Enterprises like Business Process Outstanding (BPO) Units, Telecommunication Service Providers, corporate enterprises, etc. a competitively priced DLC Service, which is fundamental for achieving a higher rate of penetration of Broadband in the country, will go a long way in transferring the socio-economic opportunities in the country particularly in rural areas.

Tariff for telecommunication services in India is one of the lowest in the world. The Indian consumer has immensely benefited from such lower tariffs which has also been a major factor for explosive growth in the sector. Considering intense competition in various segments of telecommunications sector and continuous decline in the tariff, TRAI has moved to a regime of tariff deregulation in a gradual manner. Currently, TRAI is following 'Hands Off approach in deciding tariffs except in areas where competition is found to be insufficient. As of March 2006, tariff for Cellular Services (except for roaming services), Basic Services (except for rural telephony) and NLD/ILD Services stand forborne and tariff for rural telephony, roaming services and leased lines continue to be in the regulated regime. With a view to protect the interest of subscribers on tariff related matters, the Authority has taken several initiatives by amending the Telecommunications Tariff Order (TTO) 1999 wherever necessary.

The DOT stated that "generally, price could be cost based and should allow for a reasonable rate of return on capital employed. A certain mark up for risk should also be allowed. This is particularly true for some of the new services where there is no assured market. For some services, such as leased line services, prices should be based on the earning capacity of the facility being provided. For some of the premium services e.g. ISDN, IN services etc. higher tariffs can be charged as compared to basic telephone service".

The DOT also pointed out that a tariff setting involved more nuances than could be captured by emphasis only on cost orientation. For a number of services "opportunity cost" principle, or the principle of "what the service can earn", would be relevant for fixing tariffs; sometimes tariffs had to be set on the basis of "value of service to the customer"; promotional tariffs might be required in case of new telecom services; and that "ability to pay" principle could not be entirely done away with in the context of the country's social policy.

The Telecom Pricing Consultation should be widened to include all types of telecom services available to a citizen such as cellular radio, trunk mobile radio, radio raging, etc. It should also include the aspects of Spectrum Fee, Wireless Licence Fee, which a service provider is required to pay, in addition to DOT's licence fee; and in due course, the TRAI should also look into the "pricing" aspects of Global Mobile Personal Communication Service. The Telecom tariffs effective from January, 2003 are presented in Annexure 5.1

Basic One India Plan

Particulars		
Fixed Monthly Charges		Rs.180
Free calls		50
Unit call rate		Rupee One
Particulars	**Pulse in Sec.**	**Call Charges**
Own Network Fixed, WLL	180	Rs. 1.00/3min.*
Own Network Cellular (94)	60	Rs. 1.00/min.
Other Network (Fixed)	180	Rs. 1.00/3min.
Other Network (WLL, Cellular)	60	Rs. 1.00/min.
Intra Circle calls more than 50 kms and Inter Circle Calls (Own and Other Network)		
Fixed, WLL, Cellular	60	Rs. 1.00/min.
Calls made from SDCA adjoining Delhi and terminating in Delhi (Gurgaon/Faridabad/Bahadurgarh/ Ballabhgarh/Sonepat (Kundli) SDCA of Haryana Circle and Ghaziabad/Noida/Loni/Meerut/ Modinagar/Sikandrabad SDCAs of UP circle)		
Particulars	**Pulse in sec.**	**Call charges**
Any Fixed and MTNL's WLL	120	Rs. 1.00/2min.
Any Cellular	60	Rs. 1.00/min.
WLL (Other network)	60	Rs. 1.00/min
Calls made from Gurgaon/ Faridabad/Bahadurgarh/ Ballabhgarh/Sonepat (Kundli) SDCA of Haryana Circle to Ghaziabad/Noida/Loni/Meerut/ Modinagar/Sikandrabad SDCAs of UP circle and Vice versa		
Particulars	**Pulse in sec.**	**Call Charges**
0-50 kms (Own network)		
Fixed/WLL	180	Rs. 1.00/3min.
0-50 kms (Other network)		
Fixed/WLL/Mobile	60	Rs. 1.00/min.
more than 50 kms (All network)	60	Rs. 1.00/min.

Average rate for ISD calls per minute in Rs. : Uniform across all plans PSTN Charges for Dail up internet access under BSNL ONE INDIA		
Time Band	**Pulse**	**Charges per hour**
0730-2230 Peak Hours	375 sec	Rs. 9.60
2230-0730 Off peak hours	750 sec	Rs. 4.80

Note:

* Local and Intra circle calls up to 50 kms are chargeable at Rupee one for 3 minutes.

The above package will be applicable for both Rural and Urban subscribers.

Additional Instructions:

(*i*) The above Plan is not meant for Local/STD/ISD PCO's franchisee.

(*ii*) The change in plan shall be implemented as per existing practice.

(*iii*) Other terms and condition shall remain unchanged.

(*iv*) This order shall be effective from 16th January 2007 (Midnight of 15th January 2007 and 16th January 2007)

(*v*) Service Tax will be charged extra.

ISD Pulses (in seconds) and Timings

BSNL has decided to reduce the charges for International Calls (ISD) with effect from 01st October 2006 as under:

Country Category	**Revised rate w.e.f. 01.10.06 for all 24 hours**	
	Pulse in sec	**Rs. per minute***
USA, Canada, UK and Sri Lanka	10	7.2
Europe (other than UK), Singapore, Thailand, Malaysia, Indonesia and Hong Kong	7.5	9.6
Kuwait, Baharin, UAE, Oman, Qatar		
Rest of world	6	12.00

***Per minute rates are based on Rs.1.20 per pulse.**

Notes: The revised rates are applicable with effect from 01.10.2006 (00.00 hrs on the midnight of 30th September and 1st October, 2006) and shall apply to all calls originated from Fixed, Cellular and WLL (M) phones of BSNL and also be applicable to Trunk Calls and PCOs.

Long Distance Connections

1. Beyond the Local Area
   Actual Length

(*i*) Up to 5 km	Rental for local area + Rs. 600 p.a. for each additional km or part
(*ii*) 6-10 km	Rental as (*a*) above + Rs. 800 p.a. for each additional km or part beyond 5 kms
(*iii*) Exceeding 10 kms	Rental as (*b*) + Rs. 1500 p.a. per km or part beyond 10 kms with minimum period of hire as 3 years

Temporary Connections and Extensions

1. Telephone Connections from Temporary Exchanges or PBXs. The rate shall be the same as applicable for regular telephone
2. Charges for Extension to DELs Connections

		Annual Rental
(*i*) Internal Extension (without inter-com)/ Internal Connection	Rs. 400	
(*ii*) Internal Extension (with inter-com)	Rs. 500	
	Chargeable Distance from main connection	Annual Rental
(*iii*) External Extension to DEL/External Connection	(*a*) 1 km	Rs. 1,400
	(*b*) Exceeding 1 km but not exceeding 5 km	Rent as per (a) above + Rs. 800 per km for each additional km or part
	(*c*) Beyond 5 kms	Rent as per (b) above + Rs. 1.500 per km for each additional km or part

(Chargeable distance is 1.25 times the radial distance)

3. Temporary Extensions and Temporary Private Wires
   Temporary extensions from departmental exchange connections, from private exchanges, connections from private branch exchanges and extensions from these connections, may be given up to a maximum period of four months provided the cost involved in giving the facility does not

exceed Rs. 200 in each case. The charges for these facilities shall be levied at half appropriate annual rental/prescribed for the corresponding facility provided on regular basis.

Manual Trunk Calls

1.Trunk Calls:	
(*i*) From and to places with STD facilities	(a) Rs. 5 per call plus
(*b*)	Tariff for subscriber trunk dialed long distance calls, as applicable. Provided that the minimum tariff under this plan may be the amount applicable to a one minute subscriber trunk dialed domestic long distance call. For calls more than 1 minute duration, the time period of charging will be calculated in discrete unit of 1 minute each.
(*c*)	Rs. 1.20 per metered call to be charged uniformly.
(*ii*) From/to places without STD facilities	Tariffs shall be the same as in (*i*) above assuming as if these places have STD facilities.
2.Charges for various types of Trunk calls:	
(*i*) S.V.H. Calls	Same rate as for ordinary calls at H(1) provided that where the SVH calls issued for purpose other than that contemplated by such a call it should be charged at the highest rate applicable in the service.
(*ii*) Urgent /Demand Call	Twice the ordinary call rate at H(1)(i)(b) & (c) plus Rs. 5/- per call.
(*iii*) Lightening calls	8 times the ordinary call at H(1)(i)(b) & (c) plus Rs. 5/- per call.

(*iv*) Most immediate, Operation immediate, Immediate and important calls booked by authorized official of Govt. Departments.	4 times the ordinary call rate as at H(l)(i)(b) & (c) plus Rs. 5/- per call.

3. Supplementary charge for special services like PP, FT, SFT:

   The additional charges for a particular person facility, Fixed time call and subscriber fixed time call shall be 50% of Trunk charge for unit call (one minute trunk) of ordinary category, subject to a minimum of Re. 0.50.

4. (*i*) Press Trunk Calls	Rebate 12.5% on the basic trunk call charges and not on the International Trunk call charges.
(*ii*) Late fee per call effective or ineffective	(*a*) on trunk call Rs. 2.00 (*b*) on local calls Rs. 0.50
(*iii*) Messenger service per call effective or ineffective	Rs. 2.00
5. Charges for Special Facilities of Trunk files:	
(*i*) Cancellation Charges: Trunk Call Cancelled after booking but before maturity:	
(*a*) Ordinary Call (within one hour)	Rs. 5/-
(*b*) Others (within half an hour)	Rs. 5/-
(*ii*) Charge for ineffective trunk call:	
(*a*) No reply from the called number	no charge
(*b*) Called number closed/out of order	no charge
(*c*) Line at either end is out of order	no charge

(*d*) Called number obtained but PP not available	1 minute charge based on pulse applicable at the the time of maturity plus Rs. 5/-
(*e*) Called number given by the caller being wrong	as in ii(d) above
(*f*) Called number after being rung up refuse to accept Trunk call	as in ii(d) above
(*g*) Called person or persons being obtained refuses to talk	as in ii(d) above
(*h*) No answer from the calling number or the calling subscriber refuses to talk after the called person has been obtained.	as in ii(d) above
(*iii*) For ineffective Fixed Time/S.F.T Calls:	
(*a*) Call cancelled due to failure of service	no charge
(*b*) Call cancelled by the subscriber when not connected, within 15 minutes of fixed time/ subscription fixed time	no charge
(*c*) Call cancelled by subscriber half an hour before the required time of the FT or S.F.T.	Rs. 5/-
(*d*) Call ineffective due to no reply from called number or calling number	no charge

(*e*) Call ineffective for any reason other than above, such as called number wrongly given and caller number refuses to talk, no responsible person etc.	1 minute charge based on pulse applicable at the time of maturity plus Rs. 5/-
(*iv*) Report fee:	
(*a*) SAARC countries:	Rs. 6/-
(*b*) Other neighbouring countries	Rs. 6/-
(*c*) Countries in Africa, Europe, Gulf, Asia Oceania	Rs. 8/-
(*d*) All countries in American Continent and other places in Western places	Rs. 10/-
(*v*) Supplementary Charges for effective PP and FT calls for International Trunk Calls	

Private Exchange and Private Branch Exchanges

The charges of PMX/PMBX/Electro Mechanical PAX and PABX/ Extendable type PBXs and PABXs (Electromechanical and Electronic) and Electronic PBX and I PABX remain unchanged.

1. Rental for telephone connection from PBX and Private Exchange(Manual and automatic)

	Annual Reutal
1	2
(*a*) Internal extensions	Rs. 400
(*b*) External extension:	
(*i*) Not exceeding 1 km chargeable distance from private Exgs./PBX	Rs.1400
(*ii*) Exceeding 1 km but not exceeding 5 km of chargeable distance from the Pvt. Exgs. and PBX.	Rental as b(*i*) above plus Rs. 800 per additional km. or or fraction thereof.

1	2
(*iii*) Exceeding 5 kms of chargeable distance from the Pvt. Exgs. and PBX	Rental as b(*ii*) above plus Rs. 1500 per annum for each additional km. or fraction thereof.
2. Charges for Private Wires	
Internal Pvt. Wires	Rs.400
3. Subscribers owned group PBX/PABX/EPBAX (For office, building Hotels, and other parties)	
Monthly Rental per Junction Line	
(*a*) Rental charges for outgoing and Both ways Junction lines	Rental as per DELs (Rural or Urban as the case may be)
(*b*) Rental charges for Incoming Junction lines	Rental as per DELs (Rural or Urban as the case may be). Less a rebate of Rs. 50/- per month per incoming junction.
(*c*) Call charges	As per DELs (Rural or Urban as the case may be)
(*d*) Free Calls	As per DELs (Rural or Urban as the case may be)
(e) Additional charge of 20% on junction rental for DID facilities will be levied	
4. Service provider Owned Group PBX/PABX/EPABX (for office, building Hotels and other parties)	
Monthly Rental per Junction Line	
(a) Rental charges for outgoing and Both ways Junction line	Rs. 620 monthly
(b) Rental charges for Incoming Junction lines	Rs. 620 monthly less a rebate of Rs. 50 monthly
(c) Call charges	Rs. 1.20 per metered call
(d) Free Calls	NIL
Operator Assisted International Calls	
(i) From and to places with ISD facilities	(*a*) Rs.5 per call Plus (*b*) Tariff for ISD calls as applicable Provided that the minimum tariff under this plan may be the amount applicable to a one minute International Subscriber Trunk Dialed Call. For calls more than 1 minute duration, the time period of charging will be calculated in discrete unit of 1 minute each.

1	2
	(*c*) Rs. 1.20 per metered call to be charged uniformly.
(*ii*) From/ to places without ISD facilities	Tariff shall be the same as in (*i*) above, assuming as if these places have ISD facilities

Public Telephone

Category of PT	Charges for call between Exgs. other than parent Exgs.	Charges for call from PT to Exgs. other than parent Exgs.	Charges for calls to PT from Exgs. other than parent Exgs.
1	2	3	4
(*i*) Local PTs connected to Measured Rate Exchange System	Re. 1 irrespective of duration of the call	Trunk call charges as from parent Exgs. plus Re. 1 Pt. charge, the Pt. charge being irrespective of the duration of call	Trunk call charges to parent Exgs. of public telephones plus Re. 1 PT charge, the PT charges being irrespective of the duration of call
(*ii*) Interpolated Pts	Trunk call charges as for an Exgs. located at the same station as the PT plus 50p charge per unit duration for call or part thereof.	Trunk call charges as for an Exgs. located at the same station as the PT plus 50p charge per unit duration for call or part thereof.	Trunk call charges as for an Exgs. located at the same station as the PT plus 50p charge per unit duration for call or part thereof.
(*iii*) L.D.P.T.			
(*a*) Connected to FR Exchange/ MR Exchange	25p/50p PT charges per unit duration of call or part thereof.	50% of Trunk call charges as from parent Exgs. plus appropriate PT charge as in col. 2	Trunk call charges to parent exchange of PT plus appropriate PT charge as in col. 2

* Provided that for calls between two PTs connected to different Exchanges, the PT charges for both the Pts. will be levied in addition to the Trunk call charge between the Exchanges

* Provided further that for a call between two PTs connected separately to the same Exchange or same Pt the charge for the call shall be sum of charges for a call from each of the two Pts. to the common Exgs of common Pts.

* Provided further that in the case of a call between two LDPT connected in tandem, charge of the call shall be levied on the basis of radial distance between the two PTs as indicated in col 1 & 2 against the LDPTs

(*b*) Extension from LDPTs

Actual length from PCO	Annual rental
Upto 1 km.	Rs. 300
1 to 5 kms	Rs. 300 for 1st km plus Rs. 250 for each additional km.
More than 5 km.	Rs. 1300 for 1st 5 kms plus Rs. 1500 for each additional km with a minimum period of hire as 3 years.

Tariff of Landline/WLL PCO/VPTs
Call Charges for all type of PCOs except
Local VPT (without 95 facilitv)

1. Local, Intra and Inter Circle Calls

Particulars	Unit Rate (inclusive of service tax)	Revised Pulse in seconds			
		BSNL Network		Other Network	
		Wire line/ WLL*	Cellular	Wire line	Cellular/ WLL*
Local & Intra Circle Calls					
Local & Intra up to 50 kms	Rs. 1.00	90	60	60	60
Intra > 50 kms	Rs. 1.00	60	60	60	60
Inter Circle Calls					
0-50 kms	Rs. 1.00			30	
> 50 kms	Rs. 1.00			30	

**WLL covers both WLL (fixed) & WLL (M).*

BSNL Fixed line Packages. 1

Package Name	Monthly (Rs.) Fixed charges	Free Units (Monthly)	Units Charges (After Free Calls) Rs. Ps.
One India	180	50	1.00
Economy	300	200	1.20
Special	475	500	1.10
Special Plus	975	1100	1.00
Super	1450	1800	0.90
Premium	2450	3500	0.80
Plan-260	260	160	1.20
Plan-2250	2250	2900	0.90
Sulabh-I	120	0	O/G with ITC only
Sulabh-II	120	0	1.20
Plan-100	100	0	1.20

(this is for Apartments/Housing Complexes along with free Intercom facility)

BSNL Fixed line Packages. 2

Unlimited Plan	Monthly Charges	Unit Charges	Free Units (Monthly)
Plan 399	399	1.20	Free units 75 and Unlimited free calls within BSNL fixed network with in SCDA
Plan 599	599	1.10	Unlimited free calls within BSNL fixed network in A.P
Plan 899	899	1.00	Unlimited free calls within BSNL fixed and Cellular network in A.P

2 ISO Call Charges (Unit Rate of Rs. 1.00 inclusive of Service Tax)

Country Category	Pulse (sec.)	Rs./min. inclusive of Service Tax
USA, Canada, UK, Sri Lanka	6	10
Europe, (other than UK), Singapore, Thailand, Malaysia , Indonesia and Hong Kong, Kuwait, Bahrain, UAE, Oman, Qatar	5	12
Rest of World	4	15

Note: Service tax has already been included in Unit rate of Rupee One. Hence no additional service tax is required to be charged.

Discount allowed to PCO Operators: All type of Postpaid Landline PCOs including fixed PCOs provided on WLL & VPTs (except Local VPT without 95 facility)

Billed MCU per month	MRP per MCU	Net billed to PCO operator per MCU inclusive of ST & Cess	Discount per MCU	Return on Investment for PCO Operator (%)
Cl	C2	C3	C4=C2-C3	C5=C4/C3
< = 400	1.000	0.700	0.300	42.86
> 400 <= 800	1.000	0.680	0.320	47.06
> 800 <= 1200	1.000	0.650	0.350	53.85
> 1200 <= 1500	1.000	0.630	0.370	58.73
> 1500 <= 2500	1.000	0.615	0.385	62.60
> 2500	1.000	0.600	0.400	66.67

[**Note:** 1. MRP is defined as: Maximum limit of the price allowed to be charged to public by PCO Operator.]

LOCAL VPT without 95 facility

1. Discount Structure for Local PCO without 95 facility

Particular	Discount per MCU
Local VPTs	50%

2. Pulse Rate and Call Charges

Particular	Unit rate	Service Tax	Calls to Wire line/ WLL (except 9 level)		Calls to Cellular/ WLL (9 level)
			Local & Intra Circle upto 50 kms	Intra Circle Calls beyond 50 kms	Intra Circle Calls Including local calls
Local VPT without 95 facility	Re. 1.00	N.A.	90	N.A.	60

Other Charges

1. Reconnection Fee

   Disconnected due to default of payment.

(*i*) Telephone connection/plug point	Rs. 100
(*ii*) (*a*) For an extra bell restored within a period of 10 days	Nil
(*b*) in other cases	Rs. 30

2. Transfer Fees

(*i*) For transfer of telephone connections to near relative	Rs. 100
(*ii*) Use of land lords telephone by the tenant living in the same building	Rs. 100
(*iii*) Third party transfer	Rs. 500

3. Shifting Charge

(*i*) Telephone connection, extensions and connections to Private and Private Branch Exchanges:

	In the same room	**In all other cases**
(*a*) In Exchange system with less than 500 lines	Rs. 75/-	Rs. 150/-
(*b*) In Exchange system with 500 lines	Rs. 75/-	Rs. 600/-*

* Rebate of Rs. 300/- allowed if internal wiring is done by subscriber

(*ii*) Private & Private Branch Exchange Board	The percentage of the installation charges prescribed for corresponding PABX	
	50%	100%
(*iii*) Attendant Box of PABX	The percentage of the installation charges prescribed for corresponding PABX	
	10%	20%
(*iv*) Plug and Socket	Rs. 75/-	Rs. 150/-
(*v*) Bells	Rs. 15/-	Rs. 30/-

4. Additional Facilities (one time charge with a warranty of 3 years)

(*i*) Extra Bell	Rs. 150/-
(*ii*) Extension Bell with Switch	Rs. 200/-

(*iii*)	A Plug & Two Sockets** for one additional socket**	Rs. 100/- No charge
(*iv*)	for each additional socket** **with effect from 24.9.2003	Rs. 50/-
(*iv*)	For long cord	
(*a*)	Up to 5 meters	Rs. 75/-
(*b*)	For every additional 5 meters	Rs 30/-
(*v*)	A complete Telephone Set	Rs. 150/- p.a.
(*vi*)	Coin Collecting Box	Rs. 150/- p.a.
(*vii*)	Loud-speaking Telephone	Rs. 800/- p.a.
(*viii*)	Ampliphone	Rs. 80/- p.a. (or Rs. 10 per month)
(*ix*)	Secraphone/Ultaphones	Rs. 500 (pro-rata for a month)

5. Charge Indicators (Check Meter):

Used with	Rental Per Annuam	Check Meter Quarterly Charges	Installation Charge
(*i*) DELs	Rs. 40	Rs. 10	Rs. 40
(*ii*) PBX Junctions	Rs. 90	Rs. 22.50	Rs. 40
(*iii*) PABX Junctions	Rs. 150	—	Rs. 50

6. Fire Alarm Service

(*a*)	Rental for Fire Alarm Switch Board	75% of the rental for a PBX of equivalent capacity
	Rental for Fire Alarm Extension	75% of the rental of PBX connection of equal length
(*b*)	Rifle Range Connections Rental	Same as for Private Wires/ N.E. Lines

7. Safe Custody

(*i*) Short Duration	Minium : 7 days Maximum: 90 days	7 Full normal rental, cable pair, and days telephone number will be reserved : and restoration will be done within one week or day specified by sub, which ever is later and Rs. 20/- will be charged

(*ii*) Long Duration

(*a*) Non-Elect. Exgs. Elect. Exgs. where dynamic locking is not provided	More than 90 days	Full rental for 90 days and 40% of rent thereafter if sub. does not require cable pair and indicator reserved for him. Restoration fee Rs. 100 at the same place and full shifting charge at other places. Restoration fee on overriding priority and within a month is Rs. 100
(*b*) For Subs of Elec. Exges with Dynamic Locking Facility	Minimum 6 months	Full rental for 6 months and 40% of normal rental, thereafter if sub. does not require cable pair and indicator reserved for him. If they are to be kept reserved, full rental should be paid for entire period of safe custody. Restoration on overiridng priority and within a month is Rs. 100

Note: Normal Rental/Rental means: for urban subscribers-as applicable to low calling urban subscribers as mentioned in para C(2) for rural subscribers—as applicable to rural subscribers as mentioned in para C(1)

8. Phone Plus Facilities (Special Services)

(*i*) Abbreviated Dialing	BSNL has decided to offer all Phone Plus Services including CLIP facility free of cost to its customers
(*ii*) Call Transfer/forwarding • Call transfer facility is available only within BSNL Network-PSTN and Cellular. • Call Forwarding facility to other network (other than BSNL) mayd also be available as per mutual agreement to this effect if signed later with other operators.	subject to following conditions: • Technical feasibility and availability • First come first serve basis • The CLI facility will be provided only after production of purchase receipt of interface approved CLI indicator by subscriber
(*iii*) Hotline facility	(BSNL circular no. 106-9/2002-Comml. dated 22.1.2003)
(*iv*) Three party conferencing	
(*v*) CLIP facility	

Source: BSNL circular on tariffs, 2003

REFERENCES

1. Edward W. Candif, Richard R. Still and Norman A.P. Govani, 'Fundamentals of Modern Marketing', Prentice Hall of India, New Delhi, 1980, p. 228.
2. Sudarsana Rao, G., 'Marketing of Services—A Study of Marketing Operations of Andhra Pradesh State Electricity Broad', Unpublished Thesis, Andhra University, Visakhapatnam, 1991, p. 216.
3. Mamoria C.B. and Joshi, R.I., "Principles and Practice of Marketing in India', Kitab Mahal, Allahabad, 1984, p. 218.

DISTRIBUTION SYSTEM

Distribution is an important element in the marketing mix of any organisation. It is the facilitating function for the interaction of producer and consumer for the exchange to take place. Distribution or the place element of the marketing mix is concerned chiefly with two main issues, i.e., accessibility and availability. Accessibility must be a component of the actual service offering for it to have value. Additionally, the perishable nature of services means it is essential for the service to be available to customers — in the right place and at the right time. The services cannot be stored until a later date and must be available for consumption at the point of production[1]. Decisions about marketing channels, which help producers deliver goods and services to their target market, are among the most critical issues the management facing because the channels that are chosen intimately affect all the other marketing decisions[2].

Distribution of services differs significantly from that of manufacturing goods. Distribution of services differs significantly from that of manufacturing goods. The nature of the service both influences and shapes distribution strategy. It is through delivery systems that the supplier provides service to the customer. With mature services, improvements may take the form of incremental enhancements to improve the efficiency or attractiveness of the delivery system. The thrust of the so-called experience economy, often consists of enhancing the experience associated with delivery processes as opposed to improving the core product[3].

The special characteristics of services such as intangibility, inseparability, variability, perishability and customer participation require specific form of distribution system. Service products are mostly those where no transfer of ownership takes place and the service is simply rented or consumed. But it is essential that it must be available and accessible before its consumption. This needs a distribution system. The distribution system may be defined as the channels, or means used by which the service providers gains access to potential buyer of the service product[4]. Service characteristics limit the application of channel know-how and warrant adaptations to cope with the specific problems. Services are intangible, often inseparable from provider and cannot be stored or transported. That being so, unlike goods they cannot be produced in one place and transported to another place for sale. Therefore, services must be sold at multiple outlets which combine promotion and production activities[5].

Designing a distribution system in a services organisation (whether it be for profit or non-profit) involves two tasks. One is to select the channels of distribution, and the other is to provide physical facilities for the distribution of the services[6]. A service marketing organisation may choose either direct marketing or channels of distribution. Direct marketing involves no intermediaries and the service producer sells directly to the customers. In the case of channels of distribution, a number of intermediaries are involved between the producer and the customer. When intermediaries are involved in distribution there will be two marketers—one is a service principal and the other is a service deliverer. The service principal is the service originator and the service deliverer is the distributor. The service deliverer fulfils the promises of the service principal given to the customers. The service intermediaries, apart from fulfilling promises, also provide time, place and convenience utilities to the target customers. The intermediaries may perform services of many service principles and thereby, providing a retailing functions for customers[7].

Basically, quality in service occurs in the service encounter between customer and employee of the service firm. Maintaining standards of performance at the service outlet is always challenging to the service provider. If such job is assigned to middlemen, there may be a danger of decrease in value of offering and bad reputation to the organisation. However, if the distributor has ability and willingness to offer such services, the risk of failure and damage to the company image get minimized.[8]

BSNL follows direct marketing as well as Franchise system to serve the target market. Physical infrastructure for the distribution of service has been laid throughout country with special focus on rural distribution network. BSNL has provided villages public telephones (VPTs) in 5.18 lakh villages, out of 5.93 lakh villages in the country by the end of 2007. The total number of rural DELs is 241.31 lakh which constitute 35.22 per cent of the total DELs of the country. The company took measures to provide accessibility of all the services offered by the company to the target market. Besides telephone connections at customer premises in urban as well as rural areas, the BSNL has 19,13,182 public telephones. The public telephone services are offered through franchise services. The company has 33,206 STD stations also operated through franchise services. Table 6.1 presents the details of transmission system.

Table 6.1 : Transmission Systems and Satellite Based Services as on 30.09.08

Transmission Systems	(Route Kms)
Coaxial	6,024
Microwave	50,430
UHF	45,130
Optical Fiber	5,60,086
Satellite Based Services	
MCPC-VSATs	82
IDR Systems (2 Mb/ 8Mb)	99/38

Source : www.bsnl.co.in/network/telephone.htm

As can be seen from the table the transmission systems are laid in four deferent forms which include Coaxial, Microwave, UHF and optical fiber. The Coaxial is of 6024 route kms. The microwave is of 50,430 route kms. The UHF is of 45, 130 route kms while optical fiber is of 5.60 lakh route kms. The satellite based services are offered through 82 MCPC-VSATs and 99/38 IDR systems (2mb/8mb).

In case of mobile services, the company had a coverage of 617 district headquarters and 2,74,428 villages. The company has covered a length of 53,230 kilometers on national highways, 69,770 kilometers on state highways and 39,173 kilometers on railway routes. The BSNL has Internet connectivity in 24 telecom circles with 2,644 working connections.

The data relating to circle-wise subscriber base of services of BSNL as on 31st March 2007 are shown in Table 6.2. (see on next page) Maharshtra occupies the first position in having number of DELs. The total number of DELs in Maharshtra is 38.05 lakh. Kerala occupies second place with 36.31 lakh DELs. The third position goes to Tamil Nadu with 3.59 lakh DELs. The table further reveals that the largest number of DELs in rural areas is in Kerala. Ther are 25.26 lakhs rural DELs in Kerala Circle. The second place in this respect goes to Maharshtra with 14.52 lakh DELs in rural areas. Andhra Pradesh occupies third position with 11.68 lakh DELs in rural areas.

The data relating to the equipped switching capacity of basic services of BSNL by the end of 2006-07 are shown in Table 6.3 (see on page. 157) It can be seen from the table, Maharshtra (excluding Mumbai) has the highest switching capacity with 51.48 lakh capacity. The second place goes to Karala, which is having 42.68 lakh switching capacity. Gujarat occupies the third position in terms of having equipped switching capacity with 36.45 lakh capacity.

Table 6.2. Circle-wise subscriber base of Basic services of BSNL as on 31st March 2007

Name of the Circle/ Service Area	No. of DELs as on 31st March 2007 Fixed (Wireline)		Total DELs on 31st as March 2007
	Urban	Rural	
Andaman and Nicobar	14282	17341	31623
Andhra Pradesh	1605989	1168358	2774347
Assam	363472	138916	502388
Bihar (including Jharkand)	931960	503238	1435198
Gujarat	1566712	776283	2342995
Haryana	586416	414910	1001326
Himachal Pradesh	89981	366589	456570
Jammu and Kashmir	244314	51145	295459
Karnakata	1683408	793685	2477093
Kerala	1104255	2526312	3630567
Madya Pradesh (including Chattisgarh)	1183352	374888	1558240
Maharshtra	2352688	1451949	3804637
North East	266371	97076	363447
Orissa	477552	294644	772196
Punjab	856073	732396	1588469
Rajasthan	1036658	619525	1656183
Tamil Nadu (including Chennai)	2678089	914898	3592987
Uttar Pradesh (east)	1084988	423818	1508806
Uttar Pradesh (West including Uttranchal)	1097915	264169	1362084
West Bengal (including Kolkata)	1965052	618937	2583989

Source : http : www.trai.gov.in

Table 6.3 Details of Equipped Switching Capacity of Basic Services of BSNL as on 31st March 2007

Name of the Circle/ Service Area	Equipped Capacity
Andaman and Nicobar	59,496
Andhra Pradesh	39,42,505
Assam	7,13,208
Bihar (including Jharkand)	20,13,833
Gujarat	36,45,452
Haryana	15,41,222
Himachal Pradesh	6,44,002
Jammu and Kashmir	4,16,132
Karnakata	34,43,485
Kerala	42,67,815
Madya Pradesh (including Chattisgarh)	21,01,091
Maharshtra (excluding Mumbai)	51,47,722
North East-I	2,81,320
North East-II	2,11,392
Orissa	9,65,720
Punjab	27,69,541
Rajasthan	22,74,618
Chennai	14,30,893
Tamil Nadu (excluding Chennai)	35,06,324
Uttar Pradesh (east)	23,23,473
Uttar Pradesh (West including Uttranchal)	22,35,022
Kolkata	16,84,161
West Bengal (excluding Kolkata)	17,03,851
Total	**534,277**

Source: http : www.trai.gov.in

BSNL is an Internet service provider, providing Internet service throughout the country except in New Delhi and Mumbai, under the brand name of Sancharnet. Sancharnet provides free all India roaming and enables it's users to access their accounts, using the same access code (172233) and user ID from any where in the Country. It has a customer base of more than 27 lakh. The details of circle wise internet services are shown in Table 6.4. The table reveals Uttar Pradesh has large number of Internet Nodes (59) following by Madya Pradesh (43 Nodes) and Maharshtra (36 Nodes). In the case of working connections, Tamil Nadu takes the first position with over 2.98 lakh connections followed by Kerala with over 2.60 lakh connections and Kolcatta with over 2.19 lakh connections. In order to make Internet available throughout the length and breadth of the Country, Internet Dhabas are being commissioned at all the Block Headquarters.

Table 6.5 (see on page. 159) depicts the circle-wise Public Call Offices as on 31st March 2007. It reveals from the table that there are 55.47 lakh Public Call Offices working by the end of 2006-07. Maharshtra circle is having the highest number of public call offices (3.28lakh) followed by Tamil Nadu (3.02 lakh) and Andhra Pradesh (2.71lakh).

Table 6.4 Internet Services (As on 30.10.2006)

Name of the Telecom Circle	No. of nodes	No. of Working connections
Andaman and Nicobar	1	2851
Andhra Pradesh	23	173105
Assam	15	17005
Bihar	15	16064
Chhattisgarh	8	19990
Gujarat	22	146658
Haryana	16	63702
Himachal Pradesh	6	17758
Jammu and Kashmir	2	27342

Name of the Telecom Circle	No. of nodes	No. of Working connections
Jharkhand	7	18964
Karnataka	27	162722
Kerala	15	260799
Madhya Pradesh	43	71198
Maharashtra	36	211950
North-East-I	5	9750
North-East-II	5	11958
Orissa	13	33629
Punjab	19	122120
Rajasthan	32	96362
Tamil Nadu	31	298509
Uttaranchal	10	26381
Uttar Pradesh (East)	39	67081
Uttar Pradesh (West)	20	67883
West Bengal	12	36932
Western Telecom Region	1	291
Kolkata Telecom District	1	219202
Chennai Telecom District	1	119714
Northern Telecom Region	1	1129
Total	**427**	**2747624**

Source : www.bsnl.co.in/network/telephone.htm

Table 6.5 Circle-wise details of Public Call Offices as on 31st March 2007.

Name of the Circle/Service Area	Public Call Offices
Andaman and Nicobar	620
Andhra Pradesh	2,71,327
Assam	33,083
Bihar (including Jharkand)	92,420
Gujarat	1,24,948
Haryana	30,411
Himachal Pradesh	12,048

Name of the Circle/Service Area	Public Call Offices
Jammu and Kashmir	16,057
Karnakata	2,67,044
Kerala	1,25,316
Madya Pradesh (including Chattisgarh)	61,230
Maharshtra (including Bombai)	3,28,100
North East-I	15,635
Orissa	30,280
Punjab	33,345
Rajasthan	67,878
Tamil Nadu (including Chennai)	3,01,737
Uttar Pradesh (east)	1,10,562
Uttar Pradesh (West including Uttranchal)	62,709
West Bengal (excluding Kolkata)	1,24,633
Total	

Source: http:/www.trai.gov.in

REFERENCES

1. Shajahan. S, 'Services Marketing', Himalaya Publishing House, Mumbai, 2001, p. 34.
2. Philip Kotler, 'A Framework for Marketing Management', Pearson Education, (Singapore) Pvt. Ltd., Indian Branch, New Delhi, 2002, p. 235.
3. Christopher Lovelock, 'Services Marketing', Addition Wesley Longman (Singapore) Pvt. Ltd., Delhi, 2001, p.338.
4. Ramphal M.K. and Gupta S.I., 'Services Marketing', Galgotia Publishing Company, New Delhi, 2000, p.20.
5. Upah, Gregory, 'Mass Marketing in Service Retailing', A Review and Synthesis of Major Methods, Journal of Retailing, Pal 1980, p. 60-61.
6. William J. Stanton, Michael J. Ezel and Brace J. Walker, 'Fundamental of Marketing', Tata McGraw Hill Publishing Co. Ltd., New Delhi, 1994, p.550.
7. Rama Mohana Rao K., 'Services Marketing', Pearson Education, New Delhi, 2005.
8. *Ibid.*

INTERNAL MARKETING

The concept of internal marketing states that the employees of the organization form the first market and the goods and services as well as specific external marketing campaigns have to be marketed to employees before they are marketed externally. According to Gronross[1], the internal marketing concept states that the internal market of employee is best motivated for service mindedness and customer-oriented performance by an active marketing like approach, where a variety of activities are used internally in an active, marking like and coordinated way. Internal marketing in all its forms was recognised as an important activity in contributing to the people element of the marketing mix and in developing a customer focussed organisation. In practice, it is concerned with communications, developing responsiveness, responsibility and unity of purpose. The fundamental aims of internal marketing are to develop internal and external customer awareness and remove functional barriers to organisational effectiveness.[2]

There is concrete evidence to the effect that satisfied employees can make satisfied customers and the satisfied customers can inturn reinforce employees' sense of satisfaction in their jobs. Some have even gone so far as to suggest that unless service employees are happy in their jobs, customer satisfaction will be difficult to achieve.[3] Among the most demanding jobs in service business are the so-called boundary - spanning positions, where employees are expected to be fast and efficient in executing operational tasks and be courteous and helpful in dealing with customers. As a result, many service encounters have the potential to be a three - cornered fight among the needs of partially conflicting parties; the customer, the server and the service firm. If the job is not designed carefully or the wrong people are picked to fill it, there is a real risk that the employees may become stressed and unproductive[4]. The purpose of internal marketing is to integrate multiple functions of the firm and operate through service firm as the holistic management process. Internal marketing ensures that all employees understand and experience various business activities and campaigns and also prepare and motivate them to act in a service oriented manner. The necessary condition is that the internal exchange between the organisation and its employees must be operating effectively before facing external markets.[5] Service marketers need to develop a high level of interpersonal skills and customer-oriented attitude in employees for the reason that employees in services are key to the service experience.[6]

The kind of effort service firms put in for designing a service product for the external market to respond, they have to make efforts for designing a product for internal market too. While customer satisfaction is the orientation for external market, employee satisfaction should be orientation for internal market. The needs and wants of the employees should be studied carefully along with their expectations, to design a package of benefits that are capable of satisfying them. The internal product consists of a job and a work environment which motivates the employees to respond favourably to management's demand for customer orientation and good interactive market performance as part time marketers and which moreover attracts and retains good employees. In order to ensure proper design of internal service product, there is a need to make the concept of internal marketing as a part of the strategic management philosophy. Internal marketing is a philosophy of managing personnel and developing and enhancing a service culture systematically. The activities of internal marketing should promote service mindedness and customer orientation.

Training

Training is one of the most critical tasks of internal marketing. The employees selected for the company need to be imparted the required competencies needed for the effective performance of employees. The corporate philosophy of BSNL considers human resources as the most prized assets of the organization. Therefore, importance is given to train the employees to have employee skills, enhance their knowledge and expertise. BSNL has a vast reservoir of highly skilled and experienced workforce of about 3.57 lakh employees. Training programmes are organized regularly through several training institution established throughout the country. Training is imparted to employees on a continuous basis to meet the latest technical and managerial requirements.

Training Institutions of BSNL: The following are the institutions established for imparting training to the employees of BSNL :

- Advanced Level Telecom Training Centre
- Bharat Ratna Bhim Rao Ambedkar Institute of Telecom Training
- National Academy of Telecom Finance and Management
- Regional telecom training centres
- Circle telecom training centres
- District telecom training centres

Advanced Level Telecom Training Centre (ALTTC): The centre is located at Ghaziabad. It is the apex training institute of BSNL. ALTTC functions on the frontiers of telecom technology, finance, management and IT and imparts training to the leaders in the business.

Bharat Ratna Bhim Rao Ambedkar Institute of Telecom Training (BRBRAITT): It is one of the premier institutes of BSNL imparting training in various areas like latest technologies in field of telecommunications, computer networking, accounting, management, competency building and skill to meet the ever changing needs of customers. BRBRAITT follows ISO 9000:2000 'Quality Management System' standards.

The main objectives of this institute are:

- To conduct in-service courses relating to latest telecom technologies for participants from department of telecom, APT countries and some other government owned departments.
- To impart induction training to group A officers of department of telecom.
- To conduct seminars on latest technologies in fields of telecommunications.
- To conduct workshops on different topics concerning DOT/BSNL.
- To review existing course and develop new courses as per on the needs of BSNL.
- To exercise Technical control over all RTTC/DTTC/CTTC's in the country.
- To conduct Field training programmes.

National Academy of Telecom Finance and Management (NATFM): NATFM was established in 2001 and became a premier resource centre for telecom studies in the Asia-Pacific region. The vision of the academy is effective institution building and inculcating excellence as the "Way of Life". The internal processes are designed to work in a simple and transparent fashion towards the following objectives:

- To establish institutional relevance and credibility by undertaking activity for middle and senior management levels of BSNL/MNTL/DOT in new and topical areas of management science;

- To explore training activities for executives of other countries.

In pursuit of the first objective, NATFM has conducted more than 150 courses, workshops and seminars since inception. Employees working in various BSNL offices and field units all over India have participated in these programmes. In the international level, NAFTM has taken the challenge of training of executives of two batches of Bhutan Telecom, Royal Government of Bhutan in the third year of its functioning. Also has undertaken the task of designing and delivering and the Induction Training of Junior Accounts Officers of MNTL (Mahanagar Telephone Nigam Limited). The primary courseware for the training of Junior Accounts Officers of BSNL "BSNL Accounts and Finance"" is designed and developed by the in-house faculty of NAFTM. Apart from in-house training, the institution has ventured to far off places to conduct workshops such as BSNL Accounting for Western Zone at Pune, Eastern Zone at Calcutta and Southern Zone Chennai and for Northern region at Kurukshetra, workshop on /attitudinal Revitalization at Ahmedabad and Chennai, and work ship on "Cost Accounting Records" at Andaman islands and these are recent tasks completed as a part our programme to reach training at far ends. A journal "*Journal of Telecom Finance and Management*" is also being published by the academy.

Regional Telecom Training Centres: There are 14 Regional Telecom Training Centres established by BSNL in Ahmedabad, Bhubaneshwar, Chennai, Guwahti, Hyderabad, Jaipur, Kalyani, Lucknow, Mysore, Nagapur, Patna, Pune Rajpura, Thiruvanthapuram. The centres are established to meet the training needs of the BSNL employees at the regional level.

Circle Telcom Training Centres: The company established 19 circle telecom training centres in Ahmedabad,

Bhopal, Bhubaneshwar, Calcutta, Chennai, Guwahati, Jaipur, Jammu, Kakinada, Kurukshetra, Lucknow, Mysore, Meerut, Nasik, Patna, Rajpura, Shillong, Sunder Nagar, Thiruvanantpuram. The centres design training programmes as per the needs of the employees of the circles.

District Telecom Training Centres: There are six district telecom centres located at -Ahmedabad, Bangalore, Calcutta, Chennai, Hyderabad, and Pune. The district centres train employees of the BSNL limiting its jurisdiction to the telecom district.

BSNL has promoted formal and informal organizations and initiated measures to motivate employees and to safeguard the interests of them and their family members. The following are the details.

Staff Grievance Cell: To strengthen the employer-employee relationship BSNL has established the Staff Grievance Cell. The staff grievance officer will be available once a week to hear the grievances of the staff. As a general rule grievances of routine matters will be finalized within two weeks. The cell not only resolves the grievances of the staff but also initiated measures to see that similar grievances do not creep-up in feature.

Staff Welfare Programmes: The BSNL has initiated several welfare programmes to support employees and their family members and there by to achieve employees' satisfaction. The following are the staff welfare programs offered by BSNL.

1. Scholarships: Scholarships are provided to the wards of employees studying the following :

   (*a*) Technical / Professional Degree course (4 years and above duration) viz. MBBS / BDS/BVSc/BE/ B.Tech/BAMS/BHMS/B.Pharm.

   (*b*) Technical Diploma (3 years' Courses) in Engineering/architecture/Hospital Management/ BB A/Aircraft Mntce. Engineering Course (*c*) B.S.c., (Nursing)/BA. LLB % years, BIT/BCA/BIS/ B.S.c (Food Tech), B.S.c. (Bio Tech)/B.S.c. Bed of 4 years

(*d*) Non Technical Courses

(*e*) All ITI Courses in ITI Institutes

(*f*) Scholarships above provided to handicapped children studying in schools and colleges.

2. Book Award: Book awards are granted to school going children of the employees who have secured 75 per cent or more marks in the last annual examination.
3. Incentive to Meritorious students: The children of BSNL employees who secure top rank of annual examination of schools are given cash awards.
4. Financial Assistance to Handicapped/Mentally Retarded Children of employees for transport/hostel subsidy.
5. Financial assistance in case of death.
6. Financial assistance in cases of death due to attack by robbers, terrorists, riots, etc.
7. Financial assistance in cases of serious illness or major operations.
8. Financial assistance to employees on leave due to prolonged illness.
9. Financial assistance to victims of natural calamities/ communal riots/terrorists attacks.
10. Farewell to employees retiring from service.
11. Grant-in-Aid to recreation clubs.
12. Grant-in-Aid to telecom women welfare organisation.
13. Holiday Homes: The BSNL has developed 27 holiday homes in 12 states to facilitate stay for their employees and family members during the authorised leave period at nominal charges.

14. Medical Reimbursement: The medical expenses of present and retired employees are reimbursed as per the set eligibility criteria.

In addition to above, the employees of BSNL are provided travel allowance, dearness allowance, house rent allowance, and other allowances that are applicable for government servants.

Retirement Benefits

One of the major reasons for preferring BSNL to service is retirement benefits provided by the company. The employees are provided with pension and gratuity after the retirement.

Pension: Different types of pensions that are provided to the employees of the BSNL are as following:

1. *Superannuation Pension:* Superannuation pension is granted as like the Government servant who retires after attaining the age of superannuation viz. 60 years.
2. *Retiring Pension:* Retiring pension is granted to an officer who retires or is asked to retire, after completion 30 years of qualifying service or after completing age of 50 years — 55 years but before attaining the age of superannuation. It is also granted to an employee who opts for voluntary retirement after being declared surplus.
3. *Invalid Pension:* It is granted to the employee who retires from service on account of any bodily or mental infirmity which permanently incapacitates him/her for any further service. For persons retiring on invalidation on or after 1.12.73 the pension shall not be less then ordinary family pension.
4. *Compensation Pension:* Granted to an employee when he/she is discharged owing to reduction in establishment and could not be accommodated against a suitable job or when offer of a lower post is not accepted.

5. *Compulsory Retirement Pension:* It is granted to an employee compulsorily retired from service as a penalty by the competent authority. The employee will be allowed pension or gratuity or both admissible to him/her on the date of compulsory retirement.
6. *Compassionate Allowance:* An employee who is dismissed or removed from service normally forfeits pension and gratuity. But the competent authority may grant, due to special considerations and compassionate allowance, which will not be less then Rs. 1,275 p.m. and which shall not exceed 2/3rd of pension and/or gratuity that would have been allowed had he retired on compensation pension.
7. *Voluntary Retirement Pension:* An employee after completing 20 years of qualifying service may retire voluntarily by giving three months notice and receive pension and gratuity. The notice can be withdrawn within the date of retirement with the approval of appointing authority. Appointing authority can accept less then three month's notice also. Notice of Voluntary Retirement can be accepted from an employee already on EOL.
8. *Pension on absorption in the Company:* If an employee is permitted to be absorbed in public interest in the company can be granted pension, the date on which he/she actually joins the company.
9. *Commutation of Pension:* A maximum of 40 per cent of the pension (excluding relief on Pension and Personal Pension) can be commuted with or without medical certificate and a lump sum in lieu thereof can be obtained.

Restoration of Commutation: The portion of the amount of Pension commuted will be restored after completion of 15 years from the date of receipt of commuted value. However, if the commuted value is received within a month from the date of retirement, the restoration will be on completion of 15 years from the date following the date of retirement:

Family Pension: Family pension is offered to the family members of the deceased employees. The definition of family for the purpose shall include:

(*a*) Parents who were wholly dependent on the employee when he/she was alive provided the deceased employee had left behind neither a widow nor a child. The earnings of the parents should not exceed Rs. 2,500 p.m.

(*b*) Son/Daughter including widowed/divorced daughter (except disable daughters) till he/she attains the age of 25 years or upto the date of his/her marriage/ remarriage, whichever is earlier.

(*c*) Disabled divorced daughters are eligible for FP from the date of divorce, if divorce is legally arrived and comes back to parental home.

(*d*) Widowed disabled daughter also eligible for family pension for life from the date of death of her husband subject to fulfillment of relevant condition.

Thirty per cent pay of the deceased employee at the time of retirement subject to a minimum of Rs. 3,500 p.m. and Pay included Basic Pay, DA, DP and NPA as pension.

Gratuity: The employees of BSNL are provided gratuity in the following ways:

(*i*) Service Gratuity is payable in one lump-sum in lieu of monthly pension to a permanent employee retiring before completing 10 years of qualifying service, at the rate of half a month's emoluments drawn at the time of retirements for every completed six months service;

(*ii*) Retirement gratuity is granted to a permanent employee who retires after completion on superannuation/invalidation after 10 years of qualifying services or those who voluntarily retire after 20 years or more of continuous servicel; and (*iii*) Death Gratuity is granted in the case of death while in service of temporary/ quasi-permanent/permanent employee.

Promotional Policy

The promotional policy of BSNL provides for promotion of executives as well as Non-executives based on the experience as well as the performance reported through confidential reports. This scale up-gradation as well as position up-gradation is time bounded. The first up-gradation from executive will be on competition of four year of service. The subsequent of up-gradation will be on the competition of five years since the first up-gradation. The performance rating for different positions and also for open category and SC/ST category employees are shown in Table 7.1

Table 7.1 Performance criteria for up-gradation

Position	Category	Grading Criteria
JTO to SDE	OC SC/ST	No adverse, not more than four Average. No adverse
SDE to Sr. SDE	OC SC/ST	No adverse, not more than two Average. No adverse, not more than three Average.
Sr. SDE to STS	OC SC/ST	No adverse, not more than two Average. No adverse, not more than three Average.
STS to JAG	OC SC/ST	No adverse, not more than one Average. No adverse, not more than two Average.
JAG to NFSG	OC SC/ST	No adverse, not more than one Average. No adverse, not more than two Average.

The ACRs of the previous 5 years will be taken into consideration for assessing the fitness of eligible Executives. The fitness of eligible executives for up-gradation will be judged by a steering committee constituted for different positions as per the rules of the company. For the non-executives category the first up-gradation is allowed after putting up eight years of service. For the subsequent up-gradation also one has to complete eight years of service after the first up-gradation.

REFERENCES

1. Christian Gronroos, 'The Internal Marketing Function—Strategic Management and Marketing in the Service Sector Report', Marketing Science Institute, Cambridge, 1983, pp.83-104.
2. Adrian Payne, 'The Essence of Services Marketing', Prentice Hall of India Pvt. Ltd., New Delhi, 1998, p. 167.
3. Tleonard A. Schiesinger and James I. Heskeltt, 'The Service Driven Service Company', Harvard Business Review, Sep - Oct 1991, pp.71 -81.
4. Christopher Lovelock, 'Service Marketing', Addition Wesley Longman (Singapore) Pvt. Ltd., Delhi, 2001, p.455.
5. *Ibid.*
6. Harsha, V. Varma, 'Marketing of Services', Global Business Press, New Delhi, 1993, p.63.

EXTERNAL MARKETING

Consumers are co-producers in the service business. The quality of services will not only depend upon the performance of the service provider but also on the performance of the service consumer. Therefore, it is the responsibility of service organisations to educate and, if necessary, train customers so as to make them prepared to use the services efficiently. A well designed external marketing programme is of immense help to organizations to inform, persuade and train customers to better their experiences.

External marketing is concerned with effectively communicating the results of the marketing strategy to large audiences. It is an active, explicit form of marketing programme highlighting the marketing elements to persuade consumers and to make them committed to service.

External marketing takes place between company and customers. It is the interaction of the company with a service offer with the target market. There is a saying that 'nothing happens until somebody sells something in the market'. Unless and until a marketing organization come with a proposal, these will not be any response from the market, either positive or negative. Marketing stimulus, therefore, is necessary to generate responses in the form of demand. External marketing includes all such kinds of communication campaigns by the service provider that inform, educate, persuade, train and influence the customers to purchase the services.[1]

Services are intangible. Therefore, the psychic costs of the customers would be high in services. As there will be nothing to see, touch and perfect measurements, consumers do entertain doubts, suspicious and look for proper evidence, in the absence of relevant and effective communication campaign. The campaign through appropriate media should provide evidence to the customers. Services quality depends to a large extent on the ability and effective participation of customers. Participation ability, skill, involvement, and mind tuning for experience depends upon, apart from consumer characteristics, the way the consumers were informed, educated, training through external marketing. Thus, the efforts on external marketing influence the customer perceived quality. Most customers cannot perceive value properly even after experiencing something, in the absence of proper communication.[2]

Often, service outlets are operated under certain limitations. The uncertainty over the time involved in handling a customer, demand uncertainties, employee, equipment and infrastructural problems cannot be eliminated totally. The problems of this kind certainly cause inconvenience to the customers and may lead to the creation of negative feelings against the service provider. Through external marketing, the service provider finds an opportunity to inform and convince the customer about 192 possible problems and increase the zone of tolerance. Image building is one of the important goals of external marketing. Image acts as a guard against minor mistakes and provide an opportunity for recovery without much damage to the organisation. One of the major sources of image building is the communication campaign launched by the service provider.[3]

BSNL uses basically advertising and personal selling for communicating service offers to the consumers. The major forms of media that carry the advertisements of BSNL are Newspapers, Radio, Television, Magazines, out door and transit advertisements. Internet also is used for banner advertisements. The BSNL has opened it's website www.bsnl.com.,to facilitate customers to get all kinds of information relating to the company.

The corporate office of the BSNL takes the responsibility of external marketing strategies and programmes that covers the entire nation. Regional level campaigns are taken care of by the circle offices.

Customer Care

Customer Care is the priority area for BSNL management. Several steps have been taken by BSNL to augment the quality of customer care to international standards. The following are the steps taken for providing adequate customer care:

1. Access round the clock help through toll free numbers;
2. All BSNL Customer Service Centers (CSCs) remain open on all seven days from 8.00 AM to 8.00 PM without any break for all activities;
3. Cheque deposit machines have been installed in many cities, so that customers can make payments 24 × 7 at their convenience;
4. Customers can make payments by cheque/Demand Draft to BSNL franchisees all over the country;
5. With a view to simplify and offer customer friendly services, more than one bfone connections can be applied on a single application form. Accordingly, a single demand note would be issued to the customer in respect of all the connections applied for;
6. Shifting charges for local as well as all India shifting of fixed telephone (bfone) has been abolished;
7. Pagers are given to outdoor staff in a phased manner for speedy rectification of faults;
8. Majority of the local network is built up on jelly filled and OFC for trouble free service;
9. Internal Distribution Points (DPs) being provided in the customer premises to eliminate the faults arising out of overhead wires;
10. Extensive use of digital loop carrier (DLC)/Wireless in Local Loop (WLL) system for improving reliability of external plant;

11. Remote Line Units (RLUs). Remote subscriber Units (RSUs) are provided extensively to reduce the long lengths of copper cables;
12. Established Call Centers across the nation to provide single window solutions and convenience to customers;
13. Countrywide Network Management and Surveillance System (NMSS) to ensure uninterrupted and efficient flow of telecom traffic;
14. Application forms for new connections have been made free of charge for all services;
15. Procedure for restoration of telephones disconnected due to non-payment simplified and powers delegated to Secondary Switching Area (SSA) heads;
16. Telephone bills for payment are received on Saturday and Sunday through cheques in City Telecom Offices (CTOs);
17. More than one Public Call Office (PCO) permitted at the same premises;
18. Various application forms and procedures are simplified for new telephone connections, shifting and third party transfer.

Consumer Grievances Redressal Mechanism in BSNL

BSNL has a well structured and multilayered Public Grievances Redressal Mechanism including Dispute Resolution Mechanism. The Public Redressal setup in BSNL has been introduced right from the Corporate Office to SSA(Secondary Switching Area) levels. Subscribers having complaints or grievances can interact with the organization through the following for Public Grievance / Dispute settlements:

(*i*) Complaints are being booked on "198". This Toll Free Service of booking complaints are available in every telephone system.

(*ii*) In every office 'visiting hours' are prescribed where the subscribers having complaints or grievances can approach the officers of BSNL at various levels.

(*iii*) Public Grievance Officers are available right from Corporate Office to SSA (Secondary Switching Area) level. The complainant can approach these officers in person or through written complaints or communicate through e-mail or contact on telephones.

(*iv*) Special attention is being given to holding meetings with consumer organizations.

(*v*) Telephones Advisory Committees have been constituted.

(*vi*) Senior Officers are available for public without prior appointment during a specified hours on working days, and.

(v*ii*) Customer Service Centres have been opened for IMPCS.

Open House Session

Complaints/suggestions of general nature as regard to improving the telecom services in the area are discussed in the Open House Sessions. The basic idea of conducting such Open House sessions is to establish direct channels of communications with customers and also to enable the telecom staff to appreciate and evaluate the customers' difficulties and complaints from their point of view. A press notification is issued in leading newspapers informing the details of the Open House Session for inviting customers to attend and submit their suggestions/grievances. Participants are invited in a public hall. The session is presided over by Senior Officers i.e. Area GM/Area Manager. Customers are requested to present their general grievances and all such presentations are recorded. The concerned officers will respond on the spot. In few cases, which cannot be settled on the spot a time frame is given. Efforts are made to settle the case within the given time frame. Written reply stating the progress is sent to the customers.

Telephone Adalats

Subscribers whose grievances remained unsettled are invited to make petitions for redressal of their grievances in

Telephone Adalats. SSA(Secondary Switching Area) Level Telephone Adalats are being conducted on bimonthly periodicity and Circle level Telephone Adalats are being conducted once in three months. Customers are asked to give their grievances in writing with all supporting documents within stipulated period to District Complaint Officer (DCO). The concerned office to which the case relates examines the case received by DCO and settles the case. A speaking order settling the case is communicated to the customers. For unsettled cases, a date is fixed for holding the Telephone Adalat. The customers are invited to attend the Telephone Adalat. The Adalat is presided over by General Manager of the area. The concerned officers of the Department are also called to be present in the Adalat. The full details of the case are presented to the presiding officer. The order of the presiding officer is communicated in the Adalat after hearing the arguments from both the parties.

Appellate Jurisdiction of Telephone Adalats

Circle level adalats headed by CGMs can consider the cases of the appeals against the decisions of the adalats chaired by SSA Heads. Adalats headed by SSA Heads can consider cases of excess billing which have been rejected by them as administrative heads of SSAs.

Telecom consumers Protection and Regulation of Grievances

BSNL ensures prompt rectification of any fault or complaint booked through its extensive grassroot level online Fault Restoration System (FRS). However, in case the customer still have problem unsolved timely, BSNL has implemented a three tier consumer grievance redressal mechanism comprising of call centres for various services, nodal officers at SSA and Circle level and an appellate authority for deciding cases that the consumers may wish to appeal against. As a first step a consumer, may contact Call Centre on toll free helpline numbers.

Procedure for Handling Grievances by Call Centres

The Call Centres, immediately on receipt of complaint:

(*a*) A register complaint by allotting a unique identification number to be called the docket number;

(*b*) Communicate, at the time of lodging the complaint, the unique identification number to be called docket number, date and time of registration of the complaint, to you;

(*c*) Record details in respect of such complaint;

(*d*) Inform the customer through telephone or other electronic means or any other means and within the time limit specified the action taken on the complaint; and give the customer contact details of the Nodal Officer (including his name, telephone number and address) in case the customer is not satisfied with the redressal of the grievance or when requested by the customer.

Time Limit for redressal of Grievance of Consumers by Call Centres

All complaints relating to fault or disruption of service or disconnection of service shall be redressed within three days from the date of registration of complaint unless specified elsewhere. Unless specified elsewhere, all other complaints shall be redressed within seven days from the date of registration of complaint. Where lesser time limit has been specified by any other law for the time being in force or other regulations of TRAI or DOT or by BSNL for redressal of grievance, the Call Centres shall redress the grievances of the consumer within such specified time.

In case the customers are not satisfied with the redressal of their grievances at the Call Centre level or in case the Call Centre within the above time limit does not attend to the complaint, they may approach the Nodal Officer for redressal of such grievances.

Redressal of Consumer Grievances by Nodal Officers

Customers may approach, by a letter in writing, or through telephone, or web based online filing of complaints or through short message service or through other electronic means and any other means, the Nodal Officer of the concerned SSA of the Circle/District for redressal of grievances. In emergency situations, one can approach at the first instance itself a Nodal Officer instead of a Call Centre and the Nodal Officer shall redress the grievance.

Handling of grievances of consumers by Nodal Officers

The Nodal Officer shall be accessible to the consumers at the address made available by the public notice and telephone bills. The officer registers every complaint lodged by the consumers and communicates within three days from date of the receipt of the complaint, the unique complaint number to the consumer. The officer intimates, within the time limit, the remedial measure or decision taken, to the consumer.

Time limit for redressal of complaints by Nodal Officer

The Nodal Officer shall redress the complaints of the consumer within ten days of the registration of the complaint, provided that the complaints relating to fault or disruption of service or disconnection of service shall be redressed within three days from the date of registration of complaint. In case the consumer is still not satisfied with the redressal of his/her grievance by the Nodal Officer or in case his/her complaint is not redressed by the Nodal Officer within the time limit specified or no reply is received regarding resolution of the complaint from Nodal Officer, he/she may appeal to the appellate authority for redressal of grievance.

Appeal to appellate authority for redressal of consumer grievances

In case a consumer is not satisfied with the redressal of his grievance by the Nodal Officer in any form the consumer may, in writing, make an appeal to the appellate authority of the concerned Circle within three months. The appellate authority may entertain any appeal after the expiry of the said period of three months but before one year from the time limit of ten days of the registration of the complaint by the Nodal Officer or three days of the registration of complaint by the Nodal Officer relating to fault or disruption of service or disconnection if it is satisfied that there was sufficient cause for not filing it within that period:

Disposal of appeal by appellate authority

The appellate authority shall ensure uniformity in the procedure for deciding appeals and comply with the provisions contained in succeeding paras.

1. The appellate authority may call for, any information, document or record, from the concerned Section of the Circle office and/or the concerned SSA head and/or the concerned Nodal Officer or the appellant, which may be relevant and necessary for examination and disposal of the appeal, as the case may be.
2. The appellate authority shall, on receipt of the reply from concerned officers and after conducting such inquiry as the appellate authority may consider necessary, and after affording reasonable opportunity of hearing to the parties, dispose of the appeal by passing an order in writing and stating therein the points for determination, the decision thereon and the reasons for the decision.
3. The appellant, being consumer, may, either appear in person or authorize any of his representative to present his case or send his representation with a request to dispose of the appeal, without being present in person;
4. The appellate authority shall decide every appeal within three months from the date of filing the appeal and pass orders.
5. The order of the appellate authority shall be communicated in writing within seven days of the order to the appellant and the concerned officer. The

concerned office shall, within fifteen days from the date of receipt of the order referred to above, comply with the order of the appellate authority and report immediately compliance thereof to the appellate authority.

In order to communicate the facility to the consumers, the address and telephone numbers of officers are printed in the information pages of telephone directory as well as through notice boards in customer service centers and exchange buildings. The dates of holding of adalats are notified through local newspapers and electronic media.

Free Insurance Coverage to Customers

BSNL has entered into an agreement with M/s Bajaj Allianz General Insurance Company Ltd., and M/s United Insurance Corporation for providing free Insurance Coverage to the Landline/WLL/Post paid Mobile customers/PCO and VPT operators against accidental death and permanent total disability due to accident. The sum assured is Rs. 50,000/- per connection.

REFERENCES

1. Rama Mohana Rao, K., '*Services Marketing*', Pearson Education, New Delhi, 2005.
2. Frank Jefkins, '*Advertising*', McMillan, New Delhi, 1999, p.5.
3. Ronalt T. Markes. B., "*Personal Selling an Interactive Approach*", Allyn and Bacon Inc. Boston, 1981, p.8.

EMPLOYEES' OPINION SURVEY

To study the opinion of the employees' on work environment, interactions with colleagues, the job assigned, the work culture, promotional opportunities, training, compensation, employer-employee relationships and the problems, both internal and external, being faced by them an opinion survey was conducted. A sample of 300 employees has been selected taking 50 each from each of the six telecom circles of Andhra Pradesh for the study.

A. Demographic Profile of Respondents

The study reveals 92 per cent of the respondents are in the age group of 31 to 50 years (Table 9.1). Only two per cent of the respondents are in the age group of 21 to 30 years and six per cent of the respondents are of above 51 years of age. The mean age of the sample is 40.67 years

Table 9.1 Age of respondents

Age	Telecom Circle						Total
	Hyderabad	Warangal	Chittore	Karnool	Vijayawada	Vizag	
21-30	1 0.33%	—	2 0.67%	1 0.33%	—	2 0.67%	6 2.00%
31-40	24 8.00%	23 7.67%	28 9.33%	22 7.33%	20 6.67%	19 6.33%	136 45.33%
41-50	24 8.00%	25 8.33%	19 6.33%	25 8.33%	26 8.67%	21 7.00%	140 46.67%
51& above	10 .33%	2 0.67%	1 0.33%	2 0.67%	4 1.33%	8 2.67%	18 6.00%
Total	50 16.67%	50 16.67%	50 16.67%	50 16.67%	50 16.67%	50 16.67%	300 100.00%

Out of the total, about 87 per cent of the respondents are males and 13 per cent are females (Figure 9.1).

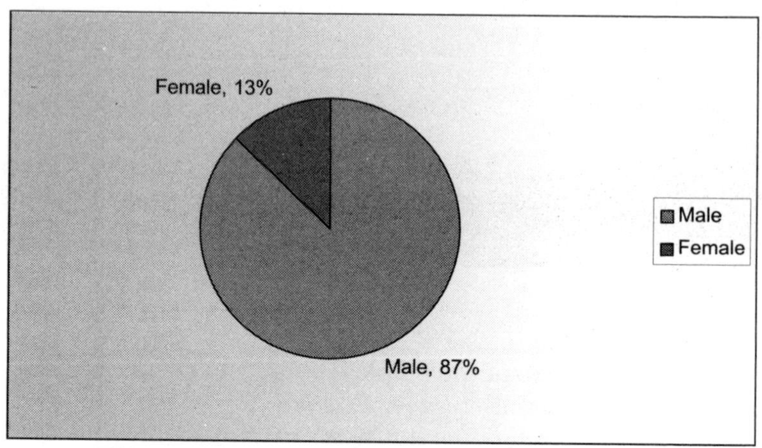

Fig. 9.1. Sex- wise distributions of respondents

The education background of the respondents is shown in Table 9.2. Out of the total, 71 per cent of the respondents are graduates. About 28 per cent of the respondents are post-graduates and only a little over one per cent are professionals.

Table 9.2 Education background

Age	Telecom Circle						Total
	Hyderabad	Warangal	Chittore	Karnool	Vijayawada	Vizag	
Graduates	36 12.00%	32 10.67%	36 12.00%	36 12.00%	35 11.67%	38 12.67%	213 71.00%
Post Graduates	1 13.67%	18 6.00%	14 4.67%	14 4.67%	15 5.00%	11 3.67%	83 27.67%
Professio-nals	3 1.00%	—	—	—	—	1 0.33%	4 1.33%
Total	**50 16.67%**	**50 16.67%**	**50 16.67%**	**50 16.67%**	**50 16.67%**	**50 16.67%**	**300 100.00%**

The annual income of the respondents varied between Rs. 1,50,000 and Rs. 6,00,000 (Table 9.3). The study reveals, as many as 109 respondents' income varied between Rs. 2,50,000 and Rs. 3,00,000. The annual income of 102 respondents representing 34 per cent of the total varied between Rs. 1,50,000 and Rs. 2,00,000. There are 30 respondents representing 10 per cent of the total with an annual income of more than Rs. 3,00,000 each. The mean of the annual income of the respondents is Rs. 2,36,166.67.

Table 9.3 Annual Income of the respondents

Annual Income Rs.	Telecom Circle						Total
	Hyderabad	Warangal	Chittore	Karnool	Vijayawada	Vizag	
150001-200000	18 6.00%	23 7.67%	13 4.33%	20 6.67%	17 5.67%	11 3.67%	102 34.00%
200001-250000	12 4.00%	5 1.67%	12 4.00%	9 3.00%	9 3.00%	12 4.00%	59 19.67%
250001-300000	18 6.00%	17 5.67%	21 7.00%	15 5.00%	18 6.00%	20 6.67%	109 36.33%
300001 & Above	2 0.67%	5 1.67%	4 41.33%	6 62.00%	6 62.00%	7 2.33%	301 0.00%
Total	50 16.67%	50 16.67%	50 16.67%	50 16.67%	50 16.67%	50 16.67%	300 100.00%

The family size of the respondents varied between two and five [Table 9.4].The family size of the majority of the respondents [59.33 per cent] is three. The size of the family for about 20 per cent of the respondents is four whereas the family size of 16.33 per cent of the respondents is two. The mean family size of the respondents is 3.02.

Table 9.4 Family Size

Size	Telecom Circle						Total
	Hyderabad	Warangal	Chittore	Karnool	Vijayawada	Vizag	
1	1 0.33%	—	1 0.33%	1 0.33%	1 0.33%	4 1.33%	8 2.67%
2	17 5.67%	4 1.33%	8 2.67%	5 1.67%	8 2.67%	7 2.33%	49 16.33%
3	2 27.33%	37 12.33%	31 10.33%	33 11.00%	30 10.00%	25 8.33%	178 59.33%
4	9 3.00%	8 2.67%	9 3.00%	10 3.33%	10 3.33%	13 4.33%	59 19.67%
5	1 0.33%	1 0.33%	1 0.33%	1 0.33%	1 0.33%	1 0.33%	6 2.00%
Total	**50 16.67%**	**50 16.67%**	**50 16.67%**	**50 16.67%**	**50 16.67%**	**50 16.67%**	**300 100.00%**

B. Relationship with BSNL

The experience of the respondents with the company varied between below five years and above 20 years. The data shown in Table 9.5 reveals, the large number of the respondents' [124] representing 41.33 per cent experience with the company varied between 11 and 15 years. About 22 per cent of the respondents had an experience of 16 to 20 years with the company. There are 40 respondents representing 13.33 per cent whose experience was more than 30 years each. In the case of 17.33 per cent of the respondents the experience varied between 6 and 10 years while 6.33 per cent of the respondents had an experience of less than five years with the company. The mean experience of the respondents is 13.92 years.

Table 9.5 Experience with the company

Annual Income Rs.	Telecom Circle						Total
	Hyderabad	Warangal	Chittore	Karnool	Vijayawada	Vizag	
Below 5	4	2	2	3	4	4	19
	1.33%	0.67%	0.67%	1.00%	1.33%	1.33%	6.33%
6-10	5	7	10	12	8	10	52
	1.67%	2.33%	3.33%	4.00%	2.67%	3.30%	17.33%
11-15	26	22	25	18	19	14	124
	8.67%	7.33%	8.33%	6.00%	6.33%	4.67%	41.33%
16-20	1	15	10	11	11	7	65
	3.67%	5.00%	3.33%	3.67%	3.67%	2.33%	21.67%
Above 20	4	4	3	6	8	15	101
	1.33%	1.33%	1.00%	2.00%	2.67%	5.00%	13.33%
Total	50	50	50	50	50	50	300
	16.67%	16.67%	16.67%	16.67%	16.67%	16.67%	100.00%

An attempt is made in the study to know the motivation factors of the respondents for joining the company. The data shown in Table 9.6 reveals the reason to join in the services of BSNL for about 62 per cent of the respondents was that the company is 'public sector company'. Career growth opportunities in the company motivated 22.33 per cent of the respondents. The other motivational factors include 'suitable to my abilities' [8.67 per cent] 'the best job I could secure [6.33 per cent] and compensation is more than my abilities' [one per cent].

Table 9.6 Motivation factors for joining the company

Particulars	Telecom Circle						Total
	Hyderabad	Warangal	Chittore	Karnool	Vijayawada	Vizag	
Public Sector Company	33 11.00%	33 11.00%	34 11.33%	28 9.33%	31 10.33%	26 8.67%	185 61.67%
Career growth opportunities	12 4.00%	7 2.33%	11 3.67%	15 5.00%	11 3.67%	11 3.67%	67 22.33%
Suitable to my abilities	4 1.33%	7 2.33%	2 0.67%	4 1.33%	3 1.00%	6 2.00%	26 8.67%
The best job I couldsecure	—	3 1.00%	3 1.00%	3 1.00%	4 1.33%	6 2.00%	19 6.33%

Compensation s more than my abilities	1 0.33%	—	—	—	1 0.33%	1 0.33%	3 1.00%
Total	50 16.67%	50 16.67%	50 16.67%	50 16.67%	50 16.67%	50 16.67%	300 100.00%

C. Work Environment

One of the important influencing factors of an employee performance is the work environment. The convenient working hours, comfortable work space, adequate and suitable furniture, suitable equipment which is well maintained and support services play the vital role on influencing the employee behaviour and attitude towards work. An attempt is made in the study to know the opinion of the respondents on work environment. Figure 9.2 reveals more than 91 per cent of the respondents are satisfied with the working hours of the company.

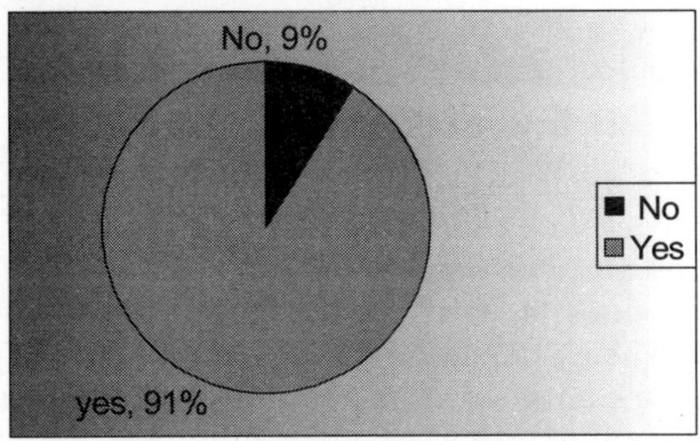

Fig. 9.2 Are the working hours convenient to you?

The respondents' rating on the work environment on a 5 point scale ranging from very good to very poor is shown in Table 9.7. The study reveals a litter over 62.34 per cent of the respondents rated 'working space' as good or very good. In the case of furniture provided at the work environment, 40 per cent of the respondents rated average, 29.33 per cent rated good and 6.33 per cent rated very good. However, 20.33 per cent rated the furniture as poor and 4 per cent of the respondents rated it as very poor. In the case equipment, 37 per cent rated equipment as average, 33.67 per cent rated it as good while 9 per cent of the respondents rated equipment as very good. The rating of 15 per cent of the respondents is poor and 5.33 per cent of the respondents are very poor for the equipment at the work place. Out of the total, 32 per cent of the respondents rated support services as good and about 20 per cent of the respondents rated the support services as very good. A little over 29 per cent of the respondents rated the support services as average while 19 per cent of the respondents rated the support service as either poor or very poor.

Table 9.7 Rating on the work Environment

Particulars	Very Good	Good	Average	Poor	Very Poor	Total
Working Space	32 10.67%	155 551.67%	52 17.33%	45 15.00%	16 5.33%	300 100.00%
Furniture	19 6.33%	88 29.33%	120 40.00%	612 20.33%	12 4.00%	300 100.00%
Equipment	27 9.00%	101 33.67%	111 37.00%	451 15.00%	16 5.33%	300 100.00%
Support Services	59 19.67%	96 32.00%	88 29.33%	37 12.33%	20 6.67%	300 100.00%

D. Opinion on Interactions

An attempt is made to know the opinion of the respondents on the interactive experience with superiors, colleagues, subordinates and customers. The data shown in Table 9.8 reveals the details. Out of the total, 116 respondents representing 38.67 per cent rated the interactive experience with superiors as good and about 18 per cent rated the interactive experience as very good. As many as 87 respondents representing 29 per cent of the total rated the interactive experience as average while about 15 per cent of the respondents rated such interactions as either poor or very poor. The majority of respondents representing 71.33 per cent rated the interactive experience with colleagues as either good or very good. The interactive experience with the subordinates was rated by 50 per cent of the respondents as good and about 15 per cent as very good. About 26 per cent of the respondents rated the interactive experience with the subordinates as average. The majority of the respondents [169] representing 56.33 per cent rated interactive experience with customers as good and 8.33 per cent of the respondents rated it as very good. The rating of 30.33 per cent of the respondents on interactive experience with customers is average.

Table 9.8 Interactive experience of the respondents.

Particulars	Very Good	Good	Average	Poor	Very Poor	Total
Superiors	53 17.67%	116 38.67%	87 29.00%	31 10.33%	13 4.33%	300 100.00%
Colleagues	89 29.67%	125 41.67%	56 18.67%	24 8.00%	6 2.00%	300 100.00%
Subordinates	44 14.67%	150 50.00%	77 25.67%	21 7.00%	8 2.67%	300 100.00%
Customers	25 8.33%	169 56.33%	91 30.33%	15 5.00%	--- —	300 100.00%

E. Opinion on Job Assigned

The respondents were asked to give their opinion on the job assigned , the suitability of the job, empowerment, team work, work culture, service orientation, promotional opportunities, inter personal trust, quality control measures, recognition and rewarding merit, transfer policy and social activities of the company organised with the participation of employees. Figure 9.3 shows the opinion of the respondents the job assigned. It reveals from that the large number of the respondents representing 38.67 per cent of the total are of the opinion that the job assigned to them is average as compared to their qualification and competences. About 35 per cent of the respondents rated the job assigned as good and 17 per cent of the respondents rated it as very good.

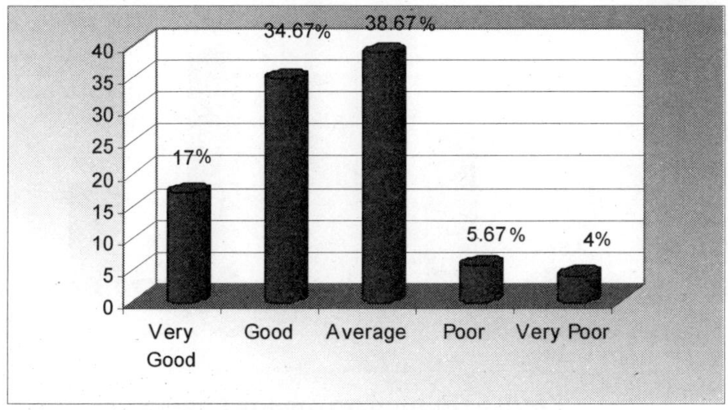

Fig. 9.3 Opinion on Job Assigned

Figure 9.4 depicts the respondents' opinion on suitability of the job to their expertise. It reveals, 37.33 per cent rated suitability of job to the expertise as average. A litter over 27 per cent of the respondents rated suitability of job as good and 19.33 per cent rated it as very good. However, there are 16 per cent of the respondents who rated the suitability of the job as either poor or very poor.

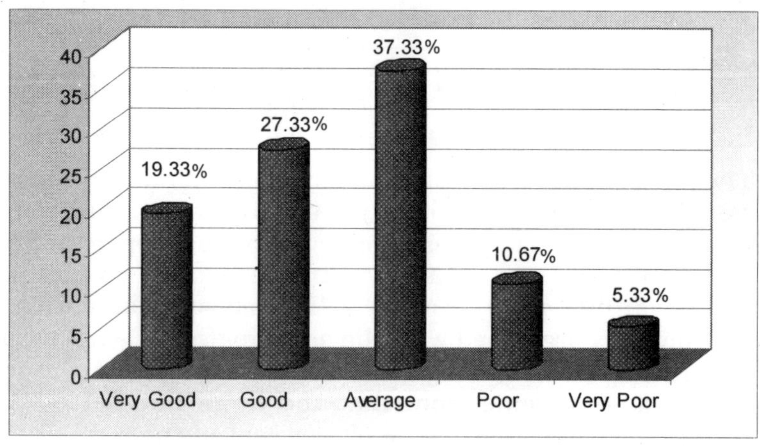

Fig. 9.4 Opinion on suitability of job

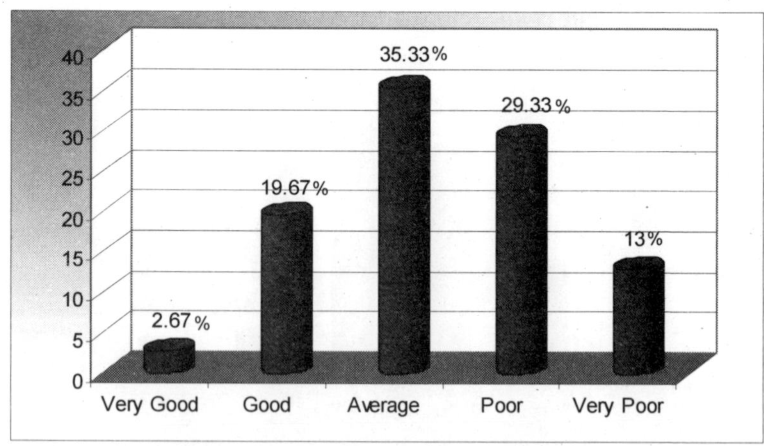

Fig. 9.5 Opinion on Empowerment

The opinion of the respondents on empowerment was shown in Figure 9.5. As many as 106 respondents representing 35.33 per cent of the total rated empowerment as average while 29.33 per cent rated empowerment as poor and 13 per cent rated it as very poor. Only a little over 22 per cent of the respondents rated empowerment as either good or very good.

Out of the total, about 35 per cent of the respondents rated team work in the company as average. About 21 per cent rated the team work as very poor and 13 per cent rated it as poor [Figure 9.6]. However, there are 24.33 per cent of the respondents who rated the team work as good and 7 per cent who rated it as very good.

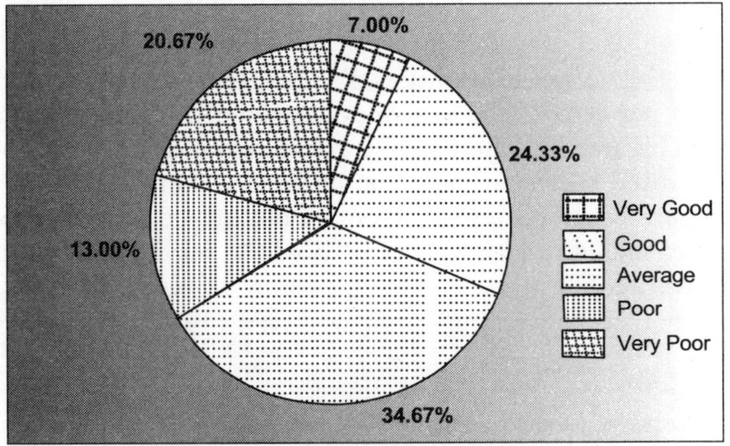

Fig. 9.6 Opinion on Team work

Figure 9.7 shows the opinion of the respondents on the work culture of the organisation. The study reveals 42 per cent of the respondents rated work culture as average. About 31 per cent of the respondents rated work culture as good and 7.33 per cent of the respondents rated it as very good. However, there are 20 per cent of the respondents who rated work culture as either poor or very poor.

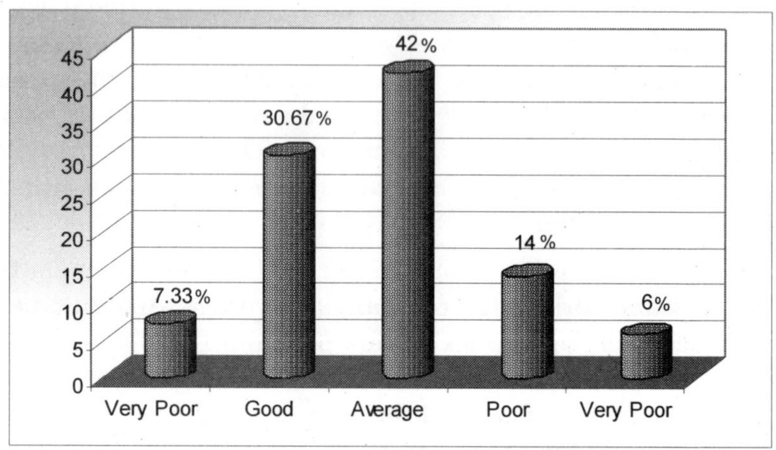

Fig. 9.7 Opinion on Work Culture

The study reveals about 40 per cent of the respondents rated the service orientation of the organisation as poor and 12.33 per cent of the respondents rated the same as very poor [Figure 9.8]. There are 24.33 per cent of the respondents who rated service orientation of the company as good and 8.33 per cent of the respondents who rated it as very good. Out of the total, 15.33 per cent rated the service orientation as average.

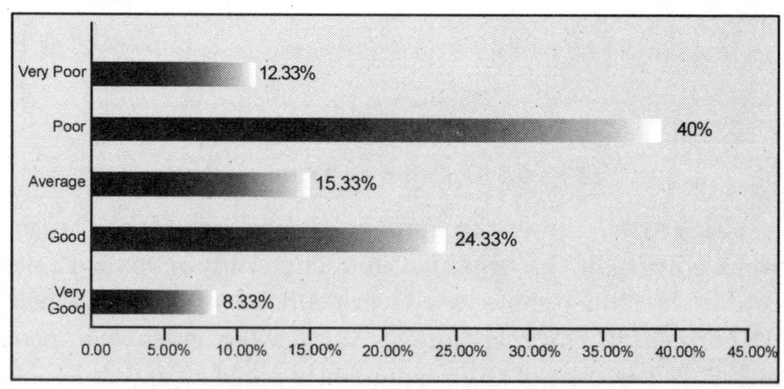

Fig. 9.8 Opinion on Service Orientation

Figure 9.9 shows the opinion of the respondents on promotional opportunities in the company. The majority of respondents representing 53 per cent of the total rated the promotional opportunities as average. Out of the total, 28 per cent of the respondents rated promotional opportunities as either poor or very poor, while 19 per cent of the respondents gave positive rating for promotional opportunities.

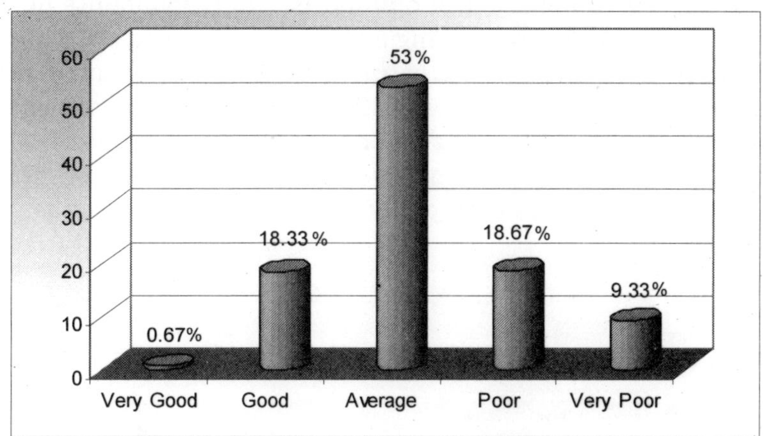

Fig. 9.9 Opinion on Promotional Opportunities

The respondents were asked to give their opinion on inter personal trust at the work environment. The data shown in Figure 9.10 reveals that as many as 145 respondents

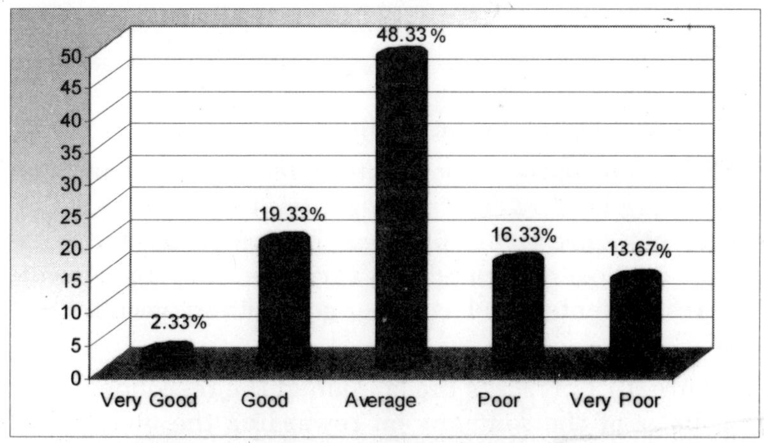

Fig. 9.10 Opinion on Inter personal trust

representing 48.33 per cent rated inter personal trust as average. The rating of 30 per cent of the respondents on inter personal trust was either poor or very poor. Only about 22 per cent of the respondents rated inter personal trust positively.

Figure 9.11 depicts the opinion of the respondents on quality control measures being adopted by the company. The study reveals 39.33 per cent of the respondents rated quality control measures as average. About 33 per cent of the respondents rated the measures as good and 2.33 per cent of the respondents rated them as very good. About 26 per cent of the respondents rated the quality control measures as either poor or very poor.

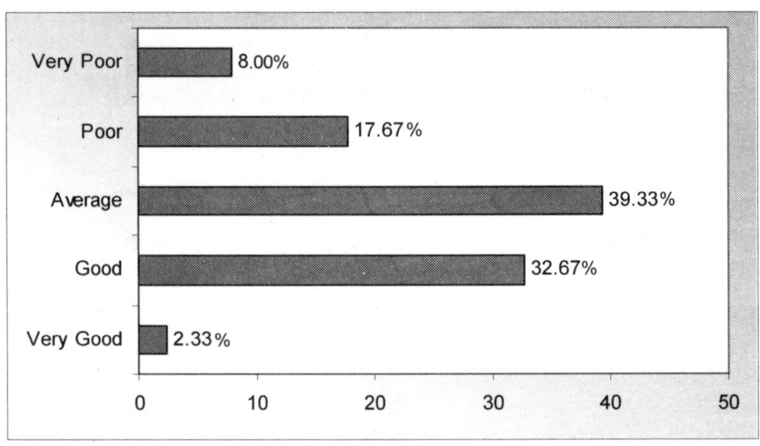

Fig. 9.11 Opinion on Quality control measures

The opinion of the respondents on recognition of merit is shown in Figure 9.12. The study reveals the majority of the respondents representing 62.33 per cent rated this factor as poor and 5.33 per cent rated it as very poor. Only 15 per cent of the respondents rated as either good or very good to this factor.

Figure 9.13 presents the opinion of the respondents on the policies of the company on rewarding the merit. The majority of the respondents representing 66.33 per cent of

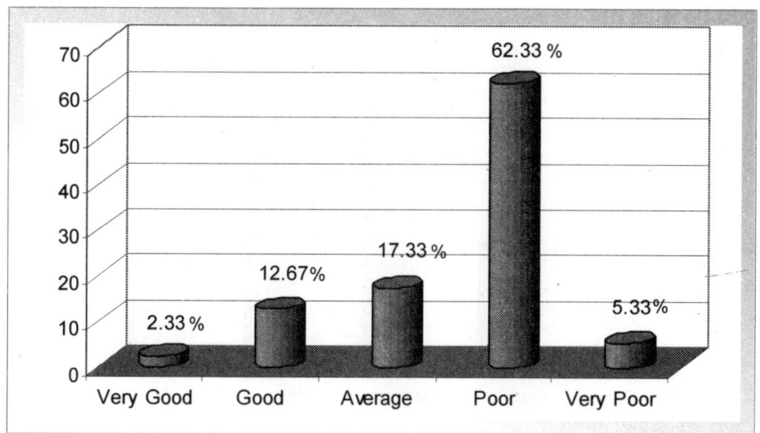

Fig. 9.12 Opinion on Recognition of merit

the total rated rewarding the merit as poor. About 18 per cent of the respondents rated it as average while only 11.33 per cent rated rewarding merit as either good or very good.

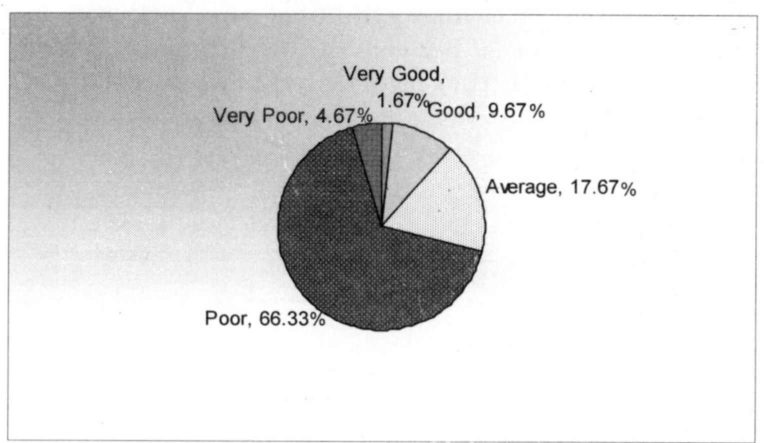

Fig. 9.13 Opinion on Rewarding the merit

Figure 9.14 shows the opinion of the respondents on transfer policy. The data presented in the figure reveals 40.33 per cent of the respondents rated transfer policies as average and an equal per cent of the respondents rated the policies as either poor or very poor.

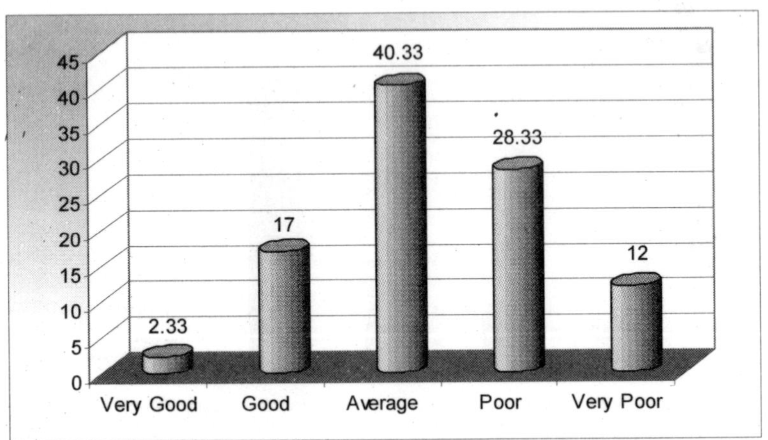

Fig. 9.14 Opinion on Transfer Policy

The rating of the respondents on the social activities of the organisation involving the employees is shown in Figure 9.15. As many as 147 respondents representing 49 per cent of the total rated the company initiated social activities as average. A little over 37 per cent of the respondents rated them as either poor or very poor. Only 13.67 per cent of the respondents rated the social activities as either good or very good.

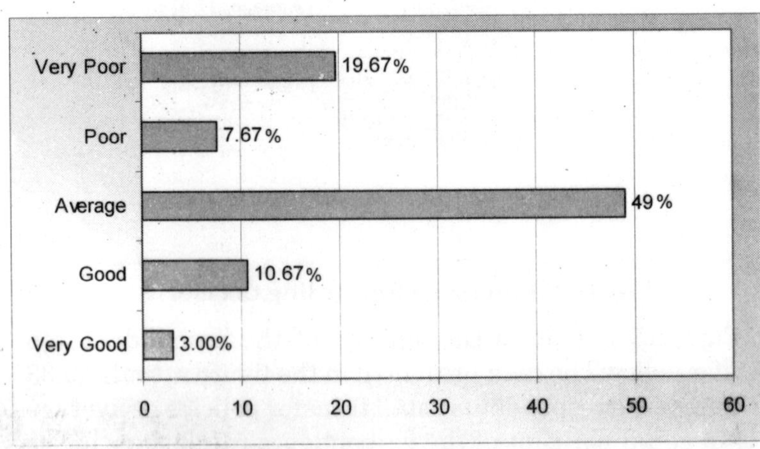

Fig. 9.15 Opinion on Social Activities

F. Opinion on Training

An attempt is made to study the opinion of respondents on induction training, on the job training and opportunities for skill development.

Figure 9.16 depicts the opinion of the respondents on induction training. About 50 per cent of the respondents rated the induction training as average. As many as 114 respondents representing 38 per cent of the total rated the induction training as good and 3.33 per cent rated the training as very good. There are only 9 per cent of the respondents who rated induction training as poor or very poor.

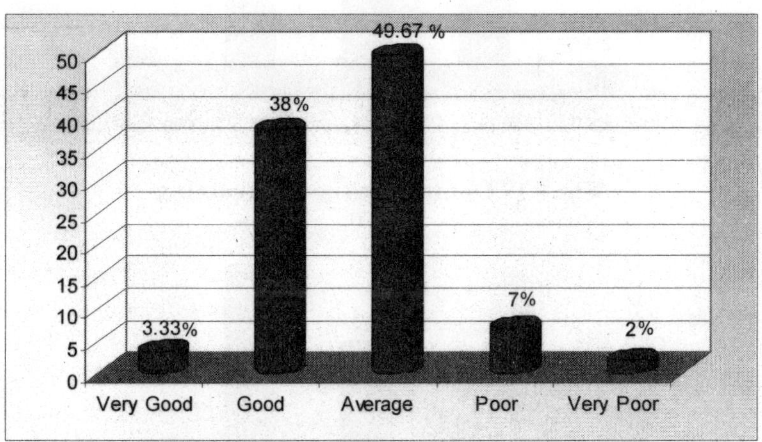

Fig. 9.16 Opinion on Induction Training

Figure 9.17 shows the rating of the respondents on 'on the job training'. As many as 138 respondents representing 46 per cent of the total rated on the job training as good. About 34 per cent of respondents rated the training as average. There are 18 per cent of the respondents who rated on the job training as either poor or very poor.

The respondents are asked to reveal their opinion on skill development opportunities prevalent in the organisation. The data shown in Figure 9.18 reveals half of the respondents rated the skill development opportunities as either poor or very poor in the company. About 30 per cent of the respondents rated average for the skill development opportunities. Only a minor part of the respondents rated good or very good for the skill development opportunities.

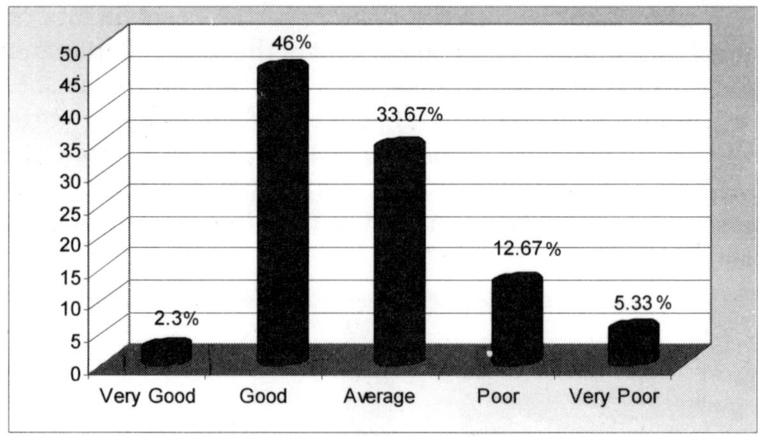

Fig. 9.17 Opinion on the Job training

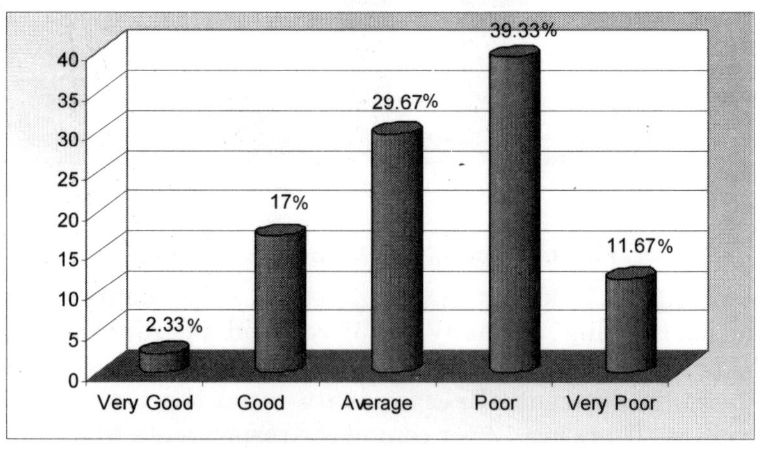

Fig. 9.18 Opinion to skill development opportunities

G. Opinion on Compensation

Compensation is identified as one of the important motivators of employees in any organisation and more particularly a service organisation. Employees shall be compensated competitively for the service rendered to satisfy their economic, social as well as psychological needs. An attempt is made in the study to know the opinion of the respondents on the compensation given to their work performance. The data shown in Figure 9.19 reveals 45.67 per cent of the respondents rated the compensation as the average. About 30 per cent of the respondents rated the compensation is good. The rating of 18 per cent of the respondents on compensation is poor.

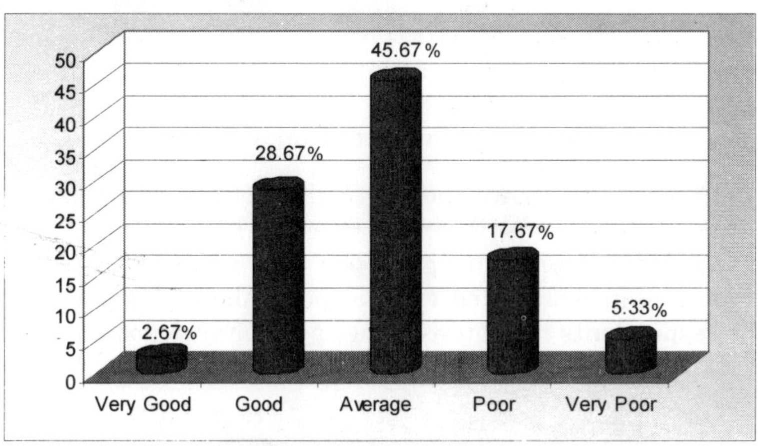

Fig. 9.19 Opinion on compensation

H. Employer–Employee Relations

An attempt is made in the study to know the opinion of the respondents on employer care on employees, the functioning of grievance redressal mechanism and the opportunities provided to the employees for their growth in career. Figure 9.20 shows the details of the opinion of the respondents on the employee care of the management of the company. As many as 117 respondents representing 39 per cent of the total rated employee care as average.

About 30 per cent of the respondents rated employee care as good while 26 per cent of the respondents rated the same as poor.

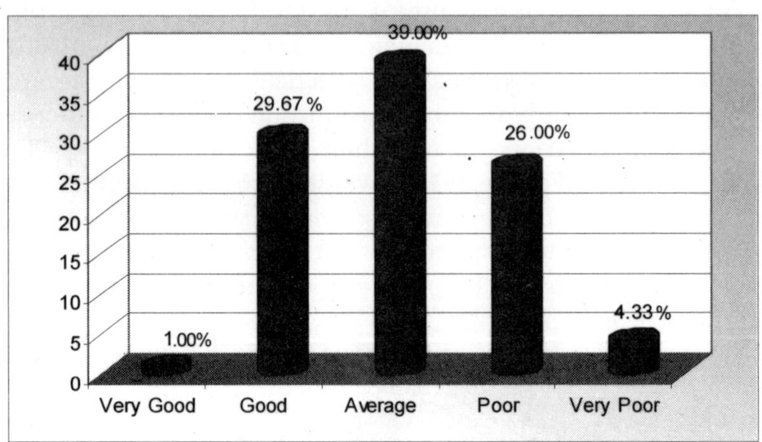

Fig. 9.20 Opinion on Employee care

Figure 9.21 shows the particulars of the respondents' rating on employee grievance redressal. The majority of the respondents representing 53 per cent of the total rated employees grievance redressal as poor. About 29 per cent of the respondents rated it as either good or very good.

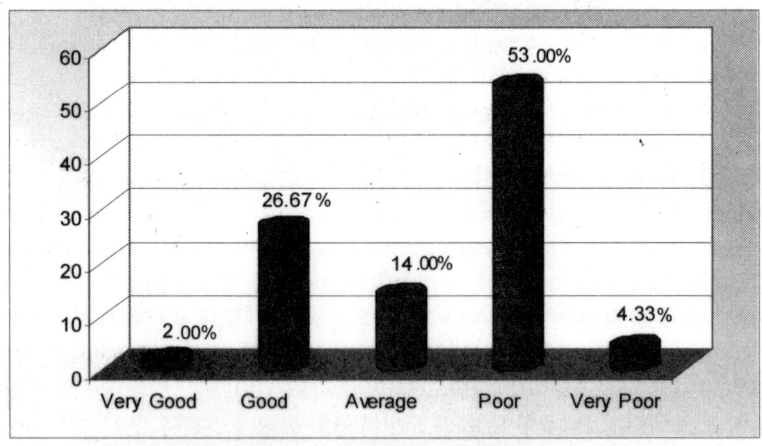

Fig. 9.21 Opinion on Employee grievance redressal

The respondents' opinion on career growth potential in the company is shown in Figure 9.22. The study reveals 141 respondents representing 47 per cent of the total rated career growth potential in the company as average. As many as 30 per cent of the respondents rated the growth potential as poor and 5.33 per cent of the respondents rated it as very poor. Only about 18 per cent of the respondents rated career potential as either good or very good.

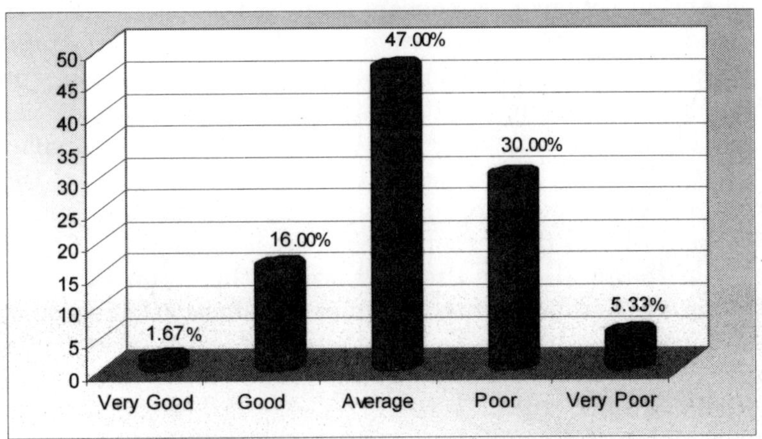

Fig. 9.22 Opinion on career growth potential

I. Impediments Faced by BSNL in Providing Customer Satisfaction

Marketing analysts, time and again, established the fact that customer satisfaction shall be the ultimate goal of any organisation for its survival and growth. In order to satisfy the ever changing needs, wants and expectations of the customers, the companies need to become customer centric and evolve the organisation system, policies, processes, operations and activities towards customer service and satisfaction. The service organisations in the public sector are often criticised on their poor performance in satisfying customers. BSNL is not an exception to this. In the fast changing competitive scenario, BSNL cannot afford to ignore or poorly handle the issues relating to customer satisfaction. Employees constitute an important resource of information and support to transform the organisation as customer oriented one.

Keeping this in view an attempt is made in the study to know the opinion of the respondents on impediments faced by the company in providing customer satisfaction. The related data are presented in Table 9.9 (see on next page).

Absence of business concept is one of the impediments in providing customer satisfaction as 65.33 per cent of the total respondents rated agree or strongly agree for the same. The large number of the respondents [129] representing 40 per cent of the total disagree to the statement 'lake of clear objectives as an impediment'. However, 33 per cent of the respondents either agree or strongly agree to the statement. The majority of the respondents representing about 64 per cent of the total opine that 'big size of the organisation' is the problem in providing customer satisfaction. Absence of autonomy required at the customer interface level is the impediment as per the opinion of about 72 per cent of the respondents.

Indifference of Top management on problems of line officers is the problem in the opinion of 62 per cent of the respondents on the way in providing customer satisfaction. Parallel administration of Unions at grassroot level was not agreed as an impediment in the process of providing customer satisfaction by 50 per cent of the respondents. The large number of respondents [45.67 per cent] took a neutral stand to the statement 'people at the top control as many decisions as possible'. The similar opinion rating was given to the statement internal disharmony and suspicion of the employees as an impediment. The vast majority of the respondents opined that government policies [67.33 per cent] and political interference [75 per cent] are impediments in the process of providing customer satisfaction. Surplus staff was not considered as reason by the majority of the respondents as a factor affecting customer satisfaction.

A little over 41 per cent of the respondents agreed that poor morale of staff is the reason standing in the way of

Table 9.9 Opinion on Impediments being faced by BSNL in providing customer satisfaction.

Particulars	Strongly Agree	Agree	Neutral	Disagree	Strongly Disagree	Total
Absence of business concept	69 23.00%	127 42.33%	63 21.00%	34 11.33%	7 2.33%	300 100%
Lack of clear objectives	43 14.33%	56 18.67%	68 22.67%	129 40.00%	4 1.33%	300 100%
The big size of the organization	48 16.00%	143 47.67%	75 25.00%	13 4.33%	21 7.0%	300 100%
Absence of autonomy required at the customer interface level	12 4.00%	203 67.67%	54 18.00%	27 9.00%	4 1.33%	300 100%
Indifference of top-management on problems of line officers	15 5.00%	171 57.00%	42 14.00%	29 9.67%	43 14.33%	300 100%
Parallel administration of unions at grassroot level	17 5.67%	52 17.33%	81 27.00%	100 33.33%	50 16.67%	300 100%
People at the top control as many decisions as possible	2 0.67%	67 22.33%	137 45.67%	87 29.00%	7 2.33%	300 100%

(Contd.)

Particulars	Strongly Agree	Agree	Neutral	Disagree	Strongly Disagree	Total
Internal disharmony and suspicion of the employees	8 2.67%	70 23.33%	133 44.33%	86 28.67%	3 1.00%	300 100%
Government Policies	104 34.67%	121 40.33%	45 15.00%	16 5.33%	14 4.67%	300 100%
Political interferences	112 37.33%	90 30.00%	67 22.33%	24 8.00%	7 2.33%	300 100%
Surplus staff	11 3.67%	41 13.67%	91 30.33%	93 31.00%	64 21.33%	300 100%
Poor morale of staff	48 16.00%	76 25.33%	94 31.33%	76 25.33%	6 2.00%	300 100%
Low motivation of the employees	93 31.00%	107 35.67%	64 21.33%	24 8.00%	12 4.00%	300 100%
Unwillingness on the part of the employees to accept responsibilities	5 1.67%	83 27.67%	82 27.33%	98 32.67%	32 10.67%	300 100%
Corruption existing at higher level	32 10.67%	101 33.67%	80 26.67%	75 25.00%	12 4.00%	300 100%

(Contd.)

Particulars	Strongly Agree	Agree	Neutral	Disagree	Strongly Disagree	Total
Corruption existing at lower level	31 10.33%	97 32.33%	87 29.00%	67 22.33%	18 6.00%	300 100%
Inter-union rivalry	5 1.67%	122 40.67%	89 29.67%	71 23.67%	13 4.33%	300 100%
Non-Availability of timely and adequate resources (viz., human, materials, finance etc.,) according to demands of operations	12 4.00%	196 65.33%	46 15.33%	39 13.00%	7 2.33%	300 100%

providing customer satisfaction while 27.33 per cent of the respondents did not agree to it. Low motivation of employees as the impediment agreed by 66.67 per cent of the respondents. The statement 'unwillingness on the part of the employees to accept responsibility' was disagreed by 43.33 per cent of the respondents and agreed by 29.33 per cent of the respondents. The statement 'corruption exiting at the higher level' was agreed by 44.33 per cent. About 43 per cent of the respondents agree to the statement 'corruption existing at the lower level'. Inter union rivalry was agreed as an impediment by 42.33 per cent of the respondents. The majority of the respondents representing 69.33 per cent of the total agreed the statement non-availability of timely and adequate resources such as human sources finance material etc., according to demands of operations as an impediment, in providing customer satisfaction.

J. Organisational Pride

The vast majority of the respondents feel proud as being employees of BSNL. The data shown in Figure 9.23 reveals 67.33 per cent of the respondents strongly agree and 21.33 per cent of the respondents agree to the statement 'I feel proud to be the employee of BSNL'.

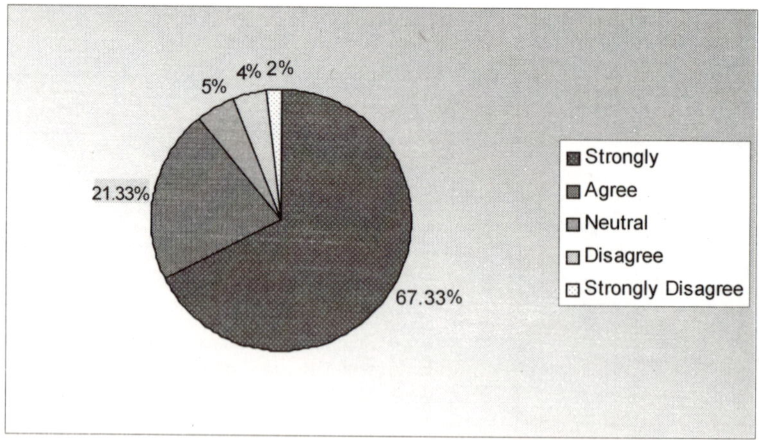

Fig. 9.23 I feel proud to be the employee of BSNL

K. Job Security

The majority of the respondents are of the view that their job is secure because BSNL is the public sector organisation. As can be seen from Figure 9.24, 42.67 per cent of the respondents agree and 42.67 per cent of the respondents strongly agree to the statement 'my job is secure because BSNL is public sector organisation'.

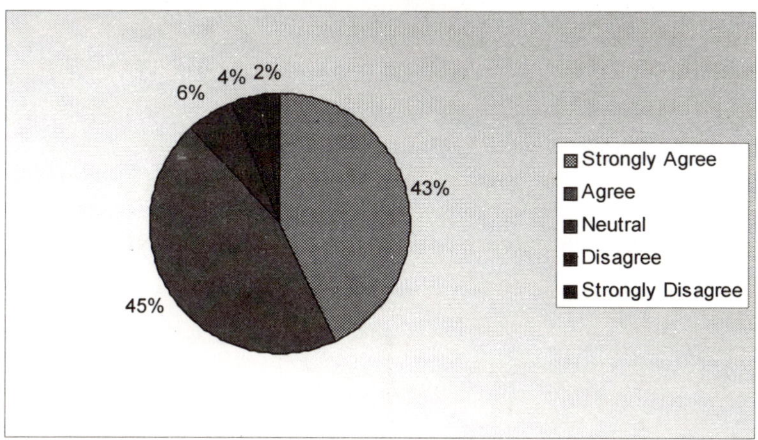

Fig. 9.24 My job is secure because BSNL is the public sector organisation

L. Competition

The opinion of the respondents on the ability of BSNL to face competition from private sector is shown in Figure 9.25. (see on next page) Out of the total, 36.67 per cent of the respondents disagree and about 8 per cent of the respondents strongly disagree to the statement 'private companies cannot beat BSNL'. Only 16.33 per cent of the respondents agreed to the statement.

M. BSNL as a Multi National Company

The majority of the respondents wish BSNL to become a Multi National Company. The data shown in Figure 9.26 (see on next page) reveals 31 per cent of the respondents agree and 28.33 per cent of the respondents strongly agree to the statement 'we wish BSNL to become a Multi National Company'.

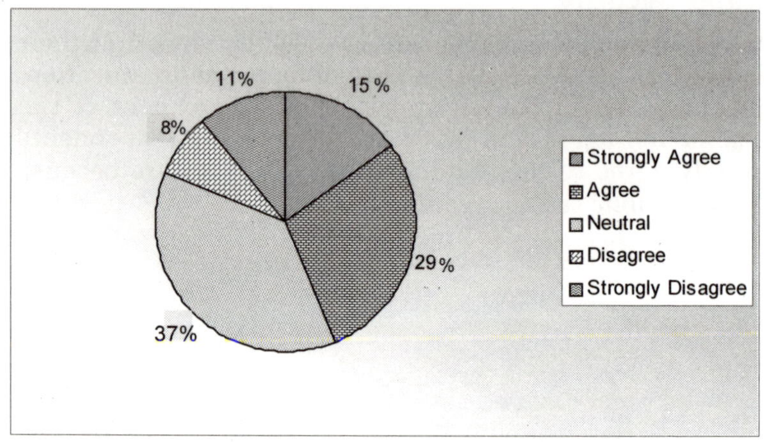

Fig. 9.25 Private companies can't beat BSNL

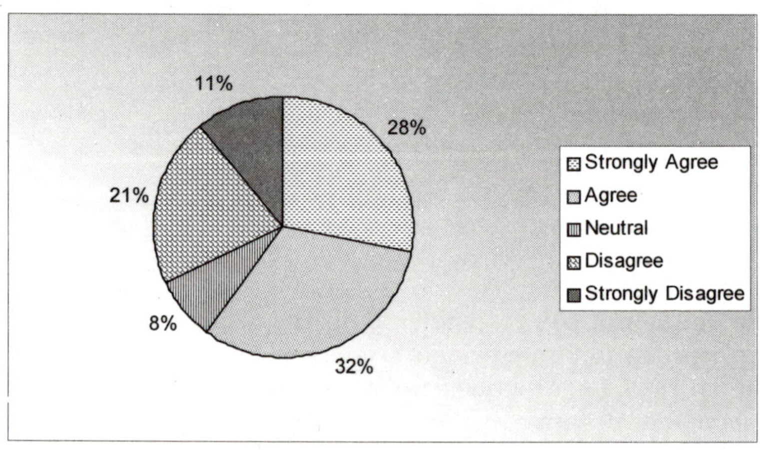

Fig. 9.26 We wish BSNL to be a Multi National Company

N. Employees as Strength

The vast majority of the respondents agreed to the statement 'the employees are the major strength of BSNL'. As can be seen from Figure 9.27, 50 per cent of the respondents strongly agree and 37 per cent of the respondents agree to the statement.

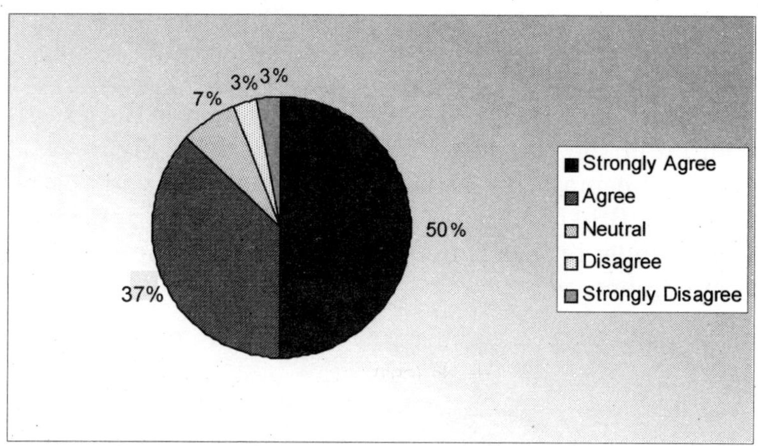

Fig. 9.27 The employees are the major strength of BSNL

O. Customer Loyalty

Figure 9.28 presents the opinion of the respondents on customer loyalty to the BSNL. As many as 128 respondents representing about 43 per cent of the total disagree and 8.33 per cent of the respondent strongly disagree to the statement 'BSNL customers continue to be loyal to the company'. They perceive grater threat from competing companies in influencing customers to switch over their loyalty.

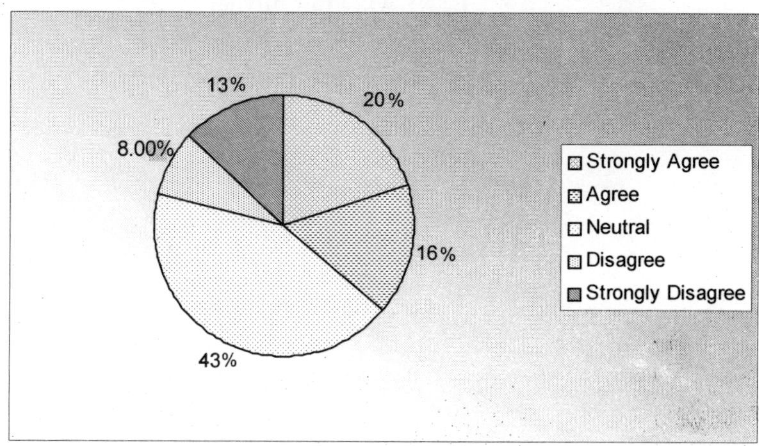

Fig. 9.28 BSNL customers continues to be loyal to the

P. Growth Potential

The respondents are asked to give their opinion on the growth potential of the company. The data shown in Figure 9.29 reveals the majority of the respondents agreed to the statement 'BSNL will grow further'. However, 41 per cent of the respondents took a neutral stand while responding to the statement.

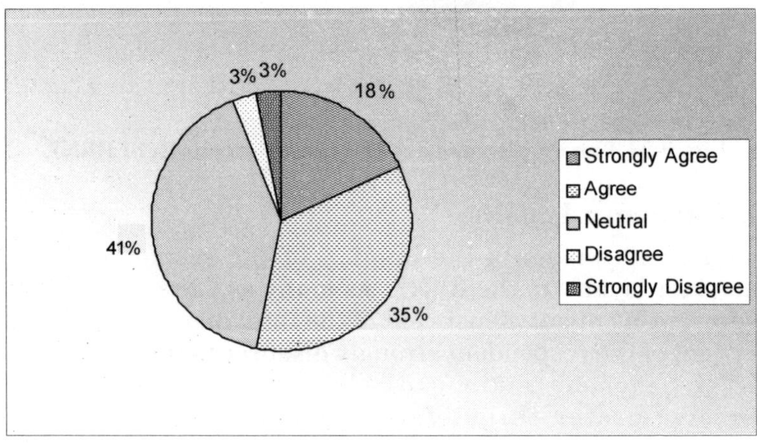

BSNL will grow further

CHAPTER 10 CUSTOMERS' OPINION SURVEY

Customers perceive quality in the service production and consumption process. Therefore, the feedback from customers should form the basis for marketing strategy of any service organisation. A systematic collection of feedback on all relevent aspects continually helps the organisation to identify problems, strengths and opportunities and to initiate measures for further development. This chapter analyses, the customers' opinion on maintenance, timeliness of service, behaviour of contact employees, pricing, service quality, responsiveness besides other marketing issues.

A. Demographic Profile of Respondents

The study covers six telecom circles of Andhra Pradesh. Seventy five customers from each circle were selected to collect opinions on telecom services of BSNL. The particulars relating to the age of the respondents are shown in Table 10.1.

The telephone users below 21 years of age are excluded from the study. The age of respondents varied between 21 years and 66 years. Out of the total, 51.33 per cent of the respondents are in the age group of 31 to 41 years. About 35 per cent of respondents are in the age group of 41 to 50 years. Out of the total, about 12 per cent are in the age group of 21 to 30 years and 2.22 per cent of the respondents are of above 50 years of age. The average age of respondents selected for the study is 37.73 years.

Table 10.1 Age of the respondents

21-30	10 2.22%	7 1.55%	18 4.00%	3 0.67%	8 1.78%	7 1.56%	53 11.78%
31-40	33 7.33%	36 8.00%	41 9.11%	35 7.78%	43 9.56%	43 9.56%	231 51.33%
41-50	31 6.89%	28 6.22%	15 3.33%	33 7.33%	24 5.33%	25 5.56%	156 34.67%
51 & above	1 0.22%	4 0.89%	1 0.22%	4 0.89%	—	—	10 2.22%
Total	**75 16.67%**	**75 16.67%**	**75 16.67%**	**75 16.67%**	**75 16.67%**	**75 16.67%**	**450 100.00%**

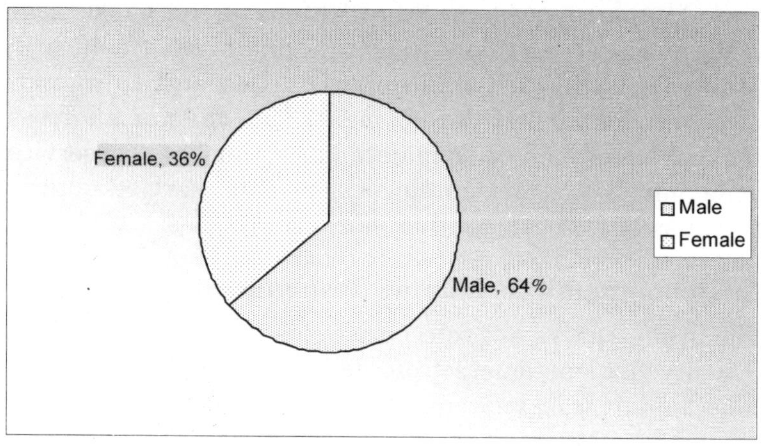

Fig. 10.1 Sex-wise distribution

Figure 10.1 Shows sex-wise distribution of respondents. Out of the total, 290 respondents representing 64.45 per cent are males. Females constitute 35.55 per cent of the total.

The particulars relating to educational qualifications of the respondents are shown in Table 10.2.

The table reveals 42 per cent of the respondents are graduates. A little over 50 per cent of the respondents are post-graduates. As many as 23.11 per cent are professionals. However, there are about 20 per cent of the respondents who had under graduate level education.

Table 10.2 Educational qualification

Age in years	Telecom Circle						Total
	Hyderabad	Karnool	Vijayawada	VSKP	Tirupati	Warangal	
Under Graduate level	12 2.67%	15 3.33%	11 2.44%	20 4.44%	14 3.11%	17 3.78%	89 19.78%
Graduation	35 7.78%	36 8.00%	26 5.78%	21 4.67%	39 8.67%	32 7.11%	189 41.99%
PG	11 2.44%	7 1.56%	16 3.56%	12 2.67%	12 2.67%	10 2.22%	68 15.11%
Professional	17 3.78%	17 3.78%	22 4.89%	22 4.89%	10 2.22%	16 3.56%	104 23.11%
Total	**75** **16.67%**	**75** **16.67%**	**75** **16.67%**	**75** **16.67%**	**75** **16.67%**	**75** **16.67%**	**450** **100.00%**

The particulars relating to occupation of the respondent are shown in Table 10.3. Out of the total, 26.89 per cent of the respondents are businessmen. As many as 25.33 per cent are employees. There are 104 respondents [23.11 per cent] who are professionals and 52 respondents [11.55 per cent] who are cultivators. Housewives constitute 13.11 per cent of the total.

Table 10.3 Occupation of the respondents

Age in years	Telecom Circle						Total
	Hyderabad	Karnool	Vijayawada	VSKP	Tirupati	Warangal	
Business	23 5.11%	15 3.33%	12 2.67%	19 4.22%	29 6.44%	23 5.11%	121 26.89%
Employee	20 4.44%	20 4.44%	17 3.78%	21 4.67%	15 3.33%	21 4.67%	114 25.33%
Professional	14 3.11%	19 4.22%	16 3.56%	24 5.33%	13 2.89%	18 4.00%	104 23.11%
Cultivation	12 2.67%	8 1.78%	10 2.22%	9 2.00%	6 1.33%	7 1.56%	52 11.55%
Housewives	6 1.33%	13 2.89%	20 4.44%	2 0.44%	12 2.67%	6 1.33%	59 13.11%
Total	**75** **16.67%**	**75** **16.67%**	**75** **16.67%**	**75** **16.67%**	**75** **16.67%**	**75** **16.67%**	**450** **100.00%**

The annual income of respondents varied between below Rs.1,00,000/- and above Rs. 5,00,000/- (Table 10.4). The

Table 10.4 Annual Incomes

Income in Rs.	Telecom Circle						Total
	Hyderabad	Karnool	Vijayawada	VSKP	Tirupati	Warangal	
1,00,000 - & Below	4 0.89%	3 0.67%	8 1.78%	7 1.56%	2 0.44%	2 0.44%	26 5.78%
1,00,001-1,50,000	15 3.33%	14 3.11%	21 4.67%	14 3.11%	16 3.56%	18 4.00%	98 21.78%
1,50,001-2,00,000	26 5.78%	24 5.33%	19 4.22%	28 6.22%	31 6.89%	30 6.67%	158 35.11%
2,00,001 - 2,50,000	10 2.22%	10 2.22%	12 2.67%	11 2.44%	12 2.67%	14 3.11%	69 15.33%
2,50,001 - 3,00,000	17 3.78%	19 4.22%	9 2.00%	10 2.22%	8 1.78%	8 1.78%	71 15.78%
3,00,001 & Above	3 0.67%	5 1.11%	6 1.33%	5 1.11%	6 1.33%	3 0.67%	28 6.22%
Total	**75 16.67%**	**75 16.67%**	**75 16.67%**	**75 16.67%**	**75 16.67%**	**75 16.67%**	**450 100.00%**

annual income of 35.11 per cent of the respondents varied between Rs. 2,00,001/- and Rs. 3,00,000/-. The annual income of 22 per cent of the respondents varied between Rs. 1,00,001/- and Rs. 2,00,000/-. A little over 31 per cent of the respondents' income varied between Rs. 3,00,001/- and 5,00,000/- each. there are 6.22 per cent of the respondents who earn an annual income of more than Rs.5,00,000/-each. The annual income of 5.77 per cent of the respondents was Rs. 1,00,001/- to Rs 2,00,000/- each. The average annual income of the respondents was Rs.1,89,666.67.

The family size of the respondents varied between one and eight (Table 10.5). It can be seen from the table, 220 respondents representing 48.88 per cent of the total are having four members in the family. The family size of 22.22 per cent of respondents is three. The family size of 18.44 per cent of respondents is five. The average family size of the sample is 3.95.

Table 10.5 Family size

Number of members	Telecom Circle						Total
	Hyderabad	Karnool	Vijayawada	VSKP	Tirupati	Warangal	
1	1 0.22%	—	—	—	—	1 0.22%	2 0.44%
2	6 1.33%	—	5 1.11%	4 0.89%	4 0.89%	3 0.67%	22 4.89%
3	15 3.33%	19 4.22%	24 5.33%	13 2.89%	15 3.33%	14 3.11%	100 22.22%
4	32 7.11%	34 7.56%	32 7.11%	42 9.33%	41 9.11%	39 8.67%	220 48.89%
5	18 4.00%	20 4.44%	11 2.44%	9 2.00%	13 2.89%	12 2.67%	83 18.44%
6 & above	3 0.67%	2 0.44%	3 0.67%	7 1.56%	2 0.44%	6 1.33%	23 5.11%
Total	**75 16.67%**	**75 16.67%**	**75 16.67%**	**75 16.67%**	**75 16.67%**	**75 16.67%**	**450 100.00%**

B. Relationship in BSNL

An attempt is made in the study to know the length of experience of the respondents with BSNL in relation to fixed line connectivity. The data shown in Table 10.6 reveals that

Table 10.6 Since how long you are having BSNL Connection?

Number of members	Telecom Circle						Total
	Hyderabad	Karnool	Vijayawada	VSKP	Tirupati	Warangal	
1 - 5	24 5.33%	20 4.44%	28 6.22%	14 3.11%	28 6.22%	27 6.00%	141 31.33%
6 - 10	31 6.89%	36 8.00%	33 7.33%	38 8.44%	25 5.56%	30 6.67%	193 42.89%
11 - 15	15 3.33%	12 2.67%	8 1.78%	18 4.00%	14 3.11%	12 2.67%	79 17.56%
16 & above	5 1.11%	7 1.56%	6 1.33%	5 1.11%	8 1.78%	6 1.33%	37 8.22%
Total	75 16.67%	75 16.67%	75 16.67%	75 16.67%	75 16.67%	75 16.7%	450 100.00%

the respondents' experience varied between one year and more than 16 years. As many as 141 respondents representing 31.33 per cent of the total had BSNL connection during the last 5 years. About 26 per cent of the respondents have more than 10 years of experience with BSNL fixed line connectivity.

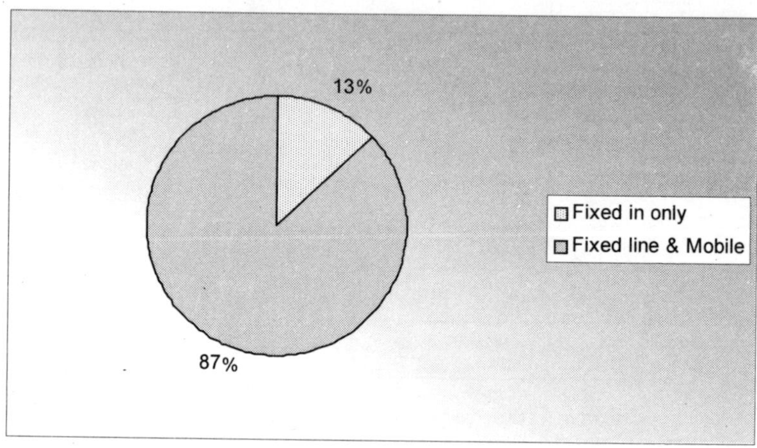

Fig. 10.2 Type of phone(s) used by the respondents

Figure 10.2 depicts the data relating to the type of phones used by the respondents. The study reveals that more than 87 per cent of the respondents are using both fixed line and mobile services. Out of the total, about 12.89 per cent of the respondents are using only fixed line services. The majority of the respondents representing 91.11 per cent are using BSNL fixed line under a price package of Rs. 500/- and below [Table 10.7].

Table 10.7 Details of the price package of the respondents

Package in Rs.	Telecom Circle						Total
	Hyderabad	Karnool	Vijayawada	VSKP	Tirupati	Warangal	
500 & Below	67 14.89%	69 15.33%	66 14.67%	68 15.11%	71 15.8%	69 15.33%	410 91.11%
501 - 1000	6 1.33%	3 0.67%	6 1.33%	5 1.11%	2 0.4%	5 1.11%	27 6.00%
1001 - 1500	2 0.44%	3 0.67%	3 0.67%	2 0.44%	2 0.4%	1 0.22%	13 2.89%
Total	**75 16.67%**	**75 16.67%**	**75 16.67%**	**75 16.67%**	**75 16.67%**	**75 16.67%**	**450 100.00%**

The price package of 6 per cent of the respondents varied between Rs.501/- and Rs.1000/-. Only about 3 per cent of the respondents have taken the price package varying between Rs.1001/- and Rs.1500/-.

An attempt is made to know the average monthly expenditure of the respondents on fixed line telephone. The study reveals that about 59.56 per cent of the respondents incur an expenditure of Rs.501/- to Rs.1000/- per month on fixed line connection [Table 10.8].

Table 10.8 Monthly Expenditure on Landline Telephone

Expen-diture in Rs.	Telecom Circle						Total
	Hydera-bad	Karnool	Vijaya-wada	VSKP	Tiru-pati	Waran-gal	
500 & Below	25 5.56%	18 4.00%	25 5.56%	20 4.44%	18 4.00%	15 3.33%	121 26.89%
501 - 1000	33 7.33%	50 11.11%	43 9.56%	47 10.44%	45 10.00%	50 11.11%	268 59.56%
1001 - 1500	17 3.78%	7 1.56%	7 1.56%	8 1.78%	12 2.67%	10 2.22%	61 13.56%
Total	**75 16.67%**	**75 16.67%**	**75 16.67%**	**75 16.67%**	**75 16.67%**	**75 16.67%**	**450 100.00%**

About 20 per cent of the respondents' expenditure was Rs. 500/- and below each per month. The monthly expenditure of 13.56 per cent of the respondents varied between Rs. 1001/- and Rs. 1500/-. The average expenditure of the respondents per month on fixed line service was Rs. 683.33.

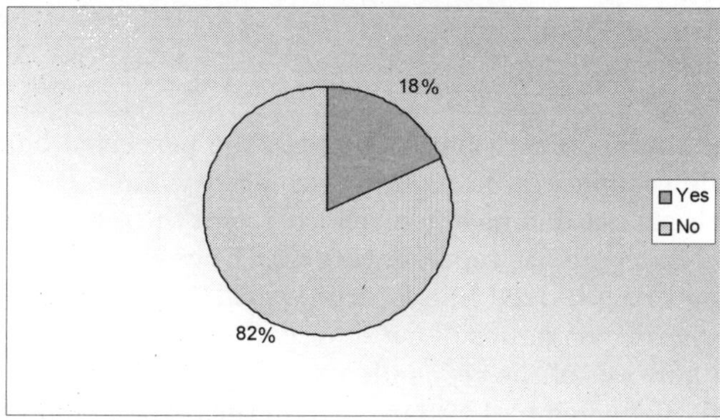

Fig. 10.3. Do you have fixed line connections of private telecom companies in addition to BSNL?

The respondents were further asked to reveal whether they are having fixed line connection of private telecom companies in addition to BSNL. The data presented in Figure 10.3 reveals, about 82 percent of the respondents do not have fixed connection of private telecom companies.

C. Perceived Benefits from BSNL Fixed Line

The respondents revealed the benefits they perceive from BSNL fixed line connectivity when compared to the other private company fixed line connections.

Table 10.9 Benefits from BSNL fixed lines connection compared to Private company fixed line connection

Particulars	Telecom Circle						Total
	Hyderabad	Karnool	Vijayawada	VSKP	Tirupati	Warangal	
Economical	30 6.67%	32 7.11%	29 6.44%	39 8.67%	30 6.67%	32 7.11%	192 42.67%
Low rent	12 2.67%	14 3.11%	9 2.00%	11 2.44%	9 2.00%	10 2.22%	65 14.44%
Voice clarity	8 1.78%	5 1.11%	10 2.22%	8 1.78%	12 2.67%	7 1.56%	50 11.11%
More Free calls	12 2.67%	10 2.22%	11 2.44%	4 0.89%	9 2.00%	11 2.44%	57 12.67%
Reliable service	11 2.44%	9 2.00%	10 2.22%	8 1.78%	9 2.00%	13 2.89%	60 13.33%
No hidden charges	2 0.44%	5 1.11%	6 1.33%	5 1.11%	6 1.33%	2 0.44%	26 5.78%
Total	**75** **16.67%**	**75** **16.67%**	**75** **16.67%**	**75** **16.67%**	**75** **16.67%**	**75** **16.67%**	**450** **100.00%**

As can be seen from Table 10.9, the perceived benefits include economical, low rent, voice clarity, more free calls, reliable service and no hidden charges. Out the total, as many as 192 respondents representing 42.67 per cent of the total revealed BSNL fixed line is 'economical' when compared to the private companies. 'Low rent' is the benefit revealed by 14.44 per cent of the respondents. 'Reliable service' was the benefit identified by 13.33 per cent of the respondents where as 'more free calls' is the benefit revealed by 12.67 per cent of the respondents. There are 11.11 per cent of the respondents who revealed 'voice clarity' as the major benefit from the BSNL while 5.78 per cent revealed that there are 'no hidden charges' in BSNL.

As mentioned already, there are 392 respondents who use mobile services along with fixed line services. The reasons revealed by the respondents for using mobile service in addition to fixed line is shown in Table 10.10.

Table 10.10 Reasons for using mobile services along with fixed line

Particulars	Telecom Circle						Total
	Hyderabad	Karnool	Vijayawada	VSKP	Tirupati	Warangal	
Communication Convenience	35 8.92%	30 7.65%	40 10.20%	38 9.69%	32 8.16%	35 8.92%	210 53.57%
Status symbol	10 2.55%	15 3.83%	14 3.57%	13 3.32%	17 4.34%	12 3.06%	81 20.67%
Privacy	5 1.28%	4 1.02%	3 0.76%	6 1.53%	6 1.53%	2 0.51%	26 6.63%
SMS facility	4 1.02%	3 0.76%	4 1.02%	5 1.28%	5 1.28%	2 0.51%	23 5.87%
Handling facility	10 2.55%	10 2.55%	9 2.30%	4 1.02%	10 2.55%	9 2.30%	52 13.26%
Total	**64** **16.33%**	**62** **15.82%**	**70** **17.86%**	**66** **16.84%**	**70** **17.86%**	**60** **15.31%**	**392** **100.00%**

Communication convenience is the major reason revealed by 53.57 per cent of the respondents for having mobile connection. For about 20.67 per cent of the respondents mobile phone is a status symbol. Handling convenience is the major reason revealed by 52 respondents representing 13.26 per cent of the total. Privacy was the reason for 6.63 per cent of the respondents while the SMS facility was the reason for 5.87 per cent of the respondents to have mobile connection.

An attempt is made to know the major reason for continuing BSNL fixed line service by the respondents. The study revealed, the majority of the respondents representing 53.33 per cent continue BSNL fixed line because of its large network connectivity even to rural areas [Table 10.11]. Low rentals was the major reason revealed by 126 respondents representing 28 per cent of the total. The other reasons identified by some respondents include Public Sector Company, free calls and reliable service.

Table 10.11 Major reason for continuing BSNL fixed line service

Particular	1	2	3	Totals
Large Network connectivity even to rural areas	75 16.67%	85 18.89%	80 17.78%	240 53.33%
Low rentals	50 11.11%	35 7.78%	41 9.11%	126 28.00%
Public sector company	7 1.56%	9 2.00%	9 2.00%	25 5.56%
Free calls	8 1.78%	6 1.33%	9 2.00%	23 5.11%
Reliable service	10 2.22%	15 3.33%	11 2.44%	36 8.00%
Total	**150** **33.33%**	**150** **33.33%**	**150** **33.33%**	**450** **100.00%**

D. Opinion on Maintenance Services

Telecom customers take fixed line connection generally to continue the service for a long period. During the period of service the customers except un interrupted service. Maintenance of service is the responsibility of the service company. The service personnel will take care of the maintenance of exchanges, distribution line and junction boxes besides attending to customers' specific maintenance problems. A failure or deficiency in maintenance service may affect seriously the customer quality perceptions of the service. The problems such as line dead, supplementary sounds or line disturbances, input /out put clarity, etc., will cause inconveniences to the customers. It is necessary, therefore, to demonstrate high level of efficiency in the maintenance of services to satisfy and retain customers. Keeping this in view an attempt is made, to know the maintenance problems faced by the respondents and their opinion on the maintenance services provided and performed by the company.

Table 10.12 Maintenance problems

Particulars	Strongly Agree	Agree	Neutral	Dis-agree	Strongly Disagree	Total
Frequent line failure	30 6.67%	157 34.89%	69 15.33%	174 38.67%	20 4.44%	450 100.00%
Voice clarity is poor	22 4.89%	48 1.67%	11 2.44%	286 63.56%	83 18.44%	450 00.00%
Supplementary sounds are often disturbing	18 4.00%	145 32.22%	63 14.00%	214 47.56%	10 2.22%	450 100.00%
Frequent wrong calls	34 7.56%	30 6.67%	54 12.00%	319 70.89%	13 2.87%	450 100.00%
Frequent instrument malfunctioning	18 4.00%	30 6.67%	56 12.44%	330 73.33%	16 3.55%	450 100.00%
Poor response to the complaints	13 2.87%	133 29.56%	36 8.00%	261 60.00%	7 1.56%	450 100.00%
Discourteous behaviour of contact employee	15 3.33%	34 7.56%	50 11.11%	333 74.00%	18 4.00%	450 100.00%
Make temporary adjust-ments on complaints	26 5.78%	168 37.33%	49 10.89%	201 44.67%	6 1.33%	450 100.00%

The data presented in Table 10.12 shows the maintenance problems of the respondents. Frequent line failure is the problem for 41.57 per cent of the respondents. The vast majority of the respondents representing 82 per cent of the total disagreed to the statement 'voice clarity is poor'. The statement 'supplementary sounds' are often disturbing, was confirmed by 36.22 per cent of the respondents where as about 50 per cent of the respondents disagreed the statement. For the statement 'frequent wrong call', only 14.23 per cent gave the agreement where as more than 73 per cent disagreed the statement. The statement 'poor response to the complaints' was rejected by 61.56 per cent of the respondents while 32.43 per cent agreed to the statement. Out of the total, 78 per cent of respondents rejected the statement 'discourteous behavior of contract employees'. The statement 'make temporary adjustments on complaints', was agreed by 43.11 per cent of the respondents whereas 46 per cent of the respondents disagreed the statement. It can be inferred from the above that frequent line failure, supplementary sounds or line disturbances, poor response to complaints and temporary solutions to the maintenances problems are the issues of concern to a sizable number of customers. BSNL should focus on these problems and take measures for rectification. The opinion of the respondents with respect to behaviour of maintenance employees, functioning of instruments and voice clarity is quite encouraging to the company.

Table 10.13 Rating on maintenance services

Particulars	Telecom Circle						Total
	Hyderabad	Karnool	Vijayawada	VSKP	Tirupati	Warangal	
Very Good	15 3.33%	13 2.87%	16 3.56%	14 3.11%	11 2.44%	16 3.56%	85 18.89%
Good	30 6.67%	27 6.00%	20 4.44%	40 8.89%	25 5.56%	36 8.00%	178 39.56%
Average	13 2.89%	9 2.00%	19 4.22%	15 3.33%	15 3.33%	20 4.44%	91 20.22%
Poor	15 3.33%	20 4.44%	18 4.00%	4 0.89%	20 4.44%	2 0.44%	126 28.00%
Very poor	2 0.44%	6 1.33%	2 0.44%	2 0.44%	4 0.89%	1 0.22%	20 4.44%
Total	**75** **16.67%**	**75** **16.67%**	**75** **16.67%**	**75** **16.67%**	**75** **16.67%**	**75** **16.67%**	**450** **100.00%**

An attempt is further made to obtain rating of the respondents on the overall maintenance service of BSNL. The data presented in Table 10.13 shows that 18.89 per cent of the respondents rated the maintainance service as very good. As many as 178 respondents representing 39.56 per cent of the total rated the maintainance services as good. The rating of 91 respondents representing 20.22 per cent is average. Out of the total, 126 respondents representing 28 per cent rated the services as poor and 20 respondents representing 4.44 per cent rated the services as very poor. It can be inferred from the above that the majority of the respondents rated the maintainance service of the company as either good or very good. However, the voice of the others can not be ignored as the percentage of the respondents who rated the service as average, poor and very poor is also significant.

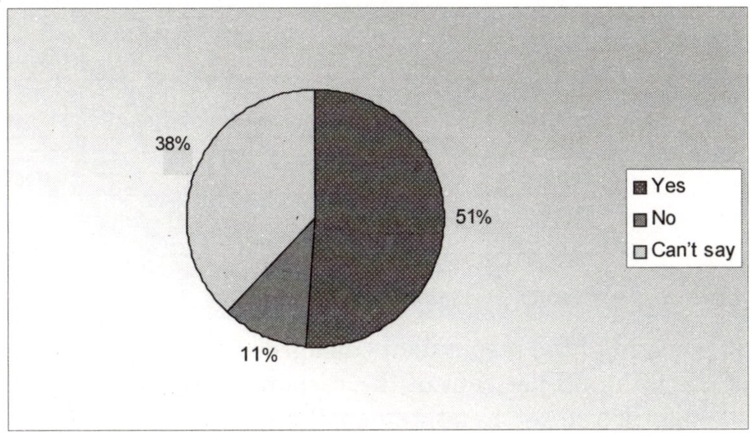

Fig. 10.4 Is BSNL Improving the quality of maintenance in recent years?

The majority of the respondents representing 51.56 per cent are of the opinion that the BSNL is improving the quality of maintenance services [Figure 10.4]. However, there are about 11 per cent of the respondents who have not accepted that there is an improvement in the quality of maintenance services. As many as 170 respondents representing 37.78 per cent of the total took a neutral stand on this issue.

The data relating to opinion of the respondents on behavior of maintenance staff of the company are presented in Table 10.14. The table reveals that 57.11 per cent of the respondents agree and 12.67 per cent of the respondents strongly agree to the statement 'the maintenance staff are courteous'. The majority of respondents [50.44 per cent] disagreed to the statement "the maintenance staff are empathetic". About 56 per cent of the respondents agree and 9.33 per cent strongly agree to the statement 'the maintenance staff are reactive'. However, a little over

Table 10.14 Opinion on the Behaviour of Maintenance staff

Particulars	Strongly Agree	Agree	Neutral	Dis-agree	Strongly Disagree	Total
Courteous	57 12.67%	257 57.11%	12 2.67%	123 27.33%	1 0.22%	450 100.00%
Empathetic	39 8.67%	154 34.22%	30 6.67%	227 50.44%	—	450 100.00%
Reactive	42 9.33%	251 55.78%	20 4.44%	137 30.44%	—	450 100.00%
Objective	34 7.56%	166 36.89%	11 2.44%	239 53.11%	—	450 100.00%
Active	28 6.22%	210 46.67%	16 3.56%	196 43.56%	—	450 100.00%
Friendliness	39 8.67%	192 42.67%	26 5.78%	192 42.67%	1 0.22%	450 100.00%

30 per cent of the respondents disagreed the statement. Out of the total, 53 per cent of the respondents either agree or strongly agree to the statement 'the maintenance staff is active'. However, about 44 per cent of the respondents disagreed the statement. 'Friendly behavior' is felt by about 52 per cent of the respondents while 43 per cent of the respondents did not find friendly behavior from the maintenance staff. It can be inferred from the above, that there is inconsistency in the interactive behaviour of maintenance staff with customers. The maintenance staffs of the BSNL are large in number and there is a possibility of differing behavior patterns in customer interactions. The variance in the behaviour is more likely to take place when the employees are not properly trained and directed. As the maintenance employees are the customer contact employees, their role in shaping consumer quality perceptions and image building cannot be overemphasized. Taking the respondents opinion in to consideration, it is suggested that the maintenance staff shall be given training on interactive skills and social behaviour.

Table 10.15 presents the data on frequency of 'out of order' problem faced by the respondents. It can be seen from the table, a little over 51.33 per cent of the respondents

Table 10.15 Frequency of 'out of order' problem

Parti-	Telecom Circle						Total
culars	Hydera-bad	Karnool	Vijaya-wada	VSKP	Tiru-pati	Waran-gal	
At least once in six months	30 6.67%	32 7.11%	27 6.00%	32 7.11%	20 4.44%	19 4.22%	160 35.56%
On an average once in a year	40 8.89%	35 7.78%	30 6.67%	35 7.78%	51 11.33%	40 8.89%	231 51.33%
Frequently	5 1.11%	8 1.78%	18 4.00%	8 1.78%	4 0.89%	16 3.56%	59 13.11%
Total	**75** **16.67%**	**75** **16.67%**	**75** **16.67%**	**75** **16.67%**	**75** **16.67%**	**75** **16.67%**	**450** **100.00%**

experience 'out of order' problem on an average once in a year. As many as 160 respondents representing 35.56 per cent experience the problem at least once a six months. However, in the case of 59 respondents representing 13.11 per cent, 'out of order' problem is frequent.

Table10.16 Time taken by the maintenances staff for undertaking repair work

Parti-	Telecom Circle						Total
culars	Hydera-bad	Karnool	Vijaya-wada	VSKP	Tiru-pati	Waran-gal	
Same day	10 2.22%	11 2.44%	8 1.78%	12 2.67%	14 3.11%	12 2.67%	67 14.89%
Next day	35 7.78%	41 9.11%	40 8.89%	37 8.22%	33 7.33%	44 9.78%	230 51.11%
Within a week	30 6.67%	23 5.11%	27 6.00%	26 5.78%	28 6.22%	19 4.22%	153 34.00%
Total	**75** **16.67%**	**75** **16.67%**	**75** **16.67%**	**75** **16.67%**	**75** **16.67%**	**75** **16.67%**	**450** **100.00%**

The respondents were asked to reveal the time taken by the maintenance personnel to rectify the problem of 'out of order'. The data presented in Table 10.16 reveals that in the case of 51.11 per cent of the respondents the problem was rectified in one day. About 15 per cent of the respondents revealed, the problem was rectified on the same day of making the complaint. However, 34 per cent of the respondents revealed, the problem was rectified within a week time.

E. OPINION ON PRICING

Price is one of the important influencing factors of customers' purchase decision process. Price of services influence customer satisfaction. An attempt is made in the study to know the opinion of the respondents on pricing of different services offered by the company. The data presented in Table 10.17

Table 10.17 Opinion on price of local calls

Parti-culars	Telecom Circle						Total
	Hydera-bad	Karnool	Vijaya-wada	VSKP	Tiru-pati	Waran-gal	
Very high	1 0.22%	— —	1 0.22%	1 0.22%	3 0.67%	2 0.44%	8 1.78%
High	4 0.89%	— —	3 0.67%	6 1.44%	5 1.11%	1 0.22%	19 4.33%
Moderate	33 7.44%	31 7.00%	37 8.33%	32 7.22%	30 6.78%	33 7.44%	196 44.11%
Low	36 8.11%	43 9.67%	32 7.22%	35 7.89%	37 8.33%	37 8.33%	220 49.56%
Very Low	1 0.22%	1 0.22%	2 0.44%	1 0.22%	— —	2 0.44%	7 1.56%
Total	**75** **16.67%**	**75** **16.67%**	**75** **16.67%**	**75** **16.67%**	**75** **16.67%**	**75** **16.67%**	**450** **100.00%**

shows the opinion of the customers on the price of local calls. The study reveals, 49.56 per cent of respondents opined that the price charge for local calls is 'low'. As many as 196 respondents representing 44.11 per cent rated the price of local call as 'moderate'. Only six per cent of the respondents consider the price as 'high or very high'.

Out of the total, 71.44 per cent rated the price of STD facility with full charges as 'moderate' [Table 10.18]. Over 21.44 per cent of respondents rated the price as 'high'. With regard to the STD services with concession, about 71 per cent of the respondents rated the price of the services as moderate while 22.33 per cent rated the price as high [Table 10.19].

Table 10.18 Opinion on price of STD with full charges

Parti-culars	Telecom Circle						Total
	Hydera-bad	Karnool	Vijaya-wada	VSKP	Tiru-pati	Waran-gal	
Very high	1 0.22%	— —	1 0.22%	2 0.44%	1 0.22%	1 0.22%	6 1.44%
High	17 3.78%	15 3.44%	15 3.44%	14 3.22%	18 4.11%	16 3.56%	95 21.44%
Moderate	53 11.89%	54 12.22%	53 11.89%	55 12.44%	52 11.67%	50 11.33%	317 71.44%
Low	4 0.89%	6 1.33%	6 1.44%	4 0.89%	4 0.89%	8 0.89%	32 7.11%
Very Low	— —	— —	— —	— —	— —	— —	— —
Total	**75** **16.67**	**75** **16.67%**	**75** **16.67%**	**75** **16.67%**	**75** **16.67%**	**75** **16.67%**	**450** **100.00%**

Table 10.19 Opinion on Price of STD with concessions

Parti-culars	Telecom Circle						Total
	Hydera-bad	Karnool	Vijaya-wada	VSKP	Tiru-pati	Waran-gal	
Very high	1 0.22%	— —	1 0.22%	1 0.22%	— —	— —	3 0.67%
High	23 5.22%	15 3.44%	12 2.67%	17 3.78%	16 3.56%	16 3.56%	99 22.33%
Moderate	49 11.11%	53 12.00%	53 12.00%	54 12.22%	53 12.00%	52 11.67%	314 70.89%
Low	2 0.44%	7 1.56%	9 2.00%	3 0.67%	6 1.44%	7 1.56%	34 7.56%
Very Low	— —	— —	— —	— —	— —	— —	— —
Total	**75** **16.67%**	**75** **16.67%**	**75** **16.67%**	**75** **16.67%**	**75** **16.67%**	**75** **16.67%**	**450** **100.00%**

The opinion of the respondents on telephone rent is divided as per the study. As can be seen from Table 10.20, 33.33 per cent of the respondents revealed that the telephone rent is 'low' while 30.11 per cent revealed that the telephone rent is 'high'. About 34 of the respondents considered telephone rent as moderate. The opinion of the respondents on the price of

Table 10.20 Opinion on Telephone rent

Particulars	Telecom Circle						Total
	Hyderabad	Karnool	Vijayawada	VSKP	Tirupati	Warangal	
Very high	2 0.44%	5 1.11%	4 0.89%	7 1.56%	6 1.44%	5 1.11%	29 6.56%
High	21 4.78%	18 4.11%	31 7.00%	25 5.67%	17 3.78%	21 4.78%	133 30.11%
Moderate	30 6.78%	16 3.56%	22 5.00%	25 5.67%	18 4.11%	21 4.78%	132 29.89%
Low	21 4.78%	36 8.11%	15 3.44%	15 3.44%	34 7.67%	26 5.89%	147 33.33%
Very Low	1 0.22%	— —	3 0.67%	3 0.67%	— —	2 0.44%	9 2.00%
Total	**75** **16.67%**	**75** **16.67%**	**75** **16.67%**	**75** **16.67%**	**75** **16.67%**	**75** **16.67%**	**450** **100.00%**

phonograms is shown in Table 10.21. The majority of the respondents representing 68 per cent of total, rated price of the service as 'moderate'. A little over 17 per cent of the respondents rated the price of phonograms as 'high' or 'very high' while others rated it as 'low or very low'.

Table 10.21 Opinion on Price of Phonograms

Particulars	Telecom Circle						Total
	Hyderabad	Karnool	Vijayawada	VSKP	Tirupati	Warangal	
Very high	2 0.44%	3 0.67%	6 1.33%	3 0.67%	3 0.67%	6 1.33%	23 5.11%
High	10 2.22%	5 1.11%	10 2.22%	13 2.89%	9 2.00%	7 1.56%	54 12.00%
Moderate	57 12.67%	55 12.22%	46 10.22%	44 9.78%	51 11.33%	53 11.78%	306 68.00%
Low	4 0.89%	8 1.78%	7 1.56%	10 2.22%	9 2.00%	7 1.56%	45 10.00%
Very Low	2 0.44%	4 0.89%	6 1.33%	5 1.11%	3 0.67%	2 0.44%	22 4.89%
Total	**75** **16.67%**	**75** **16.67%**	**75** **16.67%**	**75** **16.67%**	**75** **16.67%**	**75** **16.67%**	**450** **100.00%**

An attempt is further made to know the opinion of the respondents on the price policy of the company. The details shown in Figure.10.5 reveals, 47.56 per cent of the respondents rated the price policy as 'good' and 7.33 per cent rated it as 'very good'. As many as 189 respondents representing 42 per cent, rated the price policy as 'average' while 43.11 per cent rated it as 'poor'.

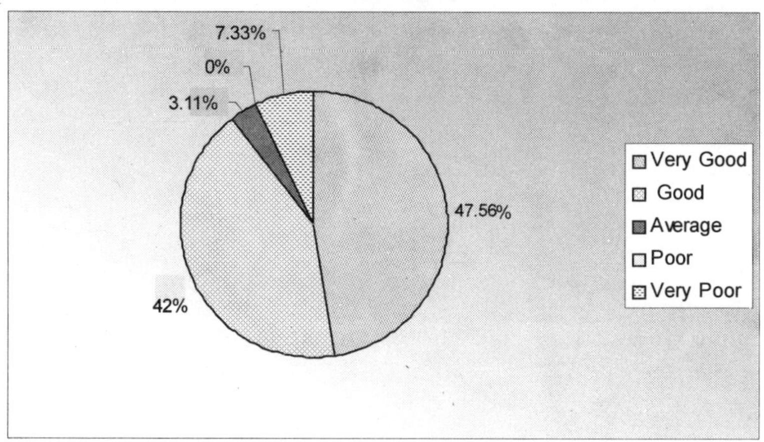

Fig. 10.5 Opinion on Price Policy

F. AWARENESS OF FIXED LINE PRE PAID SERVICES

BSNL has introduced Fixed Line Pre Paid services [FLPP] in 2006 to enable the subscribers to make calls from a prepaid account linked to respective telephone numbers. The Fixed Line Pre Paid service offers:

- Conversion of fixed line to Pre Paid in order to get rid of telephone bills;
- Easy de-linking from telephone line when prepaid is not required on any number;
- No need to dial Account number/ PIN every time the customer makes a call;
- STD/ISD Facility;
- On Line balance enquiry;

- 'Follow on feature' on no reply, busy and called party release to dial another number for subscribers other than PCO;
- Easy recharge and no problem of bills;
- Free Level 1 service like 100, 101, 102 etc.;
- Free Level 1 IN services which are free to end-customers like Free Phone, etc.

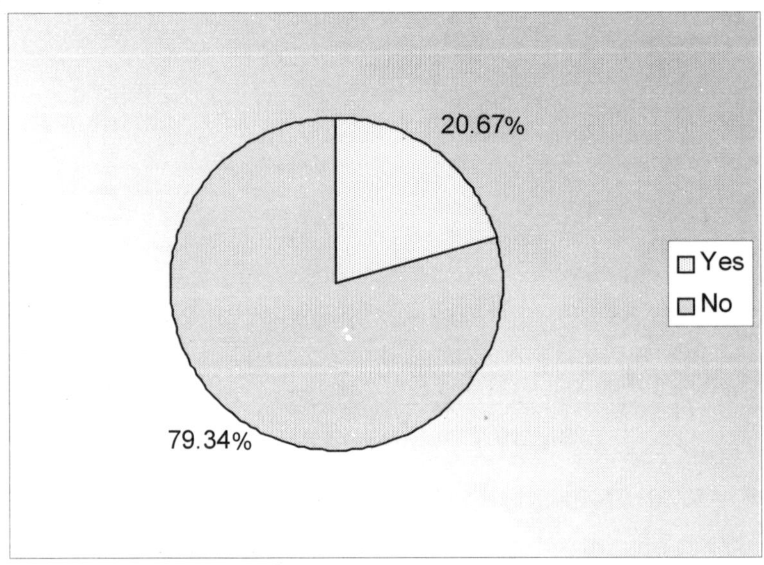

Fig. 10.6 Do you know there is fixed line Pre Paid Service?

The data presented in Figure 10.6 depicts awareness of the respondents about the details of fixedline prepaid service. It is revealed that 79.34 per cent of respondents are unaware of the availability of the service. The study further reveals, the majority of the respondents representing 74.22 per cent of total are not interested to avail this service [Figure 10.7]. The respondents revealed that there is no significant benefit out of the service and, therefore, it is a burden of paying in advance. It is suggested that the BSNL should take an awareness campaign for this service and include a significantly differentiating benefit in the service package.

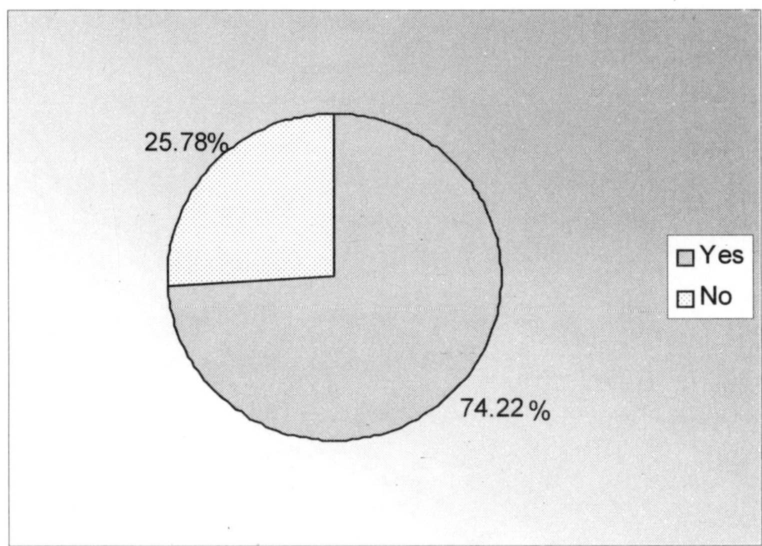

Fig. 10.7 Do you prrofer fixed prepaid to traditional bill payment System?

G. OPINION ON BILLING AND PAYMENT SYSTEMS

Billing and payment systems are important interaction points for both the company and the customers. BSNL follows monthly billing system. The monthly bill will be communicated to the customer by mail and also through electronic mode. The company has a network of payment counters including its own service units, post offices, e-seva centers, etc. The company also provides on-line payment facility to the customers. From the customers point of view it is necessary to ensure that the telephone bills are received by them on time, the billing is done accurately and the facilities of the bill payment are accessible and convenient. Therefore, an attempt is made to know the opinion of the consumers on these issues.

The data shown in Figure 10.8 reveals whether the respondents are receiving telephone bills on time. Out of the total, more than 95 per cent of the respondents revealed they are receiving the telephone bills on time. The respondents are asked to reveal whether they believe that the billing is done accurately.

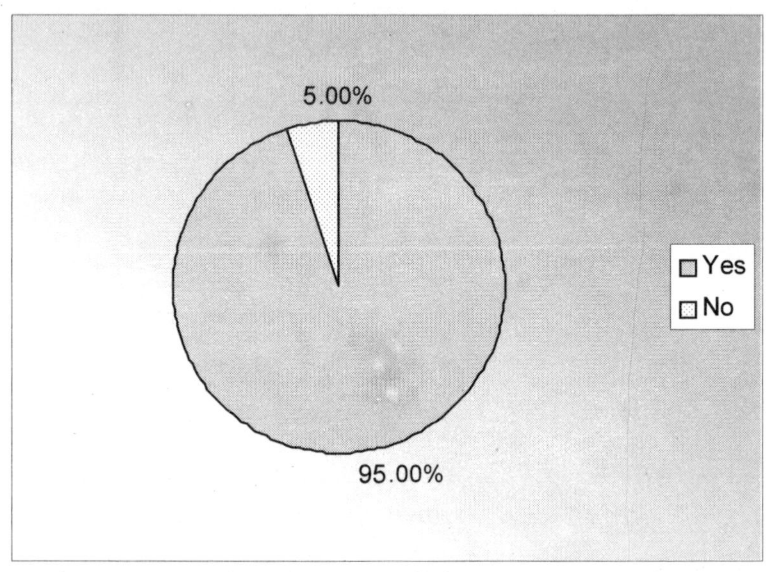

Fig. 10.8 Do you receive telephone bills on time?

Table 10.22 Do you believe that billing is done accurately?

Parti-culars	Telecom Circle						Total
	Hydera-bad	Karnool	Vijaya-wada	VSKP	Tiru-pati	Waran-gal	
Yes	66 14.56%	66 14.56%	68 15.11%	67 14.89%	61 13.56%	63 14.00%	391 86.89%
No	8 1.78%	4 0.89%	3 0.67%	3 0.67%	5 1.11%	7 1.56%	30 6.67%
Doubtful some times	1 0.22%	5 1.11%	4 0.89%	5 1.11%	9 2.00%	5 1.11%	29 6.44%
Total	**75** **16.67%**	**75** **16.67%**	**75** **16.67%**	**75** **16.67%**	**75** **16.67%**	**75** **16.67%**	**450** **100.00%**

The data presented in Table 10.22 reveals, 86.89 per cent of the respondents believe that the billing is done accurately. About 7 per cent of respondents revealed that they have some suspension over billing while 6.44 per cent of the respondents revealed the billing is doubtful some times. It can be infered from the above, BSNL enjoys credibility over billing of fixed line telecom service among customers.

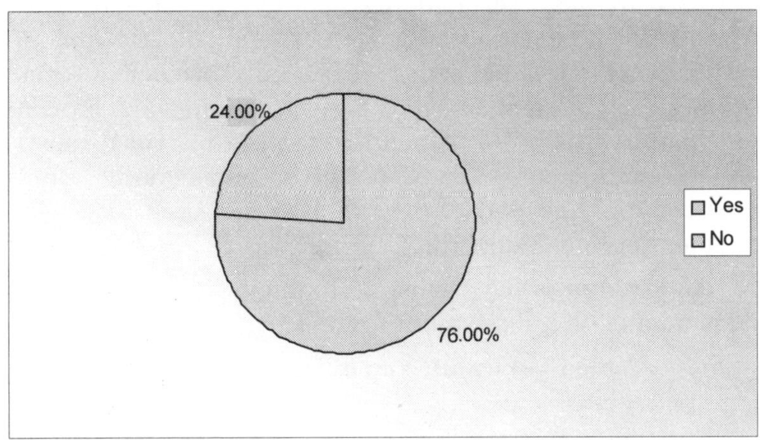

Fig. 10.9 Do you find payment of bills convenient?

The study reveals, 75.78 per cent of the respondents find convenient as far as arrangements made by the company for payment of bills are concerned [Figure 10.9]. However, 24.22 per cent of the respondents are not found the payment facilitating infrastructure convenient.

Table 10.23 Where do you pay your Bills?

Particulars	Mostly	Occasionally	Never	Total
Bank	35 7.78%	196 43.56%	219 48.67%	450 100.00%
Post Office	185 41.11%	201 44.67%	64 14.22%	450 100.00%
BSNL Service Center	157 34.89%	275 61.11%	18 4.00%	450 100.00%
e-Seva/ Internet	73 16.22%	165 36.67%	212 74.11%	450 100.00%

An attempt is made to know where the customers pay telephone bills. The data shown in Table 10.23 reveals post offices are used by 185 respondents [41.11 per cent] 'mostly' and 201 respondents [44.67 per cent] 'occasionally' to pay telephone bills. Next to post office, BSNL services centers are used by most respondents for the purpose. The study reveals 157 respondents [34.89 per cent] mostly and 275 respondents [61.11 per cent] 'occasionally' use BSNL service centers for payment of bills. E-seva/Internet are used for payment of bills by 73 respondents [16.22 per cent] 'mostly' and 165 respondents [36.67 per cent] 'occasionally'. Banks are used by 35 respondents [7.78 per cent] 'occasionally' for payment of telephone bills.

An attempt is further made to know the opinion of the respondents on bill payment system.

Table 10.24 Opinion on bill payment system

Particulars	Telecom Circle						Total
	Hyderabad	Karnool	Vijayawada	VSKP	Tirupati	Warangal	
Satisfactory	25 5.56%	21 4.67%	32 7.11%	18 4.00%	26 5.78%	19 4.22%	141 31.33%
More collection	12 2.67%	19 4.22%	5 1.11%	30 6.67%	22 4.89%	27 6.00%	115 25.56%
Consuming	23 5.11%	28 6.22%	35 7.78%	15 3.33%	13 2.87%	17 3.78%	131 29.11%
e-payment is more convenient	15 3.33%	7 1.56%	3 0.67%	12 2.67%	14 3.11%	12 2.67%	63 14.00
Total	**75 16.67%**	**75 16.67%**	**75 16.67%**	**75 16.67%**	**75 16.67%**	**75 16.67%**	**450 100.00%**

As can be seen from Table10.24, 141 respondents representing 31.33 per cent expressed their satisfaction over the exiting bill payment system. As many as 115 respondents representing 25.56 per cent revealed that there is a need for more collection centers to provide grater accessibility to the customers for payment of bills. A little over 29.11 per cent of the respondents opined, the bill payment system is consuming more time. Out of the total, 63 respondents representing 14 per cent pined that e-payment is more convenient for them.

H. CUSTOMER COMPLAINTS

An attempt is made to study the reactions of customers when they are grievous over the service provided by the company. The data presented in Table 10.25 reveals 151 respondents representing 33.56 per cent, complain their grievances orally to the company authorities. As many as 102 respondents representing 22.67 per cent express their displeasure to the service maintenance personnel. A little over 17.33 pre cent of the respondents revealed that they make a formal complaint to the company. Out of the total, 6.22 per cent of the respondents revealed that they file a case in the customer court and 8.44 per cent of the respondents revealed that they switchover to another company. However, about 11.78 per cent of respondents revealed that they will not complain any one even when they are grievous.

Table 10.25 If you are grievous with the services provided by the company, how do you react?

Parti-culars	Telecom Circle						Total
	Hydera-bad	Karnool	Vijaya-wada	VSKP	Tiru-pati	Waran-gal	
Will not complaint to any body	8 1.78%	8 1.78%	10 2.22%	9 2.00%	8 1.78%	10 2.22%	53 11.78%
Switch over to another	5 1.11%	7 1.56%	6 1.33%	7 1.56%	5 1.11%	8 1.78%	38 8.44%
Make a formal complaint	12 2.67%	14 3.11%	11 2.44%	15 3.33%	13 2.87%	13 2.87%	78 17.33%
Complain orally to the company authorities	28 6.22%	22 4.89%	25 5.56%	23 5.11%	24 5.33%	29 6.44%	151 33.56%
Express my displeasure to the service maintenance personal	21 4.67%	14 3.11%	21 4.67%	18 4.00%	19 4.22%	9 2.00%	102 22.67%
File a case in the consumer court	1 0.22%	10 2.22%	2 0.44%	3 0.67%	6 1.33%	6 1.33%	28 6.22%
Total	**75 16.67%**	**75 16.67%**	**75 16.67%**	**75 16.67%**	**75 16.67%**	**75 16.67%**	**450 100.00%**

The study revealed that out of the total, 178 respondents representing 39.55 per cent made complaints either in oral or written form. The issues of the customer complaints include line dead, wrong call, voice clarity, instrument malfunctioning, disconnection without adequate reason and cross talk. The data presented in Table 10.26 reveals line dead is the major problem which lead the customers to complain. The second major problem was wrong calls.

Table 10.26 Issues of customer complaints

Parti-culars	Telecom Circle						Total
	Hydera-bad	Karnool	Vijaya-wada	VSKP	Tiru-pati	Waran-gal	
Phone dead	23 12.92%	18 10.11%	16 8.98%	22 12.35%	18 10.11%	22 12.35%	119 66.89%
Wrong calls	7 3.89%	2 1.11%	5 2.81%	4 2.25%	— —	6 3.37%	24 13.48%
Voice clarity	— —	3 1.68%	1 0.56%	2 1.11%	— —	1 0.56%	7 3.89%
Instrument	1 0.56%	2 1.11%	2 1.11%	6 3.37%	3 1.68%	3 1.68%	17 9.45%
Disconnected without	— —	1 0.56%	— —	— —	2 1.11%	1 0.56%	4 2.22%
Cross talk	— —	2 1.12%	1 0.56%	— —	3 1.68%	1 0.56%	7 3.89%
Total	**31** **17.41%**	**28** **15.73%**	**25** **14.04%**	**34** **19.10%**	**26** **14.60%**	**34** **19.10%**	**178** **100.00%**

The respondents were asked to reveal whether they have participated in the Customer meets organized by the company [Figure 10.10]. The study revealed that only about 19 per cent have participated in customer meets organised by the company. The major reasons revealed by the respondents for not attending the customer meets include unawareness of the schedule of customer meets, disinterest and time, energy and transportation costs.

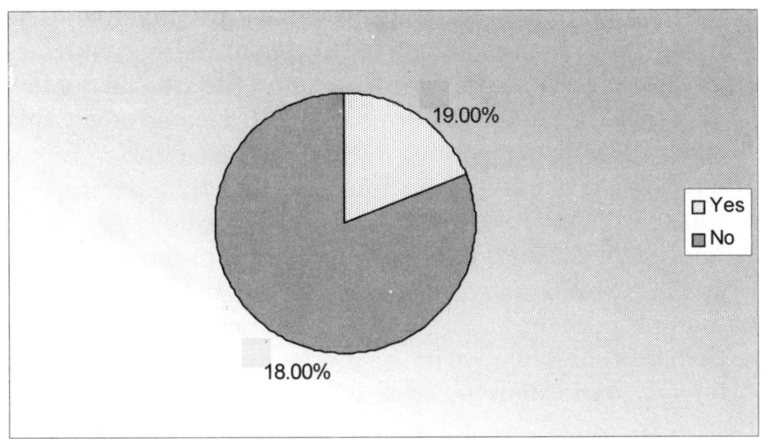

Fig. 10.10 Have you ever participated in customer meets organised by the company

Table 7.27 Reasons for not attending customers meets

Particulars	Total
Unaware of the schedule of customer meet	157 34.89%
Not interested	224 49.77%
Time, energy and transportation costs	69 15.33%
Total	**450** **100.00%**

The data presented in Table 10.27 reveals that 'no interest' is the reason for about 49.77 per cent of the respondents who have not participated in customer meets. 'Unawareness of the schedule of customer meets' is the reason for 34.89 per cent of the respondents. Some respondents revealed that attending meeting involve time, energy and transportation costs and therefore they prefer not to attend such meets.

Customer meets are important for the company to get direct feedback from the customers and also to clarify them on various issues, technical as well as managerial. The company should make efforts to involve as many customers as possible in the process. The findings of the study establish the fact that the customers are not communicated effectively about the details of customer meets and also efforts are not directed to persuade the customers to participate in such meets. It is suggested, therefore, that the company should communicate through telephone as well as other media and persuade customers to participate actively in the meets. The company should organise the meets in such a away that the participants shall involve in the process, issues are discussed objectively and follow up is taken care of by the company effectively.

Table 10.28 Are you satisfied with the following?

Particulars	Yes	No	Total
The units system of 3 min. per call	375 83.33%	75 16.67%	450 100.00%
Conversion of Andhra	359	91	450
Pradesh as local	79.78%	20.22%	100.00%
Free calls allowed on general service	207 46.00%	243 54.00%	450 100.00%

The respondents were asked to reveal whether they are satisfied with the unit system of 3 minute per call, the company decision of converting Andhra Pradesh as local and the number of free calls allowed on general services. The data presented in Table 10.28 reveals an over whelming majority of the respondents [83.33 per cent] are satisfied with the unit system of 3 minutes per call. The majority of the respondents [79.78 per cent] are also satisfied with the conversion of entire Andhra Pradesh as local for the purpose of calculating call charges. However, the majority of the respondents [54 per cent] are not satisfied with the number of free calls allowed on general services. They wanted an increase in the number of free calls.

I. SERVICE EXPECTATIONS

An attempt is made to know the service expectations of the respondents from BSNL in relation to fixed line service. The respondents were asked to reveal three of their expectations on BSNL. The data shown in Table 10.29 reveals more free calls, un interrupted quality service, quick response to maintenance calls, accurate billing, reduction in rent, adoption of modern technology, door to door bill collection facility, multiple services, attractive instruments, and reward the experienced customer are the expectations revealed by the respondents. The study reveals uninterrupted quality service is the first expectation for 34 per cent of the respondents. As many as 141 respondents representing 31.33 per cent rated uninterrupted quality service as the second expectation and 152 respondents representing 33.78 per cent rated it as the third expectation. Reduction in rent is the first expectation for 129 respondents representing 28.67 per cent. It is the second expectation for 137 respondents representing 30.44 per cent and third expectation for 112 respondents representing 24.89 per cent. Door to door bill collection facility is the first expectation for 84 respondents representing 18.67 per cent, second expectation for 79 respondents representing 17.56 per cent and third expectation for 74 respondents representing 16.44 per cent of the total.

The respondents are asked to give their opinion on some specific issues relating to BSNL on a Five point scale ranging from very good to very poor. The data presented in Table 10.30 reveals, about 70 per cent of the respondents rated the 'service package' as 'good or very good'. In the case of support services, 49.11 per cent of the respondents rated as 'good' and 4.89 per cent of the respondent as rated as 'very good'. However, 40 per cent of respondents rated support services as 'average', while 6.44 per cent of the respondents rated it as 'poor'. Out of the total, the majority of the respondents representing 52.33 per cent, rated the ability of the company to stand with competitive pressure as 'average'.

Table 10.29 What are your basic service expectations on BSNL fixed line service?

Particulars	1	2	3
More free calls	18 4.00%	23 5.11%	13 2.87%
Uninterrupted quality service	153 34.00%	141 31.33%	152 33.78%
Quick response to maintenance calls	10 2.22%	14 3.11%	20 4.44%
Accurate billing	13 2.87%	9 2.00%	15 3.33%
Reduction in rent	129 28.67%	137 30.44%	112 24.89%
Adoption of modern technology	16 3.55%	11 2.44%	22 4.89%
Door to door bill collection facility	84 18.67%	79 17.56%	74 16.44%
Multiple services	9 2.00%	8 1.78%	14 3.11%
Attractive instruments	12 2.67%	18 4.00%	9 2.00%
Reward the experienced customers	6 1.33%	10 2.22%	19 4.22%
Total	**450 100.00%**	**450 4100.00%**	**450 100.00%**

There are 177 respondents representing 39.56 per cent, rated the company on this aspect as 'good'. The majority of the respondents [51 per cent] opined that the developmental prospects for the company as 'poor'. About 39 per cent of the respondents opined that the development prospects as 'good' while 3.56 per cent of the respondents rated this factor as 'very good'. Out of the total, 208 respondents representing 46.56 per cent rated the external communication of the company as 'poor'. However, the rating of 198 respondents representing 44.44 per cent is 'good' and the rating of 19

Table 10.30 Opinion on some specific issues

Particulars	Very Good	Good	Average	Poor	Very Poor	Total
Service Package	17 3.78%	296 66.11%	132 29.55%	5 1.11%	— —	450 100.00%
Support Services	22 4.89%	220 49.11%	179 40.00%	29 6.44%	— —	450 100.00%
Ability to stand with competitive pressure	16 3.56%	177 39.56%	234 52.33%	23 5.11%	— —	450 100.00%
Development prospects	16 3.56%	174 38.89%	23 5.11%	228 51.00%	9 2.00%	450 100.00%
Effectiveness of external communications	19 4.33%	198 44.44%	18 4.00%	208 46.56%	7 1.56%	450 100.00%
Technological advancement and innovations	16 3.56%	167 37.33%	36 8.00%	231 51.56%	— —	450 100.00%
Customer care	45 10.11%	179 40.00%	52 11.56%	174 38.89%	— —	450 100.00%
Ability to change	13 2.89%	157 35.55%	47 10.44%	231 52.33%	2 0.44%	450 100.00%
Chances of holding leadership	11 2.55%	165 37.22%	29 6.44%	243 54.67%	2 0.44%	450 100.00%

respondents representing 4.33 per cent is 'very good' on external communications. On technical advancement and innovations of the company, the rating of 231 respondents representing 51.56 per cent is 'poor'. However, about 41 per cent of the respondents rated technical advancement and innovation as either 'good or very good'. With regard to customer care of the company, the rating of a little over 50 per cent of the respondents is either 'good or very good'. About 40 per cent of the respondents rated customer care as 'very poor' and 11.56 per cent of the respondents rated as 'average'. The majority of the respondents [53.33 per cent] rated the ability of the company to change as 'poor'. A little over 38 per cent of the respondents rated positively the ability of the company to change. With regard to chance of holding leadership in the changing competitive scenario, the majority of the respondents [244] representing 54.44 per cent opined that the company chances of holding leadership are 'poor'. A little over 37 per cent of respondents rated the chances as good and 2.55 per cent of the respondents rated as 'very good'.

J. SATISFACTION RATING

Marketing analysts suggest the philosophy of customer satisfaction as the ultimate goal of any business concern. All the activities of a company shall be made customer centric in order to achieve the goal of customer satisfaction. The service characteristics such as intangibility, inseparability, variability, preshability and customer participation create new challenges to service companies like BSNL to ensure customer satisfaction all the time. Service companies need to know the opinion of the customers on the service and their level of satisfaction continually to know its position and initiate required charges in the service process and performances. An attempt is made in the study to know the satisfaction rating of the respondents on BSNL fixed line service. The

Table 10.31 Are you satisfied with the service of BSNL? Please give your rating on a 10 point scale.

Rating	Number persons	Score
1	2	2
2	11	22
3	9	27
4	18	72
5	52	260
6	77	462
7	61	427
8	89	712
9	68	612
10	63	630
Total	**450**	**3226**

respondents are asked to rate on a 1-10 scale. In the scale, one represents the lowest and 10 represents the highest. The details of the satisfaction rating of the respondents are shown in Table 10.31.

The study reveals 92 respondents representing 20.44 per cent gave a rating of 5 and below. The vast majority of the respondents representing 79.56 per cent gave a rating of 6 and above.

K. MAJOR IMPEDIMENTS

The respondents are asked to reveal their opinion on the major impediments of the company on the performance and growth fronts. As can be seen from Figure 10.11, 69.11 per cent of respondents considered interference of government in company affairs is the major impediment for the company.

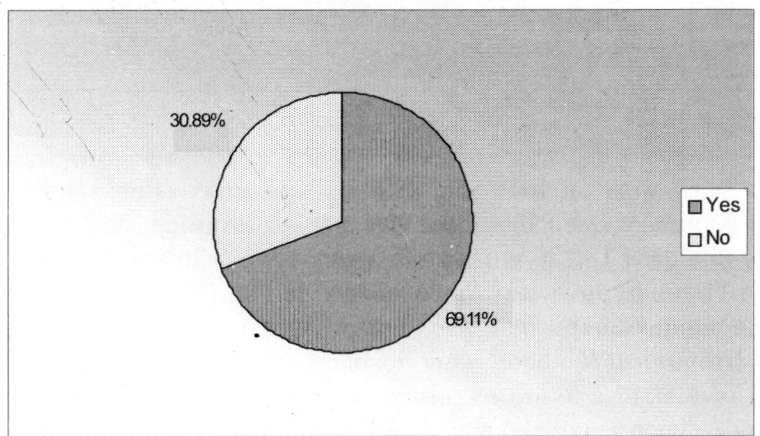

Fig. 10.11. Interference of Government

The majority of the respondents representing 55.33 per cent opined that commitment of employees of the company is not at all the major impediment. [Figure 10.12] However, 44.67 per cent consider commitment of employees of the company as one of the major impediments. Figure 10.13 reveals, old technology is the major impediment as 71.78 per cent of respondents revealed the same.

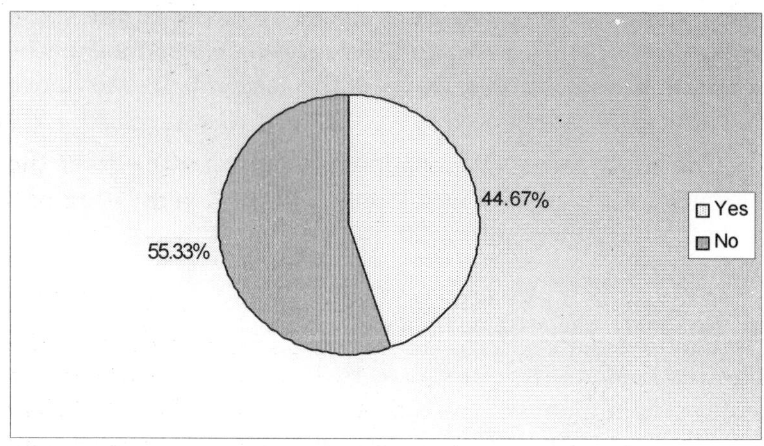

Fig. 10.12. Commitment of Employees

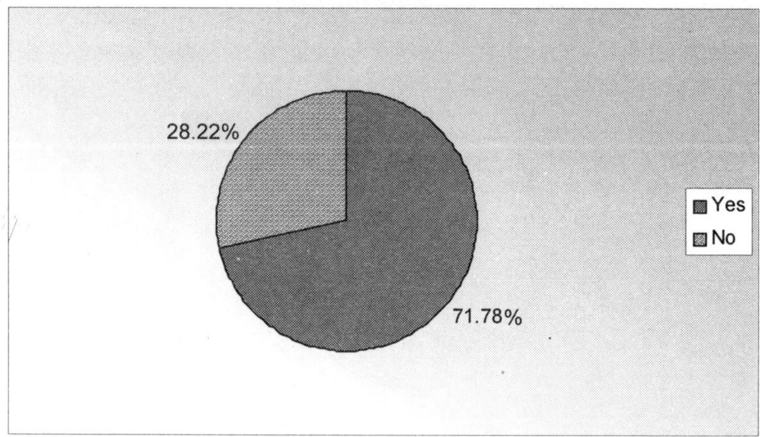

Fig. 10.13. Old Technology

L. SWOT : THE RESPONDENTS PERSPECTIVE

The opinion of the respondents on Strengths, Weaknesses, Opportunities and Threats of BSNL from their perspective are ascertained. The data presented in Figure 10.14 shows the opinion of the respondents on Strengths of BSNL.

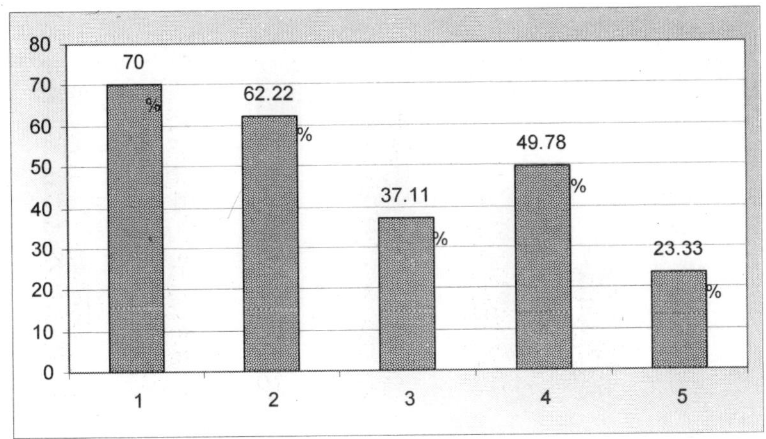

1. Public sector company
2. Long standing company
3. Large network covering rural areas
4. Loyal customer base
5. Huge organisation system to offer support services

Fig. 10.14. What is your opinion on Strengths of BSNL?

The respondents have identified five major strengths of the company. They are; 1. Public Sector Company, 2. Long Standing Company, 3. Large Network covering rural areas, 4. Loyal Customer base and 5. Huge Organisation System to offer support services. The data shown in Figure 10.15 reveals, the large number of respondents [315] representing 70 per cent recognised that being public sector company is the major strength of BSNL. Long standing company is the strength identified by 280 respondents representing 62.22 per cent. Loyal customer base is the strength of the company in the opinion of 224 respondents representing 49.78 per cent. Out of the total, 167 respondents representing 37.11per cent identified large network of BSNL covering rural areas as the strength while 105 respondents representing 23.33 per cent identified huge organisation system to offer support services as the strength of the company.

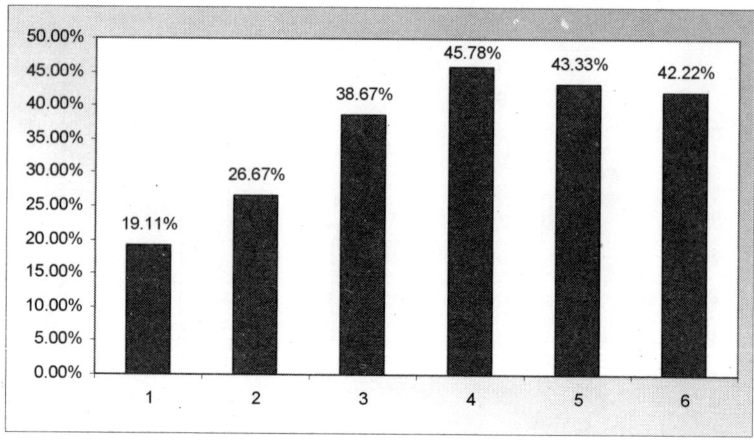

1. Inability to respond to market requirement
2. Large size employment
3. Weak support service
4. Public sector culture
5. Out dated technology
6. Government involvement

Fig. 10.15. What is your opinion on weakness of BSNL

The opinion of the respondents on the weaknesses of the company are ascertained and the data are presented in Figure 10.15 Public Sector culture is the major weakness identified by the large number of respondents followed by out dated technology and government involvement as the major weaknesses. The other weaknesses identified by the respondents include weak support services, large size employment and inability of the company to respond to market requirement.

The opinion of the respondents on the opportunities of BSNL are shown in Figure 10.16. The majority of the respondents revealed that the company has market opportunity of adding new services like cable services, tele-marking etc. [52.44 per cent of the respondents] Offering of multiple services including Internet, broadband etc., is the business opportunity for the company as per the opinion of 199 respondents representing 44.22 per cent. Out of the total, 107 respondents representing 23.78 per cent revealed that company has an opportunity of strengthening loyal customer base. In the opinion of 21.11 per cent of the respondents the company has more opportunities for development of telecom market in various parts with in out outside the Country.

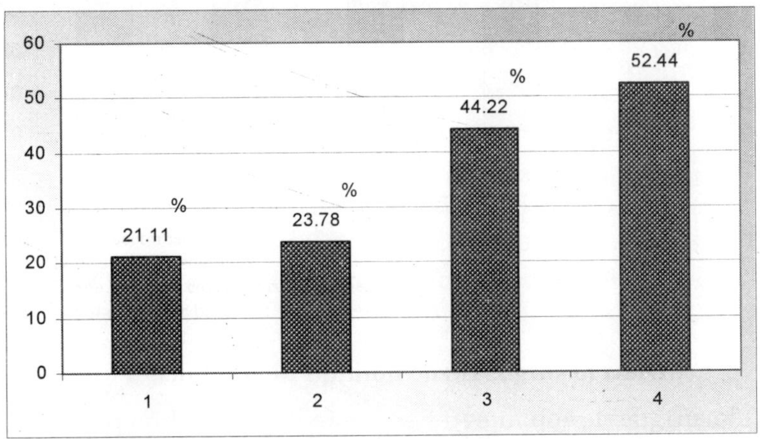

1. Market Development
2. Strenghting loyal customer base
3. Offering multiple services (Internet, broadband etc.)
4. Adding new service (cable services, telemarketing etc.

Fig. 10.16. What is your opinion on opportunities of BSNL?

Competition from private sector is the major threat for BSNL as 319 respondents representing 70.89 per cent identified this threat for the company (Figure 10.17) More demanding customers is the threat identified by 176 respondents representing 39.11per cent. Switching of customer loyalty is the threat identified by 120 respondents representing 26.67 per cent of the total.

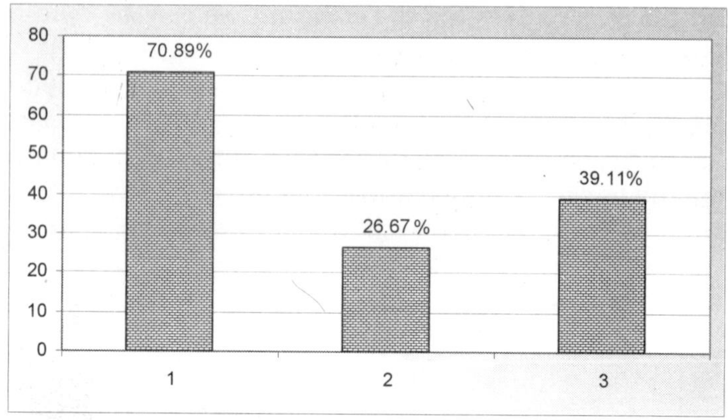

1. Competition from Private Sector
2. Switching of Customer Loyalty
3. More Demanding Customers

Fig. 10.17 What is your opinion on thereat of BSNL?

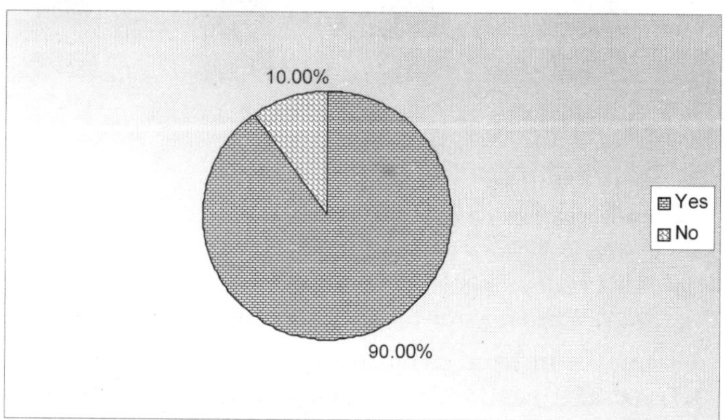

Fig. 10.18. In the light of changing competitive scenario : Do you think that there is a need to continue BSNL under public sector?

The study reveals, the vast majority of the respondents representing 90 per cent are in favour of continuation of BSNL under Public Sector in the light of changing competitive scenario [Figure 10.18].

The opinion indicates the respondents' preference to be the customers of a Public Sector company. This in fact is the major opportunity for the BSNL to reconsolidate its position and prepare the developmental plans.

CHAPTER 11 CONCLUSIONS AND SUGGESTIONS

Telecommunications is one of the fastest-growing areas of technology in the world. Because of its rapid growth, businesses and individuals can access information at electronic speed from almost anywhere in the world. By including Telecommunications in their operations, businesses can provide better services and products to their customers. For individuals, telecommunications provide access to worldwide information and services. Deregulation and new technology have created increased competition and widened the range of network services available throughout the world. This increase in telecommunication capabilities allows businesses to benefit from the information revolution in numerous ways, such as streamlining their inventories, increasing productivity, and identifying new markets and developing connectivity with customers.

India, like many other countries of the world, have adopted a gradual approach to telecom sector reform through selective privatization and managed competition in different segments of the telecom market. To begin with, India introduced private competition in value-added services in 1992 followed by opening up of cellular and basic services for local area to private competition. The Telecom Regulatory Authority of India (TRAI) was constituted in 1997 as an independent regulator in this sector. Competition was also introduced in national long distance (NLD) and international long distance (ILD) telephony at the start of the current decade.

A. TELECOM SECTOR IN INDIA

India Telecom Sector has been one of the biggest success stories of market–oriented reform, and India is now amongst the fastest growing telecom markets in the world. Supportive government policies coupled with private sector participation have fuelled the unprecedented expansion of this sector. In India, there are 18.68 million telecom subscribers in 1998, out of which 17.8 million are fixed line subscribers and 0.88 million are mobile subscribers. In other words, the fixed line subscribers account for 95.29 per cent of the total telecom subscribers in the year. The total number of telecom subscribers increased to 307.86 million in 2007 recording an increase of more than 16 times during the decade. The share of fixed line segment reduced significantly to reach 15.36 per cent in 2007. The mobile segment claimed the dominant share in the growth of telecom sector during the 1998 to 2007. The share of mobile segment increased from less than one per cent to 84.64 per cent during the period.

The telecommunication services are provided by both public sector and private sector companies in India in both fixed line and mobile segments. Public sector companies are holding 91 per cent of the ownership share in fixed line category leaving only 9 per cent share to the private companies. In the case of wireless segment, private sector dominance is well established with 81 per cent ownership share as compared to 19 per cent ownership share of the public sector.

Teledensity, the major indicator of telecom growth in a country, is on the increase year by year during 1997-1998 to 2006-2007. The teledensity which was 1.90 in 1997-1998 increased to 18.23 in 2006-2007. The gap between rural and urban teledensity is significant in the country. In urban areas the teledensity has increased from 5.80 to 45.00 during the period. In rural areas the teledensity which was 0.4. in 1997-1998 increased to 2.00 in 2006-2007. In 2006-07 the teledensity in urban areas was 45 where as it was only 2 in rural areas of the country.

The Players in Telecom Market

The telecommunications is presently operated by public sector as well as private sector companies. The public sector companies are: Bharat Sanachar Nigam Limited (BSNL) and Maharastra Telecom Nigam Limited (MTNL). The private sector companies are: Bharti Airtel, Reliance Telecom Limited, Vodafone, TATA Tele services Limited, Idea Mobile Communication, Aircel, Spice Communication, BPL Mobile, HPCL Infotel Limited, and Shyam Telelink Limited.

Organisation Setup and Regulatory Mechanism

Department of Telecommunication which is popularly known as DOT, is the principal government body that takes care of policy, licensing and co-ordination matters relating to telegrams, telephones, wireless, data, facsimile and telematic services and other like forms of communications.

The DOT takes care of International cooperation in matters connected with telecommunications including matters relating to all international bodies dealing with telecommunications such as International Telecommunication Union (ITU), its Radio Regulation Board (RRB), Radio Communication Sector (ITU-R), Telecommunication Standardization Sector (ITU-T), Development Sector (ITU-D), International Telecommunication Satellite Organization (INTELSAT), International Mobile Satellite Organization (INMARSAT), Asia Pacific Telecommunication (APT). It also looksafter the Promotion of standardization, research and development in telecommunications, Promotion of private investment in Telecommunications and financial assistance for the furtherance of research and study in telecommunications technology and for building up adequately trained manpower for telecom programme, including, assistance to institutions, assistance to scientific institutions and to universities for advanced scientific study and research; and grant of scholarships to students in educational institutions and other forms of financial aid to individuals including those going abroad for studies in the field of telecommunications.

The department is responsible for the administration of laws with respect of any of the matters specified in Indian Telegraphy Act 1985, The Indian Wireless Telegraphs Act 1933 and The Telecom Regulatory Authority of India Act 1997.

Telecom Regulatory Authority of India (TRAI)

The TRAI came in to existence as per the provisions of TRAI Act 1997. TRAI is responsible to make recommendations, either suo motu or on a request from the licensor. **TRAI** with a mission to create and nurture conditions for the growth of telecommunications including broadcasting and cable services in the country in a manner and at a pace which will enable India to play a leading role in the emerging global information society is carrying activities with goals and objectives focused towards providing a regulatory regime that facilitates achievement of the objectives of the New Telecom Policy (NTP) 1999.

National Telecom Policy 1994

The focus of the Telecom Policy 1994 was ***telecommunication for all and telecommunication within the reach of all***. This means ensuring the availability of telephone on demand as early as possible. Another objective was to achieve universal service covering all villages as early as possible and provision of access to all people for certain basic telecom services at affordable and reasonable prices. The quality of telecom services should be of world standard. Removal of consumer complaints, dispute resolution and public interface was received special attention.

The policy set certain targets of performance in Telecommunications. They include:

- Telephone should be available on demand by 1997.
- All villages should be covered by 1997.
- In the urban areas a PCO should be provided for every 500 persons by 1997
- All value-added services available internationally should be introduced in India to raise the telecom services in India to international standard well within the VIII Plan period, preferably by 1996.

The Government recognised that the result of the privatisation has so far not been entirely satisfactory. While there has been a rapid rollout of cellular mobile networks in the metros and states with over 1 million subscribers, most of the projects are facing problems. The main reason, according to the cellular and basic operators, has been the fact that the actual revenues realised by these projects have been far short of the projections and the operators are unable to arrange financing for their projects and therefore complete their projects. Basic telecom services by private operators have only just commenced in a limited way in two of the six circles where licences were awarded. As a result, some of the targets as envisaged in the objectives of the NTP 1994 have remained unfulfilled. The private sector entry has been slower than what was envisaged in the NTP 1994.

New Telecom Policy 1999

The Government of India (Government) recognizes that provision of world class telecommunications infrastructure and information is the key to rapid economic and social development of the country. It is critical not only for the development of the Information Technology industry, but also has widespread ramifications on the entire economy of the country. It is also anticipated that going forward, a major part of the GDP of the country would be contributed by this sector.

In addition to some of the objectives of NTP 1994 not being fulfilled, the far reaching developments in the telecom,

IT consumer electronics and media industries world-wide are taken into consideration. Convergence of both markets and technologies is a reality that is forcing realignment of the industry. At one level, telephone and broadcasting industries are entering each other's markets, while at another level, technology is blurring the difference between different conduit systems such as wireline and wireless. As in the case of most countries, separate licences have been issued in our country for basic, cellular, ISP, satellite and cable TV operators each with separate industry structure, terms of entry and varying requirement to create infrastructure. However, this convergence allows operators to use their facilities to deliver some services reserved for other operators, necessitating a relook into the existing policy framework. The new telecom policy framework is also required to facilitate India's vision of becoming an IT superpower and develop a world class telecom infrastructure in the country.

The Department of Telecommunication is planning to achieve a total of 650 million telephone connections (including 66 million wired and 584 million wireless connections) by the end of 2012. Concurrently, there is also a vision of providing 200 million rural telephone connections, which translates into a rural tele-density of 25 per cent. Broadband connectivity would be made available on demand, without limiting the speed. Each village would have at least one broad-band enabled kiosk. Broad-band connection would be provided to schools, health centers and panchayat offices. It is also envisaged that internet and broad-band subscribers will increase to 40 million and 20 million, respectively, by 2010.

B. BHARAT SANCHAR NIGAM LIMITED

Organisation System and Performance Perspectives

In pursuance of the New Telecom Policy 1999, the Government of India decided to corporatise the service provision functions of Department of Telecommunications

(DoT). Accordingly, Bharat Sanchar Nigam Limited (BSNL) was incorporated on 15 September 2000 as a wholly owned Central Government Company under the Companies Act, 1956.

The BSNL has a vision to become the largest telecom service provider in Asia. The mission of the company is to provide world class state-of-art technology telecom services to its customers on demand at competitive prices, to provide world class telecom infrastructure in its area of operation and to contribute to the growth of the country's economy. BSNL is carrying out the duties and responsibilities relating to establishment, maintenance and working of all types of telecommunication services in the country in accordance with and under the terms and conditions of the licence granted by the Central Government under the Indian Telegraph Act, 1885 and such other directions as may be given by the Central Government from time to time.

BSNL has installed Quality Telecom Network in the country and focusing on improving it, expanding the network, introducing new telecom services with ICT applications in villages and wining customer's confidence. BSNL is the only service provider, making focussed efforts and planned initiatives to bridge the Rural-Urban Digital Divide ICT sector. In fact, there is no telecom operator in the country to beat its reach with its wide network providing services in every nook and corner of the country and operates across India except Delhi and Mumbai. Whether it is inaccessible areas of Siachen glacier and North-eastern region of the country, BSNL serves its customers with its wide bouquet of telecom services. BSNL has set up a world class multi-gigabit, multi-protocol convergent IP infrastructure that provides convergent services like voice, data and video through the same Backbone and Broadband Access Network. At present there are 0.6 million Data One broadband customers.

The company has vast experience in Planning, Installation, Network integration and Maintenance of

Switching and Transmission Networks and also has a world class ISO 9000 certified Telecom Training Institute. The turnover, nationwide coverage, reach, comprehensive range of telecom services and the desire to excel has made BSNL the No. 1 Telecom Company of India.

Organisation Structure

The Corporate Office of Bharat Sanchar Nigam Limited is located in New Delhi. The administrative as well as the overall functional control of the company is vested with Broad of Directors headed by the Chairman and Managing Director (CMD). There are five directors in the broad looking after the functions such as finance, operations, commercial and marketing, planning and new services and human resource development.

The organisation system of the BSNL handles all the services offered by the company which include fixed line, mobile, Internet and broadband and auxiliary services. BSNL holds the lion share in fixed line segment. The growth rate of the company in the mobile segment is impressive. In broadband services, the company is unable to meet the demand and as a result losing prospective buyers to competing organisations. Inspite of its huge organisation mechanism and loyal customer base it could not make a mark in mobile service segment. The low level performance of the company helped the competitors to capture this part of the highly growing market. The organisation system is certainly responsible for the poor performance of the company in these two services. Further, there has been a decline in fixed line subscribers base year by year. The company lost sizable fixed line subscribers to the competitors.

Physical Performance

The capital structure of BSNL consists of authorised share capital and preference share capital. The authorised equity share capital is Rs. 10,000 crores, out of which Rs. 5,000 crores is the paid equity share capital. The preference share capital is Rs. 7,500 crores. While promoting the company, the government of India treated the paid up equity capital and preference share capital as investment of the government. The physical performance of the company is analysed by taking the variables such as, Telephone exchanges, equipment capacity of DELs, number of telephone connections, capacity utilisation of DELs, waiting list of prospective customers and Number of Mobile phones.

The number of telephone exchanges which was 31,589 in 2000-01 increased to 36,618 in 2003-04, recording an increase of 15.92 per cent. The growth of telephone exchanges over the previous year was highest in 2001-02 with 9.51 per cent while it was only 1.33 per cent growth over the previous year in 2003-04.The total equipped capacity of Direct Exchanges Lines (DELs) including WLL has increased from 347.93 lakh lines to 485.60 lakh lines during 2000-01 to 2003-04 recording an increase of 39.57 per cent. The growth in the equipped capacity is consistent during the period. The number of telephone connections which was 281.09 lakhs in 2000-01 increased to 363.94 lakhs recording an increase of 29.48 per cent. However, in terms of capacity utilization the trend is on the reverse side. The overall capacity utilization of exchanges went down from 81 per cent in 2000-01 to 75 per cent in 2003-04.

Despite available of equipped capacity there were persons in the waiting list for telephone connection. There were 28.71 lakh persons in waiting list in 2000-01. The number of persons in waiting was 16.49 lakhs in 2001-02 and 18.07 lakhs in 2002-03. In 2003-04, the waiting list stood at 18.15 lakh persons. The reasons for the continued waiting list, despite available of occupied capacity could be the presence of large 'technically not feasible' (TNF) areas, enhancement in equipped capacity towards the year-end leading to release of connections in subsequent years, etc.

The company started offering mobile services in 2001-02 with a modest beginning of 1.78 lakh mobile telephone connections. In one year a number of connections rose to 22.56 lakhs. In the subsequent year, the number of connections risen to 52.54 lakhs.

Business Performance

The business performance of BSNL is analysed by taking variables such as income, expenditure, profit after tax, and fixed assets. The income of the company which was Rs. 11699.47 crores in 2000-01, reached as high as Rs. 40176.58 crores in 2005-06. There was a decline in income in the subsequent two years to reach Rs. 38053.4 crores in 2007-08.

The expenditure on the other hand increased year by year except a marginal decline in 2006-07 The expenditure of the company which was Rs. 10,699.42 crores in 2000-01 increased to Rs. 33,636.43 crores in 2007-08 recording an increase of 214.38 per cent. The profit after tax of the company is fluctuative in the first four years of the period under study. The company earned a profit of Rs. 747.05 crores in 2000-01. In the subsequent year the profit after tax zoomed to Rs. 6,312.16 crores. There was a steep decline in profit in 2002-03 as the company earned only Rs. 1,444.44 crores during the year. The company jumped back in the subsequent year and made a profit of Rs. 5,976.52 crores. In 2004-05, the company earned the highest level profit of Rs.10,183.29 crores. In the subsequent two years there was a decline in profit. The decline was very sharp in the year 2007-08 as the company could make only Rs.3,009.39 crores of profit after tax. BSNL is the market leader in fixed line business in the country with 84 per cent market share. The performance of this segment became a cause of concern to the company. The subscriber growth rate is negative for the last few years. The number of fixed line subscribers decreased by 4.36 per cent in 2005-06, 16.84 per cent in 2006-07 and 21.31 per cent in 2007-08 (up to January 2008). The numbers are evident to infer that things are not seem to be hunky dory as far as the fixed line business is concerned. Over the last three years, more than a million fixed line connections were surrounded by subscribers. On the other hand, private fixed line operators like Bharati, Tata Tele services and Reliance Info com have added close to a million lines. It clearly establishes the fact that BSNL has lost business because many people are opting for a private fixed line connection.

It is true that the one of serious problems of the fixed line segment is the booming mobile market. The tariffs for mobile connection have fallen drastically making it far more accessible to the common man. The perception of fixed line for masses and mobile phone for classes has changed drastically in the recent past. Already, in the US, the growing mobile base has started to change the contours of the telecom market. According to a study by telecom solutions provider CIT-Pri Metrica, the threat posed by the wireless industry is potentially staggering. Nearly half of the US fixed line users are prepared to shift to a shared wireless phone service. But in countries like South Korea, with the advent of broadband services, earnings of the fixed service providers have actually gone up. Not surprisingly, the highest demand for bandwidth in Seoul is at 2.00p.m.when housewives start surfing the Internet on their home PCs. If operators in India play it right, the same could be replicated here.

Though BSNL is the major player in the Telecommunication Sector, it is facing severe competition from private sector. The monopoly situation enjoyed over the years and the most favourable market conditions of demand exceeding supply in almost all parts of the country lead the company to become insensitive to the customers specific needs and services. Value added services including customer services became the weakest part of the company against which the competitors are acting seriously to encourage switchovers in their favour. For the growth and development of the company market orientation is imperative. There is a need to re-engineer the service processes in order to cater to the requirements of the market. The company should learn how to offer value added services to the customers effectively than the competitors. The present study is a modest attempt to study the marketing operations of the company and service expectations of the customers in relation to fixed line services.. The finding of the study will be useful to the management to identify problems and initiate suitable measures, for further development of the company.

C. PRODUCT MIX

BSNL is the largest telecom operator in India and is known for Basic Telephony Services for over 100 years. Presently the Plain old, Countrywide telephone service is being provided through 32,000 electronic exchanges, 326 Digital Trunk Automatic Exchanges(TAX), Digitalized Public Switched Telephone Network (PSTN) all interlinked by over 2.4 lakh km of Optical Fiber Cable, with a host of Phone Plus value additions to Customers. BSNL's telephony network expands throughout the vast expanses of the country reaching to the remotest part of the country.

BSNL offers products under four product line (PL) categories. They are Fixed line services (PL-I), Mobile services (PL-II), Internet and Broadband services (PL-III) and Auxiliary services (PL-IV). The fixed line services are offered in two categories. They are permanent connections and temporary and casual connections. The permanent connections are offered under tatkal scheme. OYT. Non OYT, Sulabh scheme, WLL, FLPP and bphone for internet. Mobile services are offerd under two schemes such as prepaid and postpaid. The auxiliary services include ISDN, leased line, audio conference, video conference, web conference, enterprise solutions, telegraph, EPABX, and data communications.

D. PRICING POLICY

Telecom sector was under public sector monopoly until it is opened up to the private sector. The pricing policy reflected government policy and it was an administered one. The entry of TRAI and the emergence of competitive environment brought in several changes.

Prior to 1960, there was no tariff policy. As such, the charges were not based on any cost study. The main guiding factor was the need of balancing the budget. Subsidized rates were provided to certain categories like press, hospitals etc. The First Tariff Revision Committee was constituted in 1956 and the Committee submitted report in 1958. Tariff revision came into effect in1960. The Committee considered all relevant issues for the growth of telecom service, such as commercial character, past financial working of the department, capital structure, reserve funds, anticipated trend of revenue and the future needs of departmental expenditure. Since then, many committees have been constituted for both tariff revision as well as for recommending progressive structure of DOT, embracing all facets of telephone service and incorporating many features.

Telecom Tariff Order 1999: TRAI began the Tariff rebalancing with second consultation paper in September 1998 and specified the tariffs in the *first Telecom Tariff Order*, March 1999 ((**TTO, 99**).The modern approach to telecom tariff recognizes the existence of several objectives or criteria, that is, multi dimensional. The broad objectives can be clarified as; financial, economic and social. Social objective is to ensure that price structure takes into account policy and institutional objectives that involves provision of services at special tariffs to target groups, areas etc.For fixed services, the TTO, 99 was the first step in the process of tariff rebalancing. The tariffs were specified in terms of standard packages that all providers were obliged to offer. However, there was provision for both fixed and cellular service providers to offer alternative packages in terms of monthly rentals and per minute charges.

The TTO 99 envisaged an increase in monthly rentals and a decrease in National Long Distance and ILD tariffs to bring them near costs in three phases over a three year period. The categorization into low and general user was based on the usage in terms of metered call units (MCUs). For both the urban and rural users, low users were those who made less than or equal to 500 MCUs per month, while general users were those who belonged to neither commercial nor low user categories

Interconnections: Interconnection regulation had been in terms of interconnection charges (set up charges) and revenue share (usage charges). The basic framework was laid down in TRAI's consultation paper on Telecom Pricing (September 9, 1998) and TTO 99. Key aspects of the framework were: Interconnection prices were based on costs and usage charges were based on a percentage of revenue share. For interconnection between fixed and mobile services, the Receiving Party Pays principle was followed, with no revenue share.

The TRAI Amended the Ordinance in January 2000. This changed the composition and powers of TRAI, specifically giving TRAI the power to fix interconnectivity terms, and setting up the Telecom Dispute Settlement Appellate Tribunal (TDSAT). In addition to the scope of the disputes in the earlier act, the tribunal would also be the appeal mechanism for decisions of the TRAI. The decisions of the tribunal could be appealed against only in the Supreme Court.

In August 2000, the National Long Distance Competition policy that would allow private operators to offer long distance services was announced and it was expected that this would bring down long distance prices. A revision in the cellular air time to Rs 3 per min was also affected.

Competition in telecom services driven by regulatory initiatives and technological advancement continued to push the prices down. This trend was more visible in mobile and long distance services. The competitive pressures also made the service providers to be more innovative in their tariff offerings. Products like "2 years validity prepaid coupons" and "Life Time Validity" schemes have made telecom services more affordable and also led to large-scale subscriber acquisitions. The National Long Distance (NLD) tariff has further declined subsequent to the implementation of new ADC/IUC regime effective from 1st March 20 March 2006. Another development in the NLD segment is the launch of "One India" tariff plan by BSNL and other similar plans by other operators. This plan permits the subscribers to make long distance calls anywhere in the country at a flat rate of Rs. 1/- per minute for a fixed monthly rental of Rs. 299. The tariff for International Long Distance (ILD) service has also come down with the reduced ADC. The ILD tariffs of Rs. 7.20 per minute (to US, UK and Canada) and Rs. 9.60 per min (to South East Asia, Rest of Europe) that were initially offered as promotional tariffs have since become the standard ILD rates.

Tariff for telecommunication services in India is one of the lowest in the world. The Indian consumer has immensely benefited from such lower tariffs which has also been a major factor for explosive growth in the sector. Considering intense competition in various segments of telecommunications sector and continuous decline in the tariff, TRAI has moved to a regime of tariff deregulation in a gradual manner. Currently, TRAI is following 'Hands Off' approach in deciding tariffs except in areas where competition is found to be insufficient. As of March 2006, tariff for Cellular Services (except for roaming services), Basic Services (except for rural telephony) and NLD/ILD Services stand forborne and tariff for rural telephony, roaming services and leased lines continue to be in the regulated regime. With a view to protect the interest of subscribers on tariff related matters, the Authority has taken several initiatives by amending the Telecommunications Tariff Order (TTO) 1999 wherever necessary.

The DOT stated that "generally, price could be cost based and should allow for a reasonable rate of return on capital employed. A certain mark up for risk should also be allowed. This is particularly true for some of the new services where there is no assured market. For some services, such as leased line services, prices should be based on the earning capacity of the facility being provided. For some of the premium services e.g. ISDN, IN services etc. higher tariffs can be charged as compared to basic telephone service".

The DOT also pointed out that a tariff setting involved more nuances than could be captured by emphasis only on cost orientation. For a number of services "opportunity cost" principle, or the principle of "what the service can earn", would be relevant for fixing tariffs; sometimes tariffs had to be set on the basis of "value of service to the customer"; promotional tariffs might be required in case of new telecom services; and that "ability to pay" principle could not be entirely done away with in the context of the country's social policy.

The Telecom Pricing Consultation should be widened to include all types of telecom services available to a citizen such as cellular radio, trunk mobile radio, radio raging, etc. It should also include the aspects of Spectrum Fee, Wireless Licence Fee, which a service provider is required to pay, in addition to DOT's licence fee; and in due course, the TRAI should also look into the "pricing" aspects of Global Mobile Personal Communication Service.

E. DISTRIBUTION SYSTEM

BSNL follows direct marketing as well as franchise system to serve the target market. Physical infrastructure for the distribution of service has been laid throughout country with special focus on rural distribution network. BSNL has provided villages public telephones (VPTs) in 5.18 lakh villages, out of 5.93 lakh villages in the country by the end of 2007 . The total number of rural DELs is 241.31 lakh which constitute 35.22 per cent of the total DELs of the country. The company took measures to provide accessibility of all the services offered by the company to the target market. Besides telephone connections in urban as well as rural areas, the BSNL has 19,13,182 public telephones. The public telephone services are offered through franchise services. The company has 33,206 STD stations also operated through franchise services.

The transmission system constitute of 6,024 route kms. of Coaxial, 50,430, route kms. of Microwave, 45,130 route kms. of UHF and 5,60,086 route kms. of Optical Fiber. As regards to satellite based services BSNL has 82 MCPC-VSATs and 99/38 IDR Systems (2Mb/8Mb).

In case of mobile services, the company had a coverage of 617 district headquarters and 2,74,428 villages. The company has covered a length of 53,230 kilometers on national highway, 69,770 kilometers on state highways and 39,173 kilometers on railway routes. The BSNL has Internet connectivity in 24 telecom circles with 2,644 working connections.

There are 55.47 lakh Public Call Offices working by the end of 2006-07. Maharshtra circle is having the highest number of public call offices (3.28 lakh) followed by Tamil Nadu (3.02 lakh) and Andhra Pradesh (2.71 lakh).

F. INTERNAL MARKETING

The activities of internal marketing should promote service mindedness and customer orientation. The corporate philosophy of BSNL considers Human Resources as the most prized assets of the organization. Therefore, importance is given to train the employees to have employee skills, enhance their knowledge and expertise. BSNL has a vast reservoir of highly skilled and experienced workforce of about 3.57 lakh employees. Training programmes are organized regularly through several training institution established throughout the country. The being monitored and controlled by DDG

(Trg) at Corporate office under director (HRD). Trainings are being imparted to the employees on a continuous basis to meet the latest technical and managerial requirement. The following are the training institutions of BSNL. The following are the institutions established for imparting training to the employees of BSNL

- Advanced level telecom training centre
- Bharat Ratna Bhim Rao Ambedkar Institute of telecom training
- National Academy of Telecom Finance and Management
- Regional telecom training centers
- Circle telecom training centers
- District telecom training centers

G. EXTERNAL MARKETING

External marketing is concerned with effectively communicating the results of the marketing strategy to large audiences. It is an active, explicit form of marketing programme highlighting the marketing elements to persuade consumers and to make them committed to service.

BSNL uses basically advertising and personal selling for communicating service offers to the consumers. The major forms of media that carry the advertisement of BSNL are Newspapers, Radio, Television, Magazines, outdoor and transit advertisements. Internet also is used for banner advertisements. The BSNL has opened it's website www.bsnl.com.,to facilitate customers to get all kinds of information relating to the company.

The corporate office of the BSNL takes the responsibility of external marketing strategies and programmes that covers the entire nation. Regional level campaigns are taken care of by the circle offices.

Customer Care: Customer Care is the priority area for BSNL management. Several steps have been taken by BSNL to augment the quality of customer care to international standards.

Consumer Grievances Redressal Mechanism: BSNL has a well structured and multilayered Public Grievances Redressal Mechanism including Dispute Resolution Mechanism. The Public Redressal setup in BSNL has been introduced right from the Corporate Office to SSA(Secondary Switching Area) levels. Subscribers having complaints or grievances can interact with the organization.

Open House Session: Complaints/suggestions of general nature as regard to improving the telecom services in the area are discussed in the Open House Sessions. The basic idea of conducting such Open House Sessions is to establish direct channels of communications with customers and also to enable the telecom staff to appreciate and evaluate the customers difficulties and complaints from their point of view.

Telephone Adalats: Subscribers whose grievances remained unsettled are invited to make petitions for redressal of their grievances in Telephone Adalats.

Telecom consumers Protection and Regulation of Grievances: BSNL ensures prompt rectification of any fault or complaint booked through its extensive grass root level online fault restoration system (FRS). However, in case the customer still have problem unsolved timely, BSNL has implemented a three tier consumer grievance redressal mechanism comprising of call centres for various services, nodal officers at SSA and Circle level and an appellate authority for deciding cases that the consumers may wish to appeal .

BSNL has entered into an agreement with M/s Bajaj Allianz General Insurance Company Ltd., and M/s United Insurance Corporation for providing free Insurance Coverage to our Landline/WLL/Post-paid Mobile customers/PCO and VPT operators against accidental death and permanent total disability due to accident. The sum assured is Rs. 50,000/- per connection.

H. FINDINGS OF EMPLOYEES' OPINION SURVEY

The employees opinion survey was conducted to know the opinion of the select employees on issues like work environment, interactions, job assigned, work culture, internal relationships, problems etc.

The following are the major findings of the survey.

- The reason for joining in the service of BSNL for about 62 per cent of the respondents was that the company is a public sector company.
- More than 91 per cent of the respondents are satisfied with the working hours of the company.
- About 62 per cent of the respondents gave positive rating for working space. As many as 40 per cent rated furniture at work place as 'average'. The rating of 37 per cent of the respondents on equipment is 'average'. About 50 per cent rated support services as either 'good or very good'.
- The majority of the respondents rated their interactions with superiors, colleagues, subordinates and customers as either good or very good. About 19 to 31 per cent of the respondents rated these interactions as 'average'.
- About 39 per cent rated the job assigned to them as 'average'. About 35 per cent rated their job as 'good'.
- A little over, 37 per cent rated 'average' when they are asked to give their opinion on suitability of the job. The opinion of about 46 per cent of the respondents on this issue is 'positive'.
- In respect of empowerment in job, 35.33 per cent rated 'average', 29.33 per cent rated 'poor' and 13 per cent rated 'very poor'.
- The respondents rating on team work in the organisation was, seven per cent 'very good' , 24.33 per cent 'good', 34.67 per cent 'average', 13 per cent 'poor' and 20.67 per cent 'very poor'.

- As many as 42 per cent of the respondents rated work culture of the organisation as 'average'. Only 38 per cent rated positively the work culture.
- About 40 per cent of the respondents rated 'poor' on service orientation of the company. More than 12 per cent rated the same as 'very poor'. Only about 33 per cent rated it positively.
- The majority of the respondents rated 'average' for the promotional opportunities and interpersonal trust in the work environment.
- More than 62 per cent of the respondents rated 'poor' when they were asked to give their opinion on recognition of merit. The opinion is similar in case of rewarding the merit.
- With regard to transfer policy, 40.33 per cent rated the policy as 'average', 28.33 per cent rated it poor and 12 per cent rated the policy as 'very poor'.
- As many a 49 per cent of the respondents rated 'average' for the social activities organised by the company.
- The opinion of the majority of the respondents is not positive on induction training.
- The majority are satisfied with on the job training.
- The majority of the respondents rated either 'poor or very poor' for the skill development opportunities available in the organisation.
- About 46 per cent of the respondents rated 'average' for the compensation.
- As far as employer-employee relations are concerned, the opinion of 39 per cent of the respondents is 'average' 26 per cent 'poor' and 4.33 per cent 'very poor'.
- As many as 53 per cent of the respondents rated the mechanism for employee grievance reddressal as 'poor'.

- The majority of the respondents opined that absence of business concept, big size of the organisation, absence of autonomy required at the customer interface level, Indifference of top management on problems of line officers, government policies, political interferences, low motivation of employees and non availability of timely and adequate resources according to the demands of operations are the major impediments in providing services to the satisfaction of customers.
- The majority of the respondents feel proud to be the employees of BSNL.
- The overwhelming majority feels job security because the company is in the public sector. The majority of the respondents believe that the company is vulnerable for competitive attacks.
- The majority of the respondents wish BSNL to become a Multi National Company.
- The majority of the respondents disagree the statement 'BSNL customers continue to be loyal to the company. However, the majority agreed that the company has high growth potential.

I. FINDINGS OF CUSTOMERS' OPINION SURVEY

The customers' opinion survey was conducted to know the customers" opinion on various issues like maintenance, price, employee behaviour, service quality etc. The following are the major findings of the survey:

- Out of the total, 31.33 per cent had BSNL connection during the last five years. About 26 per cent of the respondents have more than 10 years of experience with BSNL fixed line connectivity
- More than 87 per cent of the respondents use both fixed and mobile services.

- The majority of the respondents (91.11 per cent) are in the fixed line price package of Rs. 500 and below.
- The average monthly expenditure of about 60 per cent of the respondents vary between Rs. 501 and Rs. 1,000, on fixed line.
- About 43 per cent of the respondents consider BSNL is economical compared to private companies.
- Communication convenience is the major reason revealed by 53.57 per cent of the respondents for having mobile connection.
- Largest Network covering rural areas is the major reason for continuing BSNL fixed line for 53.33 per cent of the respondents. Low rentals is the second reason.
- Frequent line failure, Supplementary sounds and temporary adjustments on complaints are the maintenance problems expressed by large number of respondents.
- The rating of the majority of the respondents on maintenance of fixed line services is positive.
- More than 50 per cent of the respondents observed improvement in the quality of maintenance in recent years.
- The majority of the respondents stated that the behaviour of maintenance staff is courteous, non-reactive and friendly. However, the majority stated that the employees are not empathetic and objective at work.
- Out of the total, 51.33 per cent experience out of order problem in fixed line.
- About 50 per cent of the respondents revealed that the prices charged by BSNL are low.
- The majority of the respondents rated the price policy of the company positively.

- As many as 79.34 per cent of the respondents are not aware of the availability of Fixed Prepaid Service.
- More than 95 per cent of the respondents receive telephone bills in time. About 87 per cent believe the accuracy of the billing.
- Out of the total, 75.78 per cent find convenient as far as arrangements made by the company for payment of bills are concerned.
- Post offices are mostly used for bill payment followed by BSNL Customer Service Centres.
- About 34 per cent of the respondents complain orally to the company personnel when they are grievous with the services provided by the company.
- Phone dead is the major issue of complaint followed by wrong calls.
- More than 80 per cent of the respondents did not participate in customer meets organised by the company. 'No interest' is the reason for the majority for non-participation in such meets.
- Un- nterrupted quality service is the major expectation of the respondents from the company. Reduction in rent and door to door bill collection are the other expectations.
- The opinion of the majority of the respondents is positive on service package, support services and customer care. The respondents are not happy with the company's ability to stand with competitive pressures, development prospects, effectiveness of external communications, ability to change and chances of holding leadership.
- The satisfaction rating of the respondents stands at 71.69 per cent on 1-10 scale.
- Interference of Government and old Technology are the major impediments for the growth of BSNL according to the majority of the respondents.

- Being public sector company, long standing and loyal customers base are the strengths of the company identified by the majority.
- Public sector culture, out dated technology and government involvement are the major weaknesses identified.
- The identified opportunities are: adding new services like cable services, tele-marketing, offering multiple services including Internet, broadband, etc.
- Competition by private sector companies is the major threat identified by the majority of the respondents followed by more demanding consumers and switching customer loyalty.
- Out of the total, 90 per cent of the respondents wanted BSNL to be continued as Public Sector Company.

J. SUGGESTIONS

Taking the findings of the study into consideration, it is felt that there is need for re-organising the management system of the company. It is suggested therefore to divide BSNL into two autonomous corporate bodies such as 1. BSN (wire line and Internet and Broadband) and 2. BSNL (mobile)). As the nature of the operations, markets and marketing challenges are different for each of the services, the suggested reorganisation may yield desired results. All the two Corporations shall be continued under public sector so that the corporate responsibility and social obligations do not stand as issues of conflict. There will be competitive strategic approach to address to current problems and to execute growth plans competitively. The manpower may be shared by the two corporations. The employees will have clear orientation and direction in work when they are identified with specific services consistently.

It can be inferred from the data that the company's financial performance is not impressive. The expenditure is increasing while income is receding, the profit after tax is highly fluctuated and it is on the decline for the last three years. One of the serious problems identified is the revenue arrears. The company has been facing the problem since its inception. The outstanding arrears which was Rs. 2,946.78 in 2000-01 increased year by year and reached Rs. 4,086.97 crores in 2003-04. The dues are from Central Government, state governments and private subscribers. In all the years more than 90 per cent of dues are from private subscribers. The amount as well as the proportion of outstanding bills against private subscribers was persistently increasing every year. Therefore, BSNL should make concerted efforts to recover dues outstanding from the private subscribers. Not only from telephone subscribers, the arrears of revenue has been increasing on renting of telegraph, teleprinter and telephone circuits and telex/intelex connections in the various categories of subscribers. It is necessary therefore, to identify the reasons for low level performance in recovery of arrears and initiate necessary measures for the same.

BSNL has to gear itself to meet competition in various segments – basic services, long distance (LD), and International Long Distance (ILD), and Internet Service Provision (ISP), and Mobile services. With the advent of competition, the private operators have been impacting the strategic matrix by influencing regulatory bodies, adopting intelligent media strategies, and by targeting the creamy layer of customers.

In changing trends, situations, and events, gaining an accurate understanding of BSNL's strengths and limitations will help in better strategic management of organization. Therefore, an attempt is made to develop SWOT analysis of BSNL taking into consideration the present business environment.

Though BSNL is an eight year old company, it has inherited many strengths and weakness from the Department of Telecommunications. There are six key strength identified which can be used for the advancement in desired directions. The company has extensive reach to both urban and rural parts of the country. No other company can have the similar reach in the near feature. The company is the time tested telecom service provider. It need not provide evidence to the customers on its capabilities of providing telecom services. The third strength is the largest customer base of the company. The customer base is not only large but also to a greater extent loyal. The company will not find any problems as far as introduction of new services of concerned. Moreover, the cost of new services would be very less compared to competing companies due to the existence of large customer base. Huge financial resources is yet another strength of the company. This strength facilitates the company to take up new projects and also to strengthen research and development activities. The company has huge optical fibre work and associated bandwidth. In this competency the company stands far ahead of competitors. Another inherited strength is transparency in billing. Very few public sector companies has this kind of competency displayed.

SWOT analysis of BSNL

STRENGTHS	WEAKNESSES
• Extensive reach to all part of the Country· • Time tested telecom service provider· • Large customer base· • Financial resources· • Huge Optical Fibre network and associated bandwidth · • Transparency in billing	• Under utilisation of network capabilities· • Poor marketing strategy· • Public Sector mindset· • Poor franchisee network· • Aged manpower· • Incumbency problem like outdated technologies, unproductive rural assets, social obligations, political interference etc.
OPPORTUNITIES	**THREATS**
• High market growth rate· • Increasing potential for broadband services· • Un-invaded VSAT market· • Exploitation of Public Sector image	• Competition from private operators· • Fast change technology· • Manpower churning· • Possible entry of Multinational

There are six major weakness identified in the company. Underutilisation of network capabilities stands in the forefront of the company's weaknesses. The company could not achieve optimum results because of its inability to exploit the network capabilities. Poor marketing strategy is considered as another weak point. The company allowed the private sector to dominate in the mobile service segment. Instead of adopting the leader strategy the company played the role of a follower. Market aggression is not seen in the company's strategy. The third weakness is the public sector mind set. The spirited motivation is lacking in the top management of the organisation. Job security, generalised policy framework for the all public sector companies, etc., have their influence on performance of the employees. Poor franchisee network is considered as another weakness of the company. The company adopted conservative approach in identifying franchisees and developing a strong franchisee network. The company is lagging behind the competing organisations in this respect. Aged manpower is one of the serious problems of the company. The company has stopped recruitment for the last three years. The majority of the employees are said to be non-conversant with the changing technology. Another weakness of the company is incumbency problems like outdated technologies, unproductive rural assets, social obligations, political interference, etc.

The company has many business opportunities in the market environment. The market growth rate particularly in mobile services is very high and company has bright chances to capture the market. High market potential for broadband services is another identified opportunity. The VSAT market is un-invaded so far and this area of business offers great potential. The company can exploit public sector image very well in India to enhance its business opportunity. The majority of the Indians prefer public sector organisations compared to private sector when the value of the offer perceived to be more or less equal.

The threats of the company are competition of private operators, fast changing technology, manpower churning and possible entry of multinational companies with state of the art technology and non-professional management practices.

The biggest challenge before BSNL is to acquire new subscribers and retain the existing ones. Price-based selling does not seem to be going very far now, as it has more or less peaked. Therefore, BSNL will have to look for newer carrots to dangle.

Effective growth of a public enterprise depends on appropriate balance between value and economic aspects of strategy. Value aspects comprise of the socio political obligations of a public sector entity while economic aspects would be considerations regarding products, markets, costs, revenues as well as technological and organizational capabilities. BSNL is still at the formative stage and is attempting to make over to the next stage i.e. to strike an appropriate balance between value and economic aspects.

BSNL should change its very strategy of acting as follower to that of leader. Instead of reacting to other operators move it should start acting proactively. BSNL should adopt greater standardization and flexibility in systems. Only then new service rollouts will be faster, and ideas will be converted into revenue streams. The overall strategy of BSNL can be of concentrating on the mobile and broadband business in near future and to immediately phase out loss making businesses like telegraph, VSAT communication etc. BSNL can leverage on its pan India reach and economies of scale to achieve overall cost leadership. At the same time capital investments can be made in next generation networks where stress should be on Wi-Max, content based data service and VOIP. Emphasis on organizational restructuring coupled with customer orientation and operational efficiency can help BSNL find place in Asian Telecom market.

The product mix of BSNL is very large and management of the product mix offers many challenges. The pace of change in telecom technology in the international scenario, affect the product mix of the company. New product development, infrastructure up-gradation, manpower building and skill development, policy restrictions, social obligations and priorities, etc. are all the critical issues need to be addressed all the time. BSNL is so far lagging behind to provide innovative leadership in introducing new products and in improving the service package of the existing products. The company moves are rather reactive to the advances of the competing private companies. BSNL should develop expertise in leading innovations to protect its leadership position or to catch the position. It is necessary to have state of the art technology as well as the motivated human resource towards the achievement of such goal.

Internal marketing is one of the serious problems of the company as identified in the study. The findings of the employees' opinion survey, throw light on some issues of concern. The work environment particularly the furniture and support services are not to the level of expectations of the employees. Suitability of Job, Empowerment, Team work, and work culture are not liked by majority of the respondents. The employees are having an opinion that the company has no service orientation. Recognition of merit and rewarding merit are not felt. Induction training is not valued well. Skill development opportunities are not found. The employees are not confident that the company can win over competition and the company has the ability to retain the existing customers. These issues are very serious in nature from the human resource management and human resource development point of view. The company shall have to pursue Internal Marketing Strategies. It is proved in service organisations that employee satisfaction precedes customer satisfaction.

If a company aims to satisfy its customers, it should first satisfy its employees. BSNL should focus on all the issues identified and take measures by involving the concerned employee groups. Measures shall be taken to motivate the employees and build confidence among employees over the activities of the company towards winning the market. It is good to know that the employees are feeling pride over serving the organisation. Such feeling is certainty the right foundation for building a committed work force.

The findings of the consumers' opinion survey reveals that the consumers are also having some problems with the company. It is found in the study that there is inconsistency in the interactive behavior of maintenance staff with customers. The maintenance staffs of the BSNL are large in number and there is a possibility of differing behaviour patterns in customer interactions. The variance in the behaviour is more likely to take place when the employees are not properly trained and directed. As the maintenance employees are the customer contact employees, their role in shaping consumer quality perceptions and image building cannot be overemphasized. Taking the respondents opinion into consideration, it is suggested that the maintenance staff shall be given training on interactive skills and social behaviour.

The awareness of the respondents about the details of fixed line pre paid service is not encouraging. The study further reveals, the majority of the respondents are not interested to avail this service. The respondents revealed that there is no significant benefit out of the service and, there fore, it is a burden of paying in advance. It is suggested that the BSNL should take an awareness campaign for this service and include a significantly differentiating benefit in the service package.

The study reveals that 'no interest' is the reason for about 49.77 per cent of the respondents who have not participated in customer meets. 'Unawareness of the schedule of customer meets' is the reason for 34.89 per cent of the respondents. Some respondents revealed that attending meeting involve time, energy and transportation costs and therefore they prefer not to attend such meets. Customer meets are important for the company to get direct feedback from the customers and also to clarify them on various issues, technical as well as managerial. The company should make efforts to involve as many customers as possible in the process. The findings of the study establish the fact that the customers are not communicated effectively about the details of customer meets and also efforts are not directed to pursue the customers to participate in such meets. It is suggested, therefore, that the company should communicate through telephone as well as other media and pursue customer to participate actively in the meets. The company should organise the meets in such a away that the participants shall involve in the process, issues are discussed objectively and follow-up is taken care of by the company effectively.

The results of the study tend to support the hypothesis. Though BSNL is the market leader in fixed line services, it is facing the problems on the marketing front. The internal marketing, external marketing and interactive marketing are the areas that offer major challenges to the organization. The suggestions offered, if followed in true spirit, will help in developing an effective marketing team and strategy to lead the organization to success.

BIBLIOGRAPHY

Ashok. V. Desai, *Indian Telecom Industry*, 1st edition, Sage Publication India Pvt. Ltd, New Delhi, 2006.

Ahluwalia, J.S *Total Quality Management, Vanity*, 1990.

Adrian Payne, '*The Essence of Services Marketing*', Prentice Hall of India Pvt. Ltd., New Delhi, 1998.

Arif Sheikh, Kaneez Fatima, *Retail Management*, Himalaya Publishing House, Mumbai, 2008.

Bagozzi, Richard, *Principle of Marketing Management*, Science Research Associates, inc, USA., 1986.

Beth G. Chung-Harrera, Nadav Goldschmidt and K. Doug Hoffman, '*Customer and Employee Views of Critical Service Incidents*', Journal of Services Marketing, Vol. 18, No.4, 2004.

Bettencourt, Lance A.; and Brown, Stephen W., 'Contact Employees: Relationships Among Workplace Fairness, *Job Satisfaction and Prosocial Service Behaviours*', Journal of Retailing, 73(1), Sep. 1997.

Bezjian-Avery and Alexandra Miranda, 'Cognitive *Processing of Interactive Marketing*', Dissertation Abstracts International Section A: Humanities and Social Sciences, 58(4-A), Oct.1997.

Courtland L Bov'ee, Jphn V. Thill, Barbara. E. Sachtzman, *Business Communication Today*, Pearson Education.Inç. New Delhi, 2003.

Cathy Parker and Philippa Ward, '*An Analysis of Role Adoptions and Scripts During Customer-to Customer Encounters*', *European Journal of Marketing*, Vol. 34, No. 3/4, 2000.

Charley Watkins *Marketing Sales and Customer Services*, 1st edition, Low Cost Textbook Publishers, New Delhi, 2002.

Christopher H. *Loverlock, Service Marketing*, 4th Edition, Pearson Edition Pte, New Delhi, 2003.

Christian Gronroos, 'Services Management and Marketing', *Max well Macllan Publishing*, Singapore Pet. Ltd., Singapore, 1990.

Christian Gronroos, *'The Internal Marketing Function – Strategic Management and Marketing in the Service Sector Report'*, Marketing Science Institute, Cambridge, 1983.

Christian Gronroos, 'The *Perceived Service Quality Concept – A Mistake*?' Managing Service Quality, Vol. 11, No. 3, 2001.

Christine Sanes, *'Employee Impact on Service Delivery', Management Development Review*, Vol. 9, No. 2, 1996.

Christo Boshoff and Janine Allen, *'The Influence of Selected Antecedents on Frontline Staff's Perceptions of Service Recovery Performance'*, International Journal of Service Industry Management, Vol. 11, No. 1, 2000.

Christopher Lovelock, *'Service Marketing'*, Addition Wesley Longman (Singapore) Pvt. Ltd., Delhi, 2001.

Collier, David. *A, Service Marketing*, Prentice Hall, Inc., Englewood, New Jersey, 1987.

Cowell Donald, *The Marketing of Service*, Hinemann, London, 1985.

Cundiff W. Edward, Still R. Richard, Govani P. Orman, *Fundamentals of Modern Marketing*, 4th Edition, Prentice Hall of India Private Limited, New Delhi, 1985.

Dwayne D. Gremler, Mary Jo Bitner, and Kenneth R. Evans, *'The Internal Service Encounter'*, International Journal of Service Industry Management, Vol. 5, No. 2, 1994.

Edward C. Malthouse, and Robert C. Blattberg, *'Relationship Marketing'*, Journal of Interactive Marketing, Vol. 19, No. 1, 2005.

Edward W. Candif, Richard R. Still and Norman A.P. Eovani, *'Fundamentals of Modern Marketing'*, Prentice Hall of India, New Delhi, 1980.

Evans, Martin; Wedande, Gamini; Ralston, Lisa; and Van t Hul, Selma, 'Consumer Interaction in the Virtual Era: Some Qualitative Insights', *Qualitative Market Research: An International Journal*, 4(3), 2001.

Feremy F. Sierra and Shaun McQuitty, 'Service Providers and Customers: Social Exchange Theory and Service Loyalty', *Journal of Services Marketing*, Vol. 19, No. 6, 2005.

Frank Jefkins, '*Advertising*', McMillan, New Delhi, 1999.

Govind Apte, Service Marketing, Oxford University Press, New Delhi, 2004.

G.Raghuram, Rekha Jain, and Sebastian Morris. Project Report on Interconnection Issues in Telecom Sector, Indian Institute of Management, Ahmedabad, 24th August, 2001.

G.S. Sureshchandar, Chandrasekharan Rajendran and R.N. Anantharaman, '*The Relationship Between Service Quality and Customer Satisfaction – A Factor Specific Approach'*, Journal of Services Marketing, Vol. 16, No. 4, 2002.

Golan–Amos, 'A *Multivariate Stochastic Theory of Size Distribution of Firms with Empirical Evidence', London, 1994.*

Gupta N.K, *The Business of Telecommunication* Tata McGraw-Hill Publishing, New Delhi, 2000.

G V Chalam: *Quality of Services in India Telecom Sector, Users' Perception – An Assessment*, the ICFAI journal of Managerial Economics, the ICFAI University Press May, 2005.

Government of India, *Economic Survey 2002-2003*, New Delhi

Harsha, V. Varma, 'Marketing of Services', Global Business Press, New Delhi, 1993. New York Times, August 27, 2003, p. W1. http.//sanjeevkumarsharma tripod/strategy_bsnl.htm http:/www.cybermedia.co.in/press/pressrelease48.html

Jap, Sandy D., Manolis, Chris., and Weitz, Barton A., 'Relationship *Quality and Buyer-seller Interactions in Channels of Distribution*', Journal of Business Research, 46(3), Nov. 1999.

John, Jeannie Denise, 'The Effects of Employee Service Quality Provision and Customer Personality Traits on Customer Participation, Satisfaction, and Repurchase Intentions', *Dissertation Abstract s International Section A: Humanities and Social Sciences. 65 (7- A)*, No Month Specified, 2005.

Jonathon R.B. Halbesleben, and M. Ronald Buckley, '*Managing Customers as Employees of the Firm*: New Challenges for Human Resources Management', Personnel Review, Vol. 33, No. 3, 2004.

K. Rama Mohana Rao, 'Services Marketing', Pearson Education, New Delhi, 2005.

K. Ashwatappa, *Essential of Business Environment*, 7th Edition, Himalaya Public House, Mumbai, 2004.

K.Karunakaran, *Marketing Management*, Himalaya Publishing House, Mumabi, 2008.

Kaisa Snellman and Tiina Vihtkari, '*Customer Complaining Behaviour in Technology-based Service Encounters*', International Journal of Service Industry Management, Vol. 14, No. 2, 2003.

Karen Maru File, Ben B. Judd, and Russ Alan Prince, '*Interactive Marketing: The Influence of Participation on Positive Word-of-Mouth and Referrals*', Journal of Services Marketing, Vol. 6, No. 4, 1992.

Karen Maru File, Judith L.Mack, and Russ Alan Prince, '*The Effect of Interactive Marketing on Commercial Customer Satisfaction in International Financial Markets*', Journal of Business and Industrial Marketing, Vol. 10, No. 2, May 1995

Keith H. Hammonds, 'Michael Porter's Big Ideas', Fast Company, March 2001.

Kulshreshtha K., '*Emerging Scenario in Banking and Finance*', R.B.S.A. Publishers, Jaipur, 1995.

Levvy and Weitz, *Retail Management*, Tata McGraw-Hill Publishing Company Ltd, New Delhi, 2002.

Lance A. Bettencourt and Kevin Gwinner, 'Customization of the *Service Experience: The Role of the Frontline Employee*', International Journal of Service Industry Management, Vol. 7, No. 2, 1996.

Mahn Hee Yoon, Jai Hyun Seo and Tae Seog Yoon, '*Effects of Contact Employee Supports on Critical Employee Responses and Customer Service Evaluation*', Journal of Services Marketing; Vol. 18, No. 5, 2004.

Mahn Hee Yoon, Sharon E. Beatty and Jaebeom Suh, '*The effect of Work Climate on Critical Employee and Customer Outcomes: An Employee-level Analysis*', International Journal of Service Industry Management, Vol. 12, No. 5, 2001.

Mamoria C.B. and Joshi, R.I., '*Principles and Practice of Marketing in India*', Kitab Mahal, Allahabad, 1984.

Mary Jo Bitner, '*Servicescapes: The Impact of Physical Surroundings on Customers and Employees*', Journal of Marketing, Vol. 56, 1992.

Mary Jo Bitner, Bernard H. Booms, and Lois A. Mohr, '*Critical Service Encounters: The Employee's Viewpoint*', Journal of Marketing, Vol. 58, 1994.

Mary Jo Bitner, Bernard H. Booms, and Mary Stanfield Tetreault, '*The Service Encounter: Diagnosing Favourable and Unfavourable Incidents*', Journal of Marketing, Vol. 54, 1990.

McColl-Kennedy, Janet R., Daus, Catherine S., Sparks, Beverley A., '*The Role of Gender in Reactions to Service Failure and Recovery*', Journal of Service Research, 6(1), Aug., 2003.

Michael D. Hartline and O.C. Ferrell, '*The Management of Customer-Contact Service Employees*: An Empirical Investigation', Journal of Marketing, Vol. 60, 1996.

Mohapatra, 'Training and Human Resource Development', *Journal of Management Development*, Vol. 17, No. 45, 46, 47 & 48, Jan-Dec 1987.

M.K. Rampal, S.L. Gupta, *Service Marketing–Concept, Application and Cases*, Galgotia Publishing Company, New Delhi, 2000.

Nimith Chowdary, Monika Chowdary, *Text Book of Marketing of Services—The Indian Experience*, MacMillan India Limited, New Delhi, 2005

Paolo Guenzi and Ottavia Pelloni, '*The Impact of Interpersonal Relationships on Customer Satisfaction and Loyalty to the Service Provider*', International Journal of Service Industry Management, Vol. 15, No. 4, 2004.

Philip Kotler; *Marketing Management, Analysis Planning, Implementation and Control*, 4th Edition, Prentice Hall of India Private Limited, New Delhi, 1981.

Philip Kotler, '*Marketing Management — Analysis, Planning, Implementation and Control*', Prentice Hall of India Pvt. Ltd., New Delhi, 1987.

Philip Kotler, *A Framework for Marketing Management*, Pearson Education, (Singapore) Pvt. Ltd., Indian Branch, New Delhi, 2002.

Philip Kotler, and Kevin Lane Keller, '*Marketing Management*', 12e, Pearson Education, New Delhi, 2006.

P.K. Sinha, S. C. Sahoo, *Services Markegting–Text and Reading*, Himalaya Publishing House, Mumbai, 1994.

Ramphal M.K. and Gupta S.I., *Services Marketing*, Galgotia Publishing Company, New Delhi, 2000.

Ravi Shankar, *Service Marketing – The Indian Prospective,* Excel Books, New Delhi, 2002-2003.

Ronald J. Burke, Jim Graham and Frank Smith, *'Effects of Re-engineering on the Employee Satisfaction-Customer Satis-Faction Relationship'*, The TQM Magazine, Vol. 17, No. 4, 2005.

Rodger Gallagher, *Driving Your Business with Customer Satisfaction Measurements,* Telecom Corporation of New Zealand Limited Publications, Wellington, New Zealand, 1992.

Ronald T. Rust, Antony J. Zoharik and Timothy I. Keming Ham, *'Services Marketing'*, Addition Wesley Longman, New Delhi, 1999.

Ronalt T. Markes. B., *'Personal Selling an Interactive Approach'*, Allyn and Bacon Inc. Boston, 1981.

Ross D. Petty, *'Interactive Marketing and the Law: The Future Rise of Unfairness'*, Journal of Interactive Marketing, Vol. 12, No. 3, 1998.

S.M.Jha, *Service Marketing*, Himalaya Publishing House, Mumabi, 2002.

S. Ramachander, *'Interactive Marketing: Boon or Nightmare?'*, www.marketing.kub

Sally Kernbach and Nicola S. Schutte, *'Impact of Service Provider Emotional Intelligence on Customer Satisfaction'*, Journal of Services Marketing, Vol. 19, No. 7, 2005.

Shajahan. S. *Services Marketing*, Himalaya Publishing House, Mumbai, 2001.

Skaggs, Bruce C. and Huffman, Tammy Ross, *'A Customer Interaction Approach to Strategy and Production Complexity Alignment in Service Firms'*, Academy of Management Journal, Vol. 46, No. 6, Dec. 2003.

Steve Sizoo, Richard Plank, Wilfried Iskat and Hendrick Serrie, *'The Effect of Intercultural Sensitivity on Employee Performance in Cross-cultural Service Encounters'*, Journal of Services Marketing, Vol. 19, No. 4, 2005.

Sudarsana Rao, G., *'Marketing of Services—A Study of Marketing Operations of Andhra Pradesh State Electricity Board'*, Unpublished Thesis, Andhra University, Visakhapatnam, 1991.

Sunil Gupta, Donald R. Lehmann, '*Consumers as Assets*', Journal of Interactive Marketing, Vol. 17, No. 1, 2003.

Dr. T.H. Chowdary, *Information and Communication Technologies for Class and Mass,* 1st Edition, Center for Telecommunication and Management and Studies, Hyderabad, 2004.

Tleonard A. Schiesinger and James I. Heskeltt, '*The Service Driven Service Company*', Harvard Business Review, Sep.–Oct., 1991.

Upah, Gregory, *Mass Marketing in Service Retailing, A Review and Synthesis of Major Methods*, Journal of Retailing, Pal 1980.

Valarie A. Zeithaml, Mary Jo Bitner, *Service Marketing, Integrating Customer Focus Across the Firm,* Tata McGraw-Hill Publishing Company Ltd. New Delhi, 2003.

Vasaanti Venugopal,, Raghu V.N. *Service Marketing*, Himalaya Publishing House, Mumbai, 2002.

Vaish M.C., *Monetary Theory,* Vikas Publishing House, New Delhi, 1973.

Van Dolen, Willemijn; de Ruyter, Ko and Lemmink, Jos, *"An Empirical Assessment of the Influence of Customer Emotions and Contact Employee Performance on Encounter and Relationship Satisfaction",* Journal of Business Research, Vol. 57, No. 4, Apr. 2004.

Vishal Sethi, Telecom Sector in India, *Law, Policy and Procedure* 1st Edition, JBA Publishers, New Delhi, 2006.

William J. Stanton, *Fundamentals of Marketing*, McGraw Hill,Kogakusha Limited, Tokyo, 1978

William J. Stanton, Michael J. Ezel and Brace J. Walker, *Fundamental of Marketing,* Tata McGraw Hill Publishing Co. Ltd., New Delhi, 1994.

William D Perreault, Jr. Jerome McCrthy, *Basic Marketing— A Global Managerial Approach*, Tata McGraw-Hill Publishing Company Ltd., New Delhi, 2002.

Yahya Melhem and Irbid, Jordan, '*The Antecedents of Customer-Contact Employees' Empowerment*' Employee Relations, Vol. 26, No. 1, 2004.

INDEX

M

N

O

P